Dishonoured
'Criminal Trib
Colonial

Revised Edition

MEENA RADHAKRISHNA

Dishonoured by History: 'Criminal Tribes' and British Colonial Policy

ORIENT LONGMAN PRIVATE LIMITED

Registered Office
3-6-752 Himayatnagar, Hyderabad 500 029 (A.P.), INDIA
e-mail : cogeneral@orientlongman.com

Other Offices
Bangalore, Bhopal, Bhubaneshwar, Chennai, Ernakulam, Guwahati, Hyderabad, Jaipur, Kolkata, Lucknow, Mumbai, New Delhi, Patna

First published 2001
This revised edition in paperback 2008

ISBN 13: 978 81 250 3403 2
ISBN 10: 81 250 3403 X

Typeset by
Scribe Consultants
New Delhi

Printed in India at
Glorious Printers
Delhi

Published by
Orient Longman Private Limited
1/24 Asaf Ali Road
New Delhi 110 002
e-mail: delgeneral@orientlongman.com

For Nasir, and for our daughters

Contents

Acknowledgements vii
Foreword by Mahasweta Devi xi
Preface to this Edition xiii
Introduction 1

1. The Criminal Tribes Act: Historical Developments 27

2. Notification and Surveillance 45

3. The Concept and Policy of Criminal Tribe Settlements 71

4. Land Reclamation, Industrial Recruitment and Settlements 98

5. From Itinerant Community to Industrial Wageworkers: Stuartpuram Settlement 127

6. Historic Memory 146

Conclusion 158
Afterword 171
Appendices 183
References and Bibliography 208
Index 220

Acknowledgements

My first and enduring debt is to Nasir Tyabji, my longest standing friend and fellow traveller, who has seen both me, and this book, through an astonishing range of trials and tribulations. His has been the most important intellectual influence during the long gestation period of this book, permeating its pages through countless unconcluded discussions. He was probably more glad than I was when the first edition of this book had finally come out. Combatively and spiritedly, he has read multiple drafts of not just the original manuscript, but of the Preface and Afterword in the current edition as well. Through these pages I would like to thank Nasir for being the way he is.

Sabyasachi Bhattacharya, the late Ravinder Kumar and the late Dharma Kumar had not just read the whole manuscript in its first, faltering phases and gave critical comments, but were also responsible for some of the earliest academic articles which came out of it. K.N. Panikkar instilled confidence and provided unstinting support for many years while the book was in the making. I sincerely and warmly thank Satish Saberwal for his easy accessibility and the friendly enthusiasm he has constantly shown for my chosen area of research.

In addition to Nasir, there were people who took the painstaking trouble to read through the entire original manuscript in its various incarnations, and offered very varied, extremely useful, (and often difficult to incorporate) comments. To this precious category belong Manorama Savur, Sumit Guha, Tanika Sarkar and the late K.S. Singh.

Years ago, Mahasweta Devi and Ganesh Devy, by including me in their practical, contemporary work with the denotified tribes, gave me a new reason to soldier on with the publication of an academic, historical work on these communities. Dilip Menon, in quite another way, had also played a more important role in this book seeing the light of day than he would imagine.

There are scholars and friends, who made themselves available at various stages of the making of this book, and were willing to discuss totally unformed ideas arising out of its concerns. I learnt as much from their support to these ideas as from their scepticism. To this very valuable category belong Shahid Amin, Rajeshwari Sunder Rajan, Stuart Blackburn, Sumit Sarkar, Kumkum Sangari, Robert Young and Anand Yang.

In the last few years, I presented versions of chapters in this book at seminars at the Nehru Memorial Museum and Library, the School of African and Oriental Studies, London, and at the Centre for South Asian Studies at Oxford and Cambridge. The participants at these seminars engaged enthusiastically with the issues presented, and this book would be a poorer one without the inputs from these scholars, too many to name individually. I would, however, still like to single out Peter Robb, Kancha Illiah, David Washbrook, the late Raj Chandavarkar, Gordon Johnson, M.S.S. Pandian and Thomas Trautmann. David Arnold was an important presence and influence during the research for this book. I thank him for all his gestures of support and encouragement. Presentation at a seminar organised by NALSAR, Hyderabad, has led to the writing of some parts of the Afterword, the ideas for which were originally explored in an article written for an edited volume on criminology. I warmly thank Kalpana Kannabiran, who has edited this book for Sage.

The Salvation Army personnel at the International Heritage Centre in London were most hospitable and allowed me free access to their library and archives. I would particularly like to thank the archivist Mr Gordon Taylor for his thoughtful help throughout my work there.

I would also like to acknowledge the role that the pleasant and stimulating environment at Teen Murti played during the revision of the manuscript. Apart from the late Ravinder Kumar, Dr O.P. Kejariwal readily granted me affiliation to NMML. This allowed me the use of Teen Murti's wonderful library and office space.

Vidya Rao, my editor for the original hardback, remains responsible for the book as it is, since the main text has not been revised. Inspite of the numerous difficulties presented by me to her as an author, she remained gracious throughout, in big ways and small. I thank Vidya for making the book what it is.

When this book was being originally prepared for publication a few years ago, Hemlata Shankar, through her numerous courtesies, considerably helped to relieve the necessary tedium which all publications entail. Recently, as the person deemed by me to be in overall charge for the revised edition, I took the liberty to approach her with a particularly difficult 'author's request'. She dealt with it with remarkable tact, grace and thoughtfulness, for which I shall remain hugely indebted to her. Satyadeep, the editor for this edition, has been a pleasure to work with and I am grateful for his punctilious eye for detail.

I must acknowledge the stabilising role that my daughters Shirali and Rushika have played all these years by their cheerful irreverence towards the entire enterprise of 'the book'. This has, all along, helped me to keep a sense of balance at those particular times when I have wanted to obsessively rework its content or inordinately worry about its future trajectory. For the cover of this book, Shirali has allowed me the use of her oil painting, *Fire*, which she made a few years ago as a school student, and which in my opinion precisely captures the current mood of the communities in question. I thank Dr Achal Bhagat of Sarthak, who thought of commissioning this work to her as a series designed for art therapy, and who is the owner of the work in original.

I would like to end by acknowledging that the communities that are the subject of this book have educated, inspired and motivated me to continue my historical searches into contemporary times. These communities are full of hope for the future while they lead a shamefully deprived subhuman existence in contemporary India. They resolutely resist and challenge a history that continues to dishonour them in the present. In the years to come, the fire of their passion shall remain my own inspiration for enduring engagement with them, and this area of research.

Foreword

I feel really honoured at being invited to write a foreword to Meena Radhakrishna's excellent work, *Dishonoured by History: 'Criminal Tribes' and British Colonial Policy.* I have gone through the entire work at least three times and frankly admit that I feel I am not the right person to do it. The communities still suffering from the stigma for once being declared as 'Criminal Tribes', have been my focus of interest for two decades or more. I knew of them in the eastern zone, Bihar, Orissa and West Bengal. Since the Lodhas are in Orissa and West Bengal, I tried, in my way to protest against the atrocities committed by the police and the neighbours. Later I entered the persecuted life of another tribe, the Kheriasabars of Purulia, West Bengal. I never thought that one day I would find younger friends taking up the cause of the denotified nomadic tribes and communities. I am very grateful to Meena Radhakrishna as she is the first person to trace the history of the Koravas (Yerukulas, Koravars and Korachas) and place them in history. Since the history of India has always been written by historians who were and still are reluctant to see the tribals as part of India, a true history is yet to be written which will give the tribals their place in history. It is not apathy. The historians are generally oblivious of tribal existence. If this be the situation, it is quite expected that they do not know that the denotified nomadic tribes exist.

But they do. And after going through this book I understand things which I did not before. I know now, only the nomadic tribes, the itinerant ones were notified by the British by the

Criminal Tribes Act. Now in West Bengal, they have been forced to accept a sedentary life, though there has been no effort to settle them as cultivators. Since West Bengal had no Stuartpuram, or Salvation Army Units, .there has been no conscious effort to invade their brain, and change their mind set. Here it is unforgivably brutal and callous total apathy. There, in the settlement area the process was equally bad, if not worse. Fourteen lakh human beings were experimented upon (see the different 'crim' songs), and story-telling, singing and riddle plays. The oral tradition, the only history left to the tribals became redundant. They were separated from their children, so there was no necessity to sing etc. A totally new oral tradition was forced upon them and the Salvation Army version of their songs try to prove that they knew they were 'crims' and now they were wage-earners, which was better. But it is good to read that they said the police were their worst enemies. And it is good to know that they protested when tobacco processing was replaced by mechanisation, as it robbed them of the only source of their livelihood. One recalls what one read of America when mechanisation was introduced and cotton workers lost their jobs.

It is of extreme importance that this book has been written at a time when increasing mechanisation is a threat to common Indian people who work with their hands.

Meena Radhakrishna writes in the Introduction that 'the focus is on the nomadic communities in general, and the Korava community in particular'. But her book has helped to cure me of my ignorance. Now I get a clear perspective and understand that only the non-sedentary nomadic tribes were targetted by the CTA of 1871, 1911, and in-between amendments. I am grateful to her; as one who works for the denotified and nomadic tribes, I will benefit by it. She too is one of the crusaders and her work will form the academic basis for further exploration into this hitherto untrodden virgin field. Perhaps others will be inspired and will write on these groups with Meena Radhakrishna's understanding, humane attitude and academic brilliance. I know that this book deserves a better foreword but I cannot do that. I became too involved in the book. Perhaps that is why I was requested to write this foreword.

MAHASWETA DEVI

Preface

Since this book was published a few years ago, historical research has continued to address some of the critical issues raised in it. While writing it a few years ago, I was still grappling with the archival material on 'criminal tribes' within the framework of colonial law. However, I am now convinced that although the Criminal Tribes Act *was* a colonial piece of legislation in spirit, laws to control the underclasses, across societies and eras, both colonial and imperial, are remarkably similar. The Afterword in this new edition will bear this out. There is contempt and suspicion surrounding all 'wandering' people, who are seen to be threatening to the existing social and moral order. The expression that this contempt takes sometimes can border on the bizarre, and the people in question are denied humanity, not to speak of equal citizenship.

Henry Mayhew, an influential English author of the mid-nineteenth century, wrote that society consists of two races, 'the wanderers and the settlers.' Of the former, he had this to say:

> Whether it is that in the mere act of wandering, there is a greater determination of blood to the surface of the body, and consequently a less quantity sent to the brain, the muscles being thus nourished at the expense of the mind, I leave physiologists to say. But certainly be the physical cause what it may, we must all allow that in each of the classes above mentioned, there is a greater development of the animal than of the intellectual or moral nature of man, and that they are

> all more or less distinguished for their high cheek-bones and protruding jaws—for their use of a slang language—for their lax ideas of property—... their repugnance for continuous labour—their disregard of female honour—their love of cruelty...—and their utter want of religion.[1]

In a similar vein, drawing on evolutionary theory, Thomas Carlyle wrote that

> ... The Nomad has his very house set on wheels; the Nomad, and *in a still higher degree the Ape,* are all for 'liberty'; the privilege to flit continually is indispensable to them... The civilised man lives not in wheeled houses. He builds stone castles, plants lands, makes life long marriage-contracts;—has long-dated hundred-fold possessions, not to be valued in the money-market; has pedigrees, libraries, law-codes; *has memories and hopes,* even for this Earth, that reach over thousands of years.[2]

As another para quoted below will show, what is interesting is not just the uniformity in the attitude of the British establishment towards the colonial nomadic tribes and English gypsies, but towards all marginalised sections. Thus, if one set of people is considered criminal, by a process of association and comparison, so are some others. Writing with John Binny, Mayhew made the following assertions in the *The Criminal Prisons of London and Scenes of Prison Life* (1862):

> If Arabia has its nomadic tribes, the British Metropolis has its vagrant hordes as well. If the Carib Islands have their savages, the English Capital has types almost as brutal and uncivilized as they. If India has its Thugs, London has its garotte men.[3]

And again,

> The pickpockets—the beggars—the prostitutes—the street-sellers—the street-performers... In each of these classes—according as they partake more or less of the purely vagabond, doing nothing whatsoever for their living, but moving from place to place preying upon the earnings of the more

> industrious portions of the community, so will the attributes of the *nomad tribes* be more or less marked in them.[4]

An important issue, however, for our immediate purposes is the way the wanderers themselves were defined by British law. A study of the vagrancy laws in England shows that they especially targeted three categories of people: the gypsy, the vagrant and the migrant.[5] These people had some important attributes in common—moving from place to place, menial and casual work, uneven phases of employment, and dire poverty—a class consisting of people who were seen to be a potential and constant threat to the established social order. When Mayhew spoke of the so-called wanderers' 'repugnance for continuous labour,' he was implicitly admitting of *non-availability* or *non-sustainability of regular work* for a large section of the people affected by the changes in the contemporary economy.

The Afterword in this edition deals specifically with the manner in which the lawmakers of the newly independent Indian state also conflated these three discrete categories of people. They associated the migratory tribes with vagrancy, on the one hand, and nomadism, on the other.

In a widely prevalent view held by lawmakers across the world, people engaged in certain occupations, like those of the nomadic tribes, are actual or would-be criminals. This is what the Afterword sets out to describe. It is instructive that both in England and India, debates on how to deal with the 'poor'—including the gypsies and the nomads—take place at historical junctures when universal citizenship is evidently still not fully acceptable to the legislators. Such commonalities amongst the members of the ruling classes across eras and societies need to be carefully analysed in order to understand how some of the issues involved are related as closely to *class* as to colonialism.

Notes

1. Henry Mayhew, *London Labour and the London Poor: the Condition and Earnings of Those that Will Work, Cannot Work, and Will Not Work,* 3 Volumes, London, 1851, quoted in Martin J. Weiner, *Reconstructing the Criminal: Culture, Law, and Policy in England, 1830–1914,* Cambridge, 1990, p. 31.

2. Thomas Carlyle, *Past and Present* (1843), Richard D. Altick (ed.), New York, 1965, p. 274, quoted in Adam Hansen, 'Exhibiting Vagrancy, 1851: Victorian London and the "Vagabond Savage"', CFP: Literary London: Interdisciplinary Studies in the Representation of London (2/28/05; e-journal) [http://cfp.english.upenn.edu/archive/Cultural-Historical/0180.html], as retrieved on 16 September 2006, emphasis added. Human attributes like memories and hopes are denied to those who are nomadic.
3. Mayhew, quoted in Adam Hansen, op. cit.
4. Mayhew, quoted in Martin J. Weiner, op. cit.
5. Meena Radhakrishna, 'Laws of Metamorphosis: From Nomad to Offender' in Kalpana Kannabiran (ed.), *The Rule(s) of Law: Critical Essays on Criminology in India*, Sage Publications, 2007 (forthcoming).

Introduction

For the British policy maker, the late nineteenth century was a difficult period of flux in both ideological and political terms. There were continental challengers to the empire; there was also a consolidated section of restive population within Britain. Moral and ethical issues were being debated afresh, Darwin's scientific discoveries looming large in the background. This inevitably led to the need for continual reformulation of social policy, in relation to the population both in Britain and in the colonies. During this period, there was also a revised perception of the colonies; 'moral and material progress' was to be at a faster pace through a set of new social and political polices. W.W. Hunter, a senior civil servant whom the British Government had asked to conduct 'a great stock-taking after a century of British rule in India' wrote of 'a more secure, more prosperous India where roads, railways, bridges, canals, schools and hospitals had been built; famines tackled; *thugi, dakaiti* and predatory castes suppressed; trade developed; barbaric social practices like widow-burning and infanticide abolished.'[1]

This book concerns itself with one of the important legislative measures in British social policy in India which dealt with the 'predatory castes' mentioned by Hunter. It traces the origins and implications of a piece of legislation, the Criminal Tribes Act, enacted by the British Indian government in 1871, and uses it as an illustration of some general aspects of British social policy in the colonies. The history of the Criminal Tribes Act (CTA) is traced with special reference to Madras Presidency: a revised version of the Act became applicable in 1911 here, affecting 14,00,000 people according to official figures. The focus is on the nomadic communities in general, and the Yerukulas, Koravars and Korachas in particular. These were three branches of the large Korava community operating in different regions of the Presidency; Yerukulas were itinerant traders in the Telugu districts, Koravars in the Tamil districts and Korachas in the ceded districts.

I

The ostensible purpose of the 1871 Act had been to suppress 'hereditary criminal' sections of Indian society. The notion of crime and criminality had, however, been changing all through the nineteenth century. There is a comprehensive discussion of the changing definition of crime over a period of time in several works.[2] These works address the problematic of differing notions of criminality in an industrialising European society, mainly England. Wiener, in his brilliant study, has pointed out that during this period, public interest in criminality was growing, and crime and criminals became the subjects of innumerable works of fiction and fact.[3] Causes of crime were variously attributed by thinkers and policy makers of the times to drunkenness, increasing poverty, increasing prosperity, rapid urbanisation, overcrowding of residential areas, universal and natural decline in morals, unsettled family life and increasing population. A strong school of thought, put forward by criminologists and scientists, and much subscribed to, held that crime was a genetic trait transmitted over generations in a family through parents or ancestors. The concept of a 'hereditary criminal class', was an important and attractive one, and a consequence was the deflection of serious enquiries into the causes of crime.

Notions of criminality were located and developed sometimes in the social, sometimes in the scientific context, the two not necessarily excluding each other. It has been shown, that British science in the nineteenth century, followed, rather than led, public opinion insofar as ideas on racism were concerned.[4] In the case of a concept like crime, this was quite likely to have happened as well, as there would always be considerable public interest in this issue, attended by questions like 'so what should be done about it/where do we go from here?' While devising a new definition of crime, or listing newly discovered causes of crime, a scientist would be under pressure to take this factor into account if new theories were to achieve any degree of public support and acceptability. Gordan has pointed out that there was vigorous public debate in Victorian England about the redeemability of the lower classes in general, and the criminal classes in particular. During the first half of the nineteenth century, public opinion had generally moved in the direction of redeemability, and both pamphleteers and politicians seem to have had definite views on what would make a 'reliable citizen'.[5]

As implied earlier, the 1880s had been deemed to be a particularly hard period by the policy maker, with economic depression, unemployment, strikes and growing political radicalism. Poverty, alcoholism, ill-health (and crime) had not disappeared in England inspite of decades of social legislation. There was great temptation for believing—preferably buttressed with scientific proof—that crime was a hereditary trait, and called for measures to reengineer society on biological, rather than social or political bases. The new concept of Eugene (good genes), coined by Francis Galton, seemed to provide an answer, among others, to the problem of criminal classes as well. One eugenicist included pauperism in his list of hereditary traits, another included criminality.[6] The social policies contemplated by eugenicists were directed against the social residuum of paupers and persistent criminal offenders. All over the world, including England, eugenics societies targetted criminals in prisons by forcibly sterilising them, so as to avoid passing on the gene for crime to the next generation.

The developing disciplines of anthropometry and anthropology also contributed to notions of hereditary criminality. These disciplines in India addressed themselves to the study of particular sections of the Indian population, mostly indigenous 'tribal' communities and itinerant groups, and contributed in a very substantial way to the conceptual outline of a criminal in the popular mind. By focusing on bizarre or exotic ritual aspects of the social lives of such communities, and at the same time also on their differential anthropometric measurements, these disciplines created categories of the civilised and the barbaric individual. In the popular ethnographic literature of the period, a sketch was drawn of a criminal who possessed not just bizarre social customs, but a strange body and psyche as well, 'which had criminality written all over'. These disciplines therefore held that criminality was a hereditary trait and one, in fact, which could actually be perceived in the physical features. The communities which were trawled under the CTA, not unexpectedly, were those which were also grist for the anthropological mill of the time.

Interestingly, as early as 1860s in England, the phrase 'our criminal tribes' was already in usage to define 'that portion of our society who have not yet conformed to civilised habits'. Such sections were likened to gypsies, who preferred to indulge their appetites when they could, resorting to plunder rather than submit to the discipline of steady work.[7] The search for practical, social causes of criminality, thus ran parallel to the marches of supposed scientific knowledge in the field of genetics or anthropometry.

The Criminal Tribes Act (CTA), however, had its conceptual origins in local systems and structures and arose out of policies of political control rather than social concern for escalating crime. In the late nineteenth century, there was a renewed interest in, and admiration for the Indian caste system in British administrative and intellectual circles: the criminal tribes seemed to belong to a definable caste of hereditary criminals within the Hindu social system. Though neither the concerned communities, nor 'the Hindus' thought of the matter in these terms, the British nevertheless transfixed these communities into an existing hierarchy. By an extension of the same logic, the communities in question also came to be perceived by the British through the yardstick of both Brahmanical and Victorian notions and norms.

Though individual crime in India was also seen to stem from a hereditary cause, the investing of entire communities with hereditary criminality was radically different in the case of India and Europe. In India it was based not on the notion of genetically transmitted crime, but on crime as a profession passed on from one generation of criminal caste to another: like a carpenter would pass on his trade to the next generation, hereditary criminal caste members would pass on this profession to their offspring.

Thus hereditary crime in India never got seriously linked to biological determinism. This happened not so much because of scepticism regarding the concept of genetically transmitted crime, but because of a particular view of Indian social structures. More immediately, however, it happened because realpolitik on the ground dictated a pragmatic policy and a need to see crime as arising out of some administratively manageable cause, such as unemployment. Genetics seemed too much out of bounds for manipulation. So while racial theorists distanced from the problem of governance might continue to adhere to some notion of the 'hereditary' criminal, a seachange was occurring in the administrative mind. By calling the trait 'hereditary', the possibility of control would be given away; the explanation had to therefore, incorporate an understanding of society which would make the process seem amenable to bureaucratic intervention. The British Indian administrator, in particular, had to pose the problem in ways which would point towards an administrative resolution, and not locate the problem in either the unquestionable superiority of the British race, or the inherent wickedness of the Indian. The preferred line of reasoning was less ideologically loaded, and attempted to pin the ungovernability of the Indian on identifiable, correctable and material causes as opposed to genetic/racial/environmentally deterministic ones.

The concept of Indian crime and its causes had, thus, changed between 1871 (when the CTA was first instituted in Northern

India) and 1911 (when a revised version was applied to the whole of British India). The needs of practical governance led to a search for a 'social scientific' explanation of crime in India, connecting Indian criminality to the introduction of the railways, the new forest policy, repeated famines and so on. Not that these material causes were seen to be reversible—in fact, the emphasis could now be on the point that the inexorable civilising processes set in motion by the British had unforeseen, unfortunate and inevitable effects on an ill-prepared section of Indian society. The new administrative rationale was that with the introduction of certain policies designed to raise revenue, some communities had irrevocably lost their means of livelihood. How else could they live except by committing crime, especially if there was no property to support them? This section which had become criminal, now needed to be treated by special legislative measures. Implicit in linking crime with a lack of means of sustenance was a corollary—the criminals were reformable, and not 'hereditary, habitual and incorrigible criminals'. The British administration would intervene in an inexorable process, and by giving these criminals employment, reverse it.

The colonial administration had, in any case, been under pressure to identify the precise causes for criminality in Indian society, which made it so ungovernable from time to time. It is within this larger context that a link was sought to be established between lack of proper means of livelihood and criminality. In this specific sense, the new concept was an advance on the old as it attributed social behaviour to social causes on the one hand, and did away with the exclusivity of Indian criminality on the other. The revised CTA, 1911, after all, sprang out of an era which prided itself on basing its social policies on an understanding that social processes were 'man-made' as opposed to God-given.[8]

Thus the concept of criminality got linked to a secular cause, and commission of crime was now directly related to lack of means of livelihood, and non-availability of work. (Even in England, by this time, lack of 'ostensible means of livelihood' made a person qualify as a potential criminal.) This implied that if honest (wage) work could be found for the affected communities, they could be weaned away from crime.[9]

However, the urge to reform these communities seems to have coincided with two other critical compulsions faced by the British Indian government: to raise revenue from land, and the administration's commitment to private enterprise. These two objective needs led the government to the unavoidable conclusion that work had to be found for a large number of CT members in order to wean them away from a life of crime, or 'reform' them. This could be achieved either by giving them work on land, or in private enterprises. Herein lay the genesis of the so-called agricultural and industrial settlements.

In the early twentieth century, while compiling records on the criminality of certain communities, the administration went back decades in time. Policies followed by the British Indian administration fifty years ago were blamed for destroying the traditional means of livelihood of a number of communities.[10] Many factors were considered responsible for the subsequent criminalisation of these communities. It was now officially recognised that the British administration's economic policies, aimed at raising revenue, had made the itinerant communities economically redundant and anachronistic.

The itinerant Korava community of Madras Presidency is the focus of this book, which discusses the trajectory of their marginalisation to the sedentary society in the late nineteenth century. Members of this community were chiefly traders in grain and salt, operating between the coastal areas of the Presidency and the interior districts.[11] They were, at one time, almost the only means of distributing salt in far-flung areas where wheel traffic could not reach. In the 1850s, road and railway networks were established throughout the Presidency, and this community's trade—carried out largely on pack bullocks or donkeys—became largely, if not wholly, redundant.

The famines of the late nineteenth century were devastating as far as their salt trade was concerned. Large numbers of their cattle died. And since the Koravas were traders in cattle, apart from using them to carry their merchandise, the death of their cattle caused them to suffer huge losses. The Koravas' grain trade also suffered drastically during this period, because famines were managed by the British administration, to the advantage of the bigger grain merchants.[12] Small traders like the Koravas found grain totally inaccessible at a time when their cattle, which carried it, were dying in large numbers.

The forest laws of the 1880s prevented the Koravas from collecting forest produce, an important item of barter in their trade. The laws also did not allow them to collect bamboo and leaves, which they used for making mats, baskets, brooms etc. Common pastureland and grazing areas were cordoned off, and not available any more to their cattle.[13] They were also crucially affected by the new salt policy of the government in the 1880s, which allowed large trading companies to enter the salt trade. A large number of retail outlets were established by the government all over the Presidency on railway routes, where salt was now sold through the agents of large company traders.[14]

As a result of the above factors, the Korava community suffered a massive economic setback in the period between the 1850s and 1890s.

Looked at another way, here was an admission by the British administration of having unleashed unsavoury social processes in India; this acknowledgement, however, could be made readily and publicly because the responsibility for this was pinned to another, earlier generation of British administrators. The duty of the current generation was seen to be the clear-headed solving of a social problem bequeathed to them by an earlier generation of administrators. To this limited extent, a study of the CTA also helps to unpeel a layer of the British perception of their own presence in India once one generation of administrators could distance itself from the ill-effects of policies introduced by another. At any rate, the CTA, 1911 conceptualised during an era when eugenics enjoyed immense popularity, embodied radically different principles: it saw crime not as a result of irreversible heredity or genes, but as arising from social causes.

II

In this book, though generalised features of the CTA are described in detail, it is the operation of the Act vis-a-vis the itinerant Korava community which is in focus. Itinerant communities were considered to be, for various reasons, more criminal than others, their 'restlessness' being a troublesome feature in a milieu where members of sedentary communities defined notions of respectability. It was believed that the itinerancy of such groups, through a process of downhill grading, becomes either 'wandering' or worse, 'vagrancy', and the only solution was to settle these communities and make them sedentary.

The relationship between itinerant and sedentary communities has become particularly problematic in modern times. The more the itinerant communities get marginalised to the main sphere of society because of transformative processes, the more they become suspect from the point of view of the sedentary society with which they interact. In real terms, their increasing marginality simply compounds the already existing prejudices against them. In Europe, gypsies became gradually marginalised to the established system with the processes of industrialisation.[16] In India, as described above, it was the colonial revenue policies which destroyed the itinerant communities' earlier trading practises.

As they become marginalised to the main system, prejudices and myths that already exist about nomads have a fresh lease of life, or come to the surface more explicitly. David Mayall has pointed out some of these in his discussion of gypsy travellers in nineteenth century England. Some of these apply to itinerant communities in general, all over the world.[17]

Firstly and most importantly, the nomads' lack of property, and supposed lack of due regard for others' property, is seen to be a threat to the established order, and their independence from rigid norms and constraints of sedentary societies is found highly objectionable. In fact, itinerancy is seen as a possible escape route for the so-called outcasts and refuse of sedentary societies—the argument being that if one is an itinerant, it is probably because he or she was not acceptable to the sedentary society. There have been other charges against gypsies, or nomadic people: they are seen as escaping from the arm of the law, or simply fleeing from hard work of any kind. In agriculture-based societies, the men resent the fact that gypsies escape the hard work of ploughing and tilling; and the women resent the gypsy' freedom from this labour and from the drudgery of housekeeping and child rearing. Itinerancy is not seen as a chosen way of life, but as an aberration of some sort. In fact, their very marginality to the established system is suspected to stem from a deliberate rejection of that system, and this offends the established members of sedentary societies. Vagrancy, wanderlust, lack of stability and general purpose in life, restlessness and aimlessness—these are accusations that plague all itinerant communities.

In addition, their superior knowledge of the world, acquired during extensive travels, is seen to endow them with greater mental resources and a potential for greater manipulation of others. But it is worth emphasising that many of the prejudices are not held so much by the local people, but by the local authorities.[18] In the Indian case, these would mean the British administration, the police establishment, the high caste sections and the village landlords.

More grievances were added to the standard list of charges against itinerants by the Indian authorities: their lack of predictability of movements implied a potential lack of control; their shifting abodes meant shifting loyalties to different patrons, and so they were seen to be perennially disloyal; the impossibility of taxing them, or raising any kind of revenue out of them, unlike their sedentary counterparts was a major irritant to the administration.[19] In addition, for the keepers of social morality, lack of visible social institutions implied complete disorder in their community life. Their lack of written codes of conduct, and absence of articulated norms of morality implied absolute licentiousness.

At another level, there were other problems. This community had amongst its members acrobats, singers, dancers, tightrope-walkers and fortune-tellers. More and more, like their counterparts all over the world, street entertainment provided by them was seen to be a threat to public order. Since they always collected a large interested crowd around themselves—and were quite a large crowd by themselves—their presence made the local authorities nervous. The British administration was increasingly inclined to favour forms of recreation which could be supervised by themselves, and would not precipitate what they called 'disorderly and riotous behaviour' on the part of the spectators.

It is worth mentioning here that in England, all laws relating to the gypsies were to protect the settled communities from itinerant ones and never the other way around.[20] Large-scale harassment of these communities by members of settled communities was a common feature in Europe, and there is evidence of this happening in Madras Presidency as well.

It is also important at this juncture to keep in mind the ambivalences and contradictions in the attitude of sedentary communities to itinerant ones. These are symptomatic of the latter's simultaneous usefulness and marginality to the established systems with which they have to interact. It was, for instance, felt that these communities must be settled somewhere, but 'not near us, not here'. This is reminiscent of a similar ambivalence: 'they should visit our village, but should not stay too long'. Further, they were expected to become a part of the mainstream, but were expected also to be segregated from the main society while this was being done, so as not to corrupt it. They were, in fact, romanticised in imagination, especially in English fiction and poetry in the case of the gypsies.[21] This was for their independent spirit; their dark attractive looks or bright clothes and jewellery as in the case of the Indian Banjaras; and their supposed healthy outdoor life. In general, there was a lot of romance and adventure associated with their travels.[22] However, when confronted in reality, there was fear and dread and they were shunned if not despised. In fact, a number of English ladies in their leisure time in India drew Banjara men and women in a romanticised light, while their law-making menfolk made the Banjara men out to be ferocious criminals.[23]

It seems inevitable that the nature of the relationship between these two different systems, and the gaps in knowledge of each other's real ways of living would lead to myth-making on both sides. While sedentary societies experience and express an overarching discomfort, a suspicion regarding itinerants which makes for fertile ground for seeing them as potential criminals, we know little, unfortunately, about the myths that itinerant people have about sedentary societies. At any rate, the prejudices that the sedentary society held formed a major strand that fed into the Criminal Tribes Act.

III

While considering some of the general prejudices about itinerant communities, it is also useful to mention some specific additional charges against Koravas which existed in the minds of the British administrators, and which contributed substantially to their being labelled a criminal tribe. Interestingly, scattered in the official records themselves, there is information collected by the administration for other purposes, which contradicts these very charges. However, since the Koravas were an itinerant community, the administrators found it difficult to shake off some of the prejudices they carried with them regarding European gypsies, and they seem to have simply superimposed some of these on the Indian counterparts. Moreover, the bulk of their own prejudices were shared by the high caste landlord sections, on whom the administration relied for first hand knowledge of Indian society.

The most convincing of the accusations was that the Koravas as itinerants had an 'insatiable lust for wandering aimlessly'. It is important here to point out that the wandering of itinerant trading communities could not have been aimless—their routes and schedules of moving and stopping were fixed and cyclic.[24] They always had fixed trade routes, depending on the demand for their wares; on the cycle of annual festivals and fairs; on the availability of raw material for making mats or baskets; and on the season in which the forest produce, or stocks of grain, which they used for barter would be available Their movements also depended on the salt manufacturing cycle, an important item of their trade, or simply on availability of casual work which they did from time to time.

The second of the significant charges was that they were idle, lazy and not keen on hard work. Booth Tucker, the head of the Salvation Army in India wrote of them, 'When we asked them to till the land, or work in a factory, they were shocked. 'Work? they said, we never work, we just sing and dance.'[25] The point that needs to emphasised however is that if indeed they did not work, neither they, nor their trade, nor their crafts would have survived for so long. So what was being discussed was not whether they worked or not, but the nature of their work. Their work was independent, not time-bound, and most important, it was not *wage* work.

The third prejudice, which had a long life, was that of their lack of any social norms, especially regarding their women. Charges of looseness of character, and even prostitution were frequent, stemming from their polygamous practises. Buying and selling of females was another charge, with origins in brideprice, which they paid at the time of marriages. The myth of their licentiousness had its roots in their unfamiliar (to the high caste sections) social organisation which included freedom in choosing of spouses, easy divorce, widow remarriage, and a marked absence of marriage of girls before puberty. Interestingly, however, this particular view about the immorality of their women prevailed with the British administrators as well, possibly because of the practice of polygamy. Ironically, in 1948, one of the high caste commentators held up the Koravas as the ideal envisioned by Indian reformers. He stated that since their social norms were what the Hindu society was aiming at through legislation, they should, in fact, 'have been left alone'[26] (as far as trying to civilise them was concerned).

The final and major charge that plagued the Koravas was that of their ostensible criminality. This had two aspects: one was that they had always been criminals—all gypsies supposedly are—and secondly, that they had become dangerous criminals once they lost their earlier means of livelihood.[27]

As far as proof of the first aspect was concerned, their own alleged folklore was used. It was claimed that 'when they asked their god Subramanya what profession they should follow, he handed them a house-breaking implement!'[28] This was supposed to be convincing evidence of their committing thefts and robberies as a profession. In actual fact, crimes attributed to them by the police were seldom proven—this generated another minor myth of their slipperiness and nimble-fingeredness![29] And yet, in the annual crime figures of Madras Presidency, their proportion in the criminal population was always lower than their proportion in the actual population. (In fact, sometimes a high caste category would account for a much higher proportion of total crime in relation to their proportion in the total population in the region).[30] Moreover, the districts through which they regularly passed, or where they stopped for relatively longer periods, did not have a higher proportion of crime than other districts with which they had little contact.[31] Incidentally, when there were genuine crimes committed in areas where they stopped, it was admitted by the police themselves that it was the handiwork of local elements, who got more active whenever an itinerant community was around—these elements were merely using an existing view of itinerants to their advantage, knowing that the crime would be blamed on the itinerants.

However, the second part of this accusation—their becoming criminals because they lost their means of livelihood—is more important. Part of this assertion was true: the Koravas *had* lost their chief means of livelihood over a period of time. As mentioned earlier, they used to be salt and grain traders, taking salt from the coastal areas of the Presidency into inland areas where wheel traffic could not reach, and bartering it for grain or forest produce. The loss of means of livelihood was correctly attributed to a network of roads and railways, which had made their trading activities redundant.[32]

What seems to have escaped the attention of the authorities was that Koravaș were not exclusively salt and grain traders. Salt was a very important source of revenue for the British administration in the nineteenth century, and the Koravas were at one time the only means of distributing it in remote areas, where only 'pack bullocks' could reach.[33] This is the reason why the British administration *officially* recognised their salt trading activities. Similarly, they helped in averting famines in far-flung areas, and that is why their grain trade was acknowledged.

At different times of the year, Koravas were cattle breeders and traders, dealers in all kinds of forest and agricultural produce, and casual workers. In addition they made baskets, mats, brooms and brushes, and were also acrobats, dancers, singers and fortune-tellers. It is precisely for this reason—that they had many other resources to fall back on—that despite being drastically marginalised as a result of British policies, they probably did not become criminals, and certainly not as a community. In the Tamil speaking region, where they were called Koravars, they continued to be called Inji, Kal or Dabbai Koravars, depending on the work they still did.[34]

IV

Once the CTA, 1911 had been instituted, the Salvation Army was put in almost exclusive charge of Indian itinerant communities notified under the CTA, while the police was entrusted with the sedentary criminals. The itinerant communities were to be reclaimed by being confined to special settlements. Interestingly, in England too, missions had played an important role from the mid-nineteenth century towards reclamation of gypsies.[35]

The Salvation Army identified itself aggressively with the imperial aims and projects of England of the time. Born in the 1870s, the heyday of British imperialism, it not only called itself the Salvation *Army*, it cashed on the popular image of romanticised imperialism by adopting marches, flags, brass bands and uniforms for its employees. Their head was called *General* Booth, they had *officers* who signed *articles of war*, and their newspaper was called *The War Cry*. They had open-air *bombardments*, not meetings. They would not say that they were going to start work in a new region, but *occupy a new territory*, and *declare war* (on ungodliness or whatever).[36] In short, the Salvation Army was a shadow imperial body, and self-consciously so.

Two other important aspects regarding the Salvation Army are explored in Chapter 3. Firstly, its founder Bramwell Booth, even in contemporary opinion, was deemed to be more a businessman than a missionary. 'He is before everything else a superb man of business, far-seeing, practical, hardheaded... Instead of a text over his mantelpiece, one might expect to find the commercial legend, "Business is Business" ...I am perfectly confident that [at the Salvation Army Headquarters] the pleasure experienced at the sight of all those ninety and nine cheques from wealthy subscribers has its rise in the knowledge that money is power.'[37] Clearly, the Salvation Army had wide financial support from the elite of the society (a state of affairs which continues to this day all over the world).[38]

There is no doubt about the high credentials of the Salvation Army vis-a-vis the government as far as their work with supposedly criminal communities was concerned. The prestige of the Salvation Army with the government was such that by 1913, the Viceroy, in recognition of his services, had already awarded one of its most influential officers, Booth Tucker, with a 'Kaiser-I-Hind.'[39] There is also the additional factor of Salvation Army's powerful position in early twentieth century social life in England, quite apart from the ideological affinity that it felt with the British Indian administration.

The Salvation Army had been working with released prisoners in India a few years before the CTA was instituted, and the government took this organisation very seriously. It played a significant role in shaping not just criminal legislation, but also public perceptions of criminality of the groups with whom it worked. What constituted 'crime' and 'immorality' for them was the inverse of what Victorian (and some times Brahmanical) values conceded. In fact, they were able, over a period of time, and with some authority, to define for administrations all over the world what constituted criminality, and in different social contexts, even pointed out who these criminals were - paupers in England, tribals or nomads in India, aborigines in Australia or New Zealand, native Americans in North America and so on. They also offered solutions for such problematic sections.

The Salvation Army officials had evolved categories of criminals like incorrigible, habitual, hereditary, ordinary, worst character, would-be-good, won't-be-good, *badmash*, *nekmash* and so on in a metaphorical 'crimdom', and differential treatment was suggested for varying degrees of Indian criminality to transform criminals in another idealised 'curedom'. The treatment, to be meted out according to ailment, had to be punitive, deterrent, preventive or curative—the experiment was aptly called 'crimnocurology'.[40]

There were unmistakable parallels between the schemes visualised in William Booth's *Darkest England* for 'the starving, the criminals, the lunatics, the paupers, the homeless, the drunkards and the harlots' and those actually run later by the British Indian government for the CT members. There is, in fact, evidence that the Salvation Army had influenced the British Indian administration regarding policy on CT settlements, as described in Chapter 3. This would be logical as the Salvation Army had a robust commercial interest in the criminal tribe settlements, and through the provisions of the Criminal Tribes Act, managed to legally control the products churned out by the 'damaged labour' under their charge.

The notion of Indian criminality as reversible (as opposed to a fixed, hereditary trait) had at least one immediate advantage: a programme of reformation could be immediately set afoot not just through moral upliftment with the help of missionaries, but through *wage* work. In the meantime, the CTA itself could be posed as a social reform measure in public proclamations. Not only would a new man or woman be made out of an erstwhile criminal, but society would also be rid of the pestilential and predatory activities of a criminal section, and the 'rising' generation would join the mainstream of society as law-abiding citizens, either as peasants or wageworkers in private enterprises.

Interestingly, the people in question themselves began to

believe that they had become *nekmashes* (as opposed to *badmashes*) as a result of this intervention. A possibility of this is glimpsed in a song that the women of a criminal tribe settlement were reported to be singing, soon after it was estalished in north India. The Salvation Army claimed that the song had been composed by the settlers themselves:

We are nekmashes upto date,
    see our certificates, sir!
We work sewing machines, we make cloth,
    we prepare warps of various kinds.
We grow silkworms, we produce cocoons of silk,
    we make bricks, we make tiles.
We cultivate fields of Fazalpur,
    we build halls, we build houses,
    we make carpets of the best kinds...'[41]

The point to emphasise here is that the category of a criminal tribe was not a sudden development. Different strands of social and political opinions and considerations had been shaping the category of 'Indian criminal' for several decades. The complexity of these converging currents has not been explored in this book. A criminal could, for instance, be any one who resisted the British, or even resisted a local oppressive landlord or high caste member. In addition, the plethora of new legislation that the British introduced created new criminals all the time. These were either people ignorant of the new laws, or those wilfully defiant of the ones which encroached on their traditional rights—for instance, the new forest laws. To give an example of the broadness and flexibility of the term 'criminal', and the open ended uses to which the Criminal Tribes Act could be put, it was suggested that the Act could be used profitably 'for combating secret societies, political preachers who might create unrest and so on' to combat the newly emerging nationalist movement.[42]

V

Essentially, the itinerant communities fitted into the category of undesirables of Indian society quite naturally, but this phenomenon needs more study.[43] The subaltern school has implicitly changed the very definition of crime by challenging the British notion of criminality which saw each episode of resistance, protest or action on the part of the subaltern groups of Indian society as crime. Some work has been done on the general notion of criminality of Indian 'lower orders' as perceived by the British administrators. The most notable contribution here is of Anand Yang who brings together a number of essays relating to Indian crime and criminality.[44] David Arnold also deals, in several articles and books, in both direct and indirect ways, with the concept of Indian criminality in British India while dealing with famine crime or the Madras police.[45] In one of the earliest seminal studies, Stuart Blackburn had pointed out that the Kallars acquired a certain image with the Madras administration because they resisted attempts by the British to annex Kallar dominated areas. It has subsequently been confirmed that the division of the Indian population into pliable and resistant groups became the epistemological basis of the classification as criminal of whole groups by the British.[46]

Sandria Freitag has argued that the CTA itself was a result of 'certain leaps of legal logic' provided by the thuggee precedent. She has also suggested that the British imperial regime established a legal system that dealt simultaneously but differently with individuals and with groups. Sanjay Nigam, in an important study, has also discussed the deliberate parallels drawn by the British between thugs and the so-called criminal tribes as a rationale for institution of the CTA in 1871. According to him, enactment of the CTA was the logical development of a number of coercive measures already in operation for the control of supposedly criminal communities.[47] On the whole, the literature on the British perception of law, authority and collective crime relating to this period is quite rich, though rather sparse.

In this book, an attempt is made to link issues of colonial law with those of colonial ethnography, in the backdrop of social and political imperatives on the ground. Chapter 1 looks into the historical compulsions behind the category of criminal tribes. It deals with the origins of the CTA, 1871 in the northern provinces, and explains the reasons why it was not applied to Madras Presidency till 1911. The subjective as well as objective reasons for the declaration of Koravas as a criminal tribe in 1911 are discussed in some detail.

Chapter 2 discusses the notification and surveillance policy under the CTA. It describes the procedures adopted by the administration for identifying criminal groups, which were kept flexible and open-ended, so that a large number of non-criminals qualified for registration under the Act. A part of the chapter discusses the political imperatives implicit in making headmen the agency for the surveillance of a large number of criminal tribe members. The chapter also traces reasons for a shift in emphasis for conduct of surveillance procedures from the headmen to the police in the 1920s.

Chapter 3 concentrates on the administrative policy of forming reformatory settlements for criminal tribe members. In this chapter, the origins of the concept of criminal tribe settlements are described and it is shown that the concept was incorporated into the CTA as a result of the influence of the Salvation Army. This chapter sets out the official rationale for forming criminal tribe settlements, and handing them over to the missionaries. Salvation Army as an organisation, with its own particular ideology, is discussed in some detail.

In Chapter 4, the concept behind the agricultural and the industrial settlements is discussed. This chapter shows how in the context of failure of agricultural settlements, the Madras administration decided to follow the example of Bombay Presidency, and settled large numbers of criminal tribe members in the vicinity of private enterprises in need of a regular workforce.

In Chapter 5, the main features of a criminal tribe settlement called Stuartpuram are discussed where a section of the Korava community lives and has lived for decades. This chapter discusses the processes by which the Yerukulas from the Telugu speaking regions were first sedentarised under the Criminal Tribes Act, then made to work on land owned by the Salvation Army, and finally turned into regular wage workers in a tobacco factory. It describes the way social and cultural aspects of Yerukulas' community life were transformed in the Stuartpuram settlement under the supervision of the Salvation Army. This seems to have been an inevitable result of the logic of work on land, or in a factory. The general point to be emphasised, however, is the complexity of the process of turning an itinerant community into regular wage workers and the pain involved in this forced transformation. The chequered career that this section of workers followed, and their special vulnerability as criminal tribe workers—which, quite amazingly, they sometimes managed to turn into strengths—is the focus of Chapter 5.

The above chapter also studies the making of a working class out of the 'thievish raw material' that the itinerant community of Yerukulas was supposed to be. The Yerukulas became highly class conscious workers in a short span of twenty five years, precisely as a result of some of the processes set into motion jointly by the Salvation Army and the ILTD factory management—something quite unforeseen by both. The process itself, however, was a warped one due to the medium through which it was achieved, viz. the Criminal Tribes Act. The processes of changing from an itinerant community to a forcedly settled one; from being considered useful members of society to being declared predators and criminals; and then transition from agricultural workers to industrial workers was a severely traumatic one for the community in question. The social and cultural resources gathered over generations were wiped out with the violence of change that each of these stages implied, in terms of a system of relationships and other social balances which sustain community life.

Within this context, Chapter 6 discusses the 'historic memory' of the Yerukulas, and their perception of their ancestors as dangerous criminals, reformed by the wage work provided by the Salvation Army and the administration. The frequent, coerced interventions in their lived community life seem to have led to irreparable breaches again and again, resulting in blanking out of the collective memory of the community's past. The memory of the past in the current generation's mind is a version that was introduced by the Salvation Army, and blots out the resistance that the community actually offered to each of the phases of sedentarisation, break up of the community, work on land, and finally wage work. Interestingly and ironically, it is from the records of the factories, the Salvation Army and the British administration that a more unmediated version has had to be retrieved; the oral culture of the community as of today represents the 'official' version and is devoid of the nuances, complexity and richness of the lived past.

Notes

1. W.W. Hunter, *England's Work in India,* London, 1881, p. 2.
2. Clive Emsley, *Crime and Society in England 1750-1800,* London & New York, 1987; Anand A Yang (ed.) *Crime and Criminality in British India,* Arizona, 1985; David Jones, *Crime, Protest, Community and Police in Nineteenth Century Britain,* London, 1982.
3. Martin J. Wiener, *Reconstructing the Criminal: Culture, lAw, and Policy in England, 1830-1914,* CUP, Cambridge, 1990, p. 15.
4. Nancy Stepan, *Idea of Race in Science: Great Britain, 1800-1960,* Oxford, 1982.
5. Stewart N. Gordan, 'Bhils and the Idea of a Criminal Tribe in Nineteenth Century India' in Yang 1985: 137.
6. Stepan 1982: 123.
7. Henry Mayhew and John Binny, *The Criminal Prisons of London and Scenes of Prison Life,* Griffin, Bohn and Company, London, 1862, p. 384 quoted in Wiener 1990: 24.
8. This trend of thinking in England was possibly a reaction to some of those very causes, which had made eugenics so attractive: poverty and urban distress. At any rate, this distress strengthened the resolve of some like J.A. Hobson and L.T. Hobhouse to reject biological determinism, and believe in an evolution of society which allowed scope for 'moral choice of social action'. Ibid. p.145.
9. This essentially meant that the CT members, as government policy, were to be parcelled out to owners of mills, factories, mines, quarries as workers, as also to plantation owners. Meena Radhakrishna, 'The

Criminal Tribes Act in Madras Presidency: Implications for Itinerant Communities', *The Indian Economic and Social History Review,* 26, 3 (1989).

10. Radhakrishna 1989: 271-75.
11. For an account of their trading activities, see Meena Radhakrishna (1989).
12. Government of Madras, *A Memorandum on the Madras Famine of 1866*, Madras, 1867, Appdx, viii; Government of India, *Report of the Indian Famine Commission*, 1878, Parts I, II and III, Vol. I, p. 49. Also see Sabyasachi Bhattacharya, 'Laissez Faire in India', *Indian Economic and Social History Review,* Vol. II, No. 1, January 1965 and S. Ambirajan 'Political Economy and Indian Famines', *South Asian Studies*, No. 1, August 1971.
13. Government of Madras, *Administration Report of the Forest Department (Southern and Northern Circles)*, Madras Presidency for 1889-90, Madras, p. 27. Revenue for grazing went up from Rs. 40,138 in 1883-84 to Rs. 1,43,845 in 1889-90, Government of Madras, *Report of the Forest Committee*, Madras, 1912, Vol. II, pp. 7, 32.
14. A detailed analysis of the *Report of the Salt Commission 1876* makes this fact clear.
15. For a detailed discussion of some of the currents which went into the making of the discipline of Anthropology, see Meena Radhakrishna, 'Colonialism, Evolutionism and Anthropology—A Critique of the History of Ideas 1850-1930', Research in Progress Papers, *History and Society*, Nehru Memorial Museum and Library, New Delhi, June, 1997.
16. For an excellent account of gypsies in England, see David Mayall, *Gypsy Travellers in Nineteenth Century*, Cambridge, 1988.
17. The following paragraph draws largely from Mayall (1988).
18. The local people must find the nomads quite useful for the unusual wares they bring periodically. Their various skills of weaving mats or making baskets or playing musical instruments, and more dramatically in the case of acrobats and dancers make them a colourful and interesting presence, in all probability providing relief and diversion from the tedium of daily routine.
19. I am grateful to David Washbrook for bringing to my notice the point about taxing.
20. Mayall 1988: 180.
21. Mayall 1988: 87.

22. It has been pointed out that the 'gypsies' exotic potential' is frequently exploited by writers in general. See Okley 1983:7, *The Traveller-Gypsies*, Cambridge University Press, Cambridge, 1983, p. 7.
23. Banjaras were a community much more in evidence all over India, unlike the Yerukulas who operated only in the limited Telugu regions of Madras Presidency. In fact, Banjaras were called the 'exporters' of grain and salt to distant provinces and regions by the Madras administration, and Yerukulas were termed 'local' traders. Essentially, Banjaras were a numerically larger community, operating on a much bigger scale, traversing a greater geographic area. For the same reason, they escaped the Criminal Tribes Act for a longer period compared to the Yerukulas, being relatively less vulnerable. Yet even they were declared a criminal tribe by the British administration.
24. Judl. 239, 24.9.1918; In fact this is now a well-recognised fact by researchers on nomads in general. There is reference to the traditional trade routes of the Gaduliya Lohars, also a criminal tribe, which depended on a host of factors. Satya Pal Ruhela, *The Children of Indian Nomads*, New Delhi, 1984, p. 57; 'it-rah' of another nomadic community is also mentioned in Frederik Barth, *Nomads of South Persia—the Basseri Tribe of Khamesh Confederacy*, Oslo, 1961.
25. F. Booth Tucker, *Criminocurology or the Indian Crim and What to Do with Him—A Report of the Work of the Salvation Army among the Criminal Tribes, Habituals and Released Prisoners in India*, London, n.d. p. 43.
26. A. Aiyyappan, *Report on the Socio-economic Conditions of the Aboriginal Tribes of the Province of Madras*, 1948, p. 47
27. See Radhakrishna 1989: 271-75
28. Government of Madras, *Note showing the Progress made in the Settlement of Criminal Tribes in the Madras Presidency upto January, 1925*, Madras, 1926, p. 63 (Hereafter *Note, 1925*).
29. Ibid.
30. Ibid.
31. Judl. GO 1071, Back nos. 51-53, dt. 10.8.1870. IGP to Chief Secretary to Government, Fort St. George, Madras, 19.5.1870, No. 3016.
32. For a detailed discussion of the process by which the Yerukulas lost

their varied means of livelihood, because of a set of colonial economic policies, see Radhakrishna (1989).

33. Ibid.
34. PWL GO 225L, 26.2.1929.
35. Mayall 1988: 129.
36. Gerald Parsons, *Religion in Victorian Britain, Vol. I (Traditions), Vol. II (Controversies)*, Manchester and New York, vol. I (1988), p. 22. The close association of missions with colonialism has been explored at length in Jean Comaroff and John Comaroff, *Of Revelation and Revolution: Christianity, Colonialism and Consciousness in South Africa*, Vol. I, Chicago and London, 1991.
37. A Gentleman with a duster (author), *Painted Windows: A Study in Religious Personality*, London, 1922, pp. 149-151.
38. As recently as September, 1998, the McDonald fast food chain heiress Joan Kroc has donated a staggering $80 million to the Salvation Army. *Japan Times*, 25.9.1998. I am grateful to Jai Sen for a clipping of this news item.
39. Solveig Smith, *By Love Compelled*, London, p.111.
40. F Booth Tucker, *Criminocurology*, p. 43.
41. English translation in Salvation Army, *The War Cry*, November, 1918, Vol. XXIV, No. 1.
42. Home (Judl.) 2764, 23.11.1916.
43. The work on contemporary Indian 'gypsies' has tended to concentrate largely on their poor socio-economic situation. D.P. Singhal, *Gypsies: Indians in Exile*, Folklore Institute, Meerut, 1982; V. Raghaviah, *Nomads*, Secunderabad, 1968; Chaman Lal, *Gypsies, Forgotten Children of India*, 1962; Satya Pal Ruhela, *The Children of Indian Nomads*, New Delhi, 1984.
44. Yang 1985. See essays by Anand Yang, Stewart Gordan and Edith S. Brandstadter that explore the concept of criminal tribe.
45. David Arnold, 'Bureaucratic Recruitment and Subordination in Colonial India: The Madras Constabulary, 1859-1947' in Ranajit Guha (ed.) *Subaltern Studies IV: Writings on South Asian History and Society*, Delhi, 1985; *Police Power and Colonial Rule, Madras 1859-1947*, Delhi, 1986; *Famine: Social Crisis and Historical Change*, Basil Blackwell, 1988.
46. Stuart H. Blackburn, 'The Kallars: A Tamil "Criminal Tribe" Reconsidered'. *Journal of South Asian Studies*, March, 1978; Shail Mayaram, 'Criminality or Community? Alternative Constructions

of the Mev Narrative of Darya Khan', *Contributions to Indian Sociology* (n.s.), 25, 1 (1991), p. 59.

47. Sandria B. Freitag, 'Crime in the Social Order of Colonial North India', *Modern Asian Studies*, 25, 2 (1991), p. 244 and 'Sansiahs and the State: The Changing Nature of "Crime" and "Justice" in Nineteenth Century British India', unpublished SOAS/Nehru Library conference paper, March 1994, Introduction; Sanjay Nigam, 'Disciplining and Policing the "Criminal by Birth",' Part I, *The Indian Economic and Social History Review*, 27,2, (1990).

CHAPTER 1

The Criminal Tribes Act: Historical Developments

The 'Wandering Tribes' of Madras Presidency were declared Criminal Tribes in 1913 under the Criminal Tribes Act (CTA) 1911. Yerukulas, Koravars, Korachas, Lambadis and Brinjaries who fell into this category were primarily grain and salt traders. For decades, they had been carrying salt from coastal districts to inland districts and bartering it for grain or forest produce.

The CTA which came into force throughout the Presidency in 1911, had replaced an earlier Act of 1871 which was restricted in its application and extended only to certain provinces in Northern India. The new Act of 1911, which applied to the whole of India, drew substantially from the earlier Act with some important modifications. This chapter traces the history of the CTA in Madras Presidency with special reference to the Korava community. It discusses the factors which led to its institution, the provisions of the Act, and the reasons for declaring the Koravas as a Criminal Tribe.

I

One of the first attempts to formally declare some communities criminal came from the Punjab and the North West Provinces (NWP), where the itinerant communities—'wandering tribes' —were beginning to be deemed criminal by the middle of the nineteenth century. In these two provinces, the police administration had been confining sections of these communities to specific areas and limiting their movements. This system had been in force for decades with 'very good results' from the point of view of the police. However, in the 1860s the Chief Court held this procedure to be illegal. The provincial governments of the Punjab and the NWP now approached the Government of India for appropriate legislation on this subject, seeking legislative enactment which would make registration of all itinerant communities compulsory, and breach of this rule a penal offence. It was in this context that the Government of India approached the local governments, including the Madras administration, to determine whether a special legislative enactment to control itinerant sections of society was necessary.[1]

During the proceedings of the Council to consider the bill on the subject, discontinuing of the initiatives taken by the police administration since the ruling of the Chief Court was regretted, and the objections raised by the Court to the draft bill were discussed and rejected. The Council consisted, among others, of the chief officers of the Punjab province which had an extremely important and influential set of administrators.

One of the main objections was that the proposed law would lead to oppression by the police. To this, the view expressed was that 'when it came to the question whether the criminals were to be annoyed by the police, or the police annoyed by the criminals, (the government) would prefer the first...' The second objection raised by the Courts was that ordinary law was sufficient to deal with these communities. To this the retort was that 'to suppose that ordinary processes of law would ever put down crime was like supposing that sportsmen would exterminate game.'[2]

In fact, at the time of consideration of the Criminal Tribes Bill it was recognised within the Council itself that itinerant communities were exceedingly useful members of society in some provinces, and it was debated whether it was wise to include them in the purview of the proposed bill. Depending on the views of the local governments on the subject, the bill was applied selectively to three provinces. And thus the Criminal

Tribes Act, 1871 was instituted by the government of India, and came into force in the NWP, the Punjab and Oudh. The Act originated from the fact that the Courts declined to accord legality to some of the practices of the police administration. This led to authorising by law of the very same practices.

In essence, the 1871 Act gave the police considerable power over a large number of people. Under this sweeping piece of legislation, individuals from communities declared criminal were to register themselves and their families with the police. They were not to leave the village without obtaining a temporary licence from the police which was valid only within the limits of the district. They were to notify change of residential village to the police, and the licence was to be shown to all police stations on the way to another village. Any member of a Criminal Tribe (CT) community found absent from the village without a licence a second time was to be punished with rigorous imprisonment upto three years. Zamindars were made responsible for the correctness of registration of the CT members and also for the whereabouts of the registered members.[3] An important provision of the Act was that the administration could not proclaim a community criminal and register it, unless its members were first settled and provided with a means of livelihood by the government. These settlements, visualised on the lines of those established by the Thuggee Department in the 1820s in the north, were expected to be very successful.

There were a number of reasons why the Criminal Tribes Act of 1871 was unacceptable to the Madras administration. Firstly, the Madras Inspector General of Police denied at that time that there was a problem of any magnitude regarding criminal sections in his province. He was firmly opposed to the declaration of itinerant communities as criminal tribes as he doubted whether these communities were seriously criminal. He presented statistics, showing that dacoities in those districts of the Presidency, with which the trading communities had regular contact, were much fewer than in one single district with which they had no contact at all.[4] The Madras Police Administration declined to be party to the draft bill submitted by the Inspector General of Police, NWP, regarding criminal tribes.[5]

Several other objections were clubbed together to challenge the need for exceptional legislative restriction upon the movements of itinerant trading communities in the Presidency. These included, firstly, the impossibility of operationalising the proposed law honestly and efficiently with a low paid police force; it was pointed out that oppression and misuse of powers by the police would follow. Secondly, the formation of government rehabilitation settlements, a statutory requirement in case of restriction of a particular group's movements, was not seen to be practicable, as the 'gypsy' carriers were expected to resist 'settling down to the plough and the sickle'. In addition, the imposition of the proposed law in British territory, it was felt, would tend to drive these communities into the princely states and thus defeat the purpose of the legislation.[6]

The underlying reason, however, was the fact that the Madras administration recognised the usefulness of the trading communities. They were practically the only means of trade within the interior, given the conditions of the roads at that time.[7] No cart traffic was possible, and these groups who used bullocks and donkeys kept up considerable trading intercourse between inland districts and the coast. Of direct interest to the Government was the fact that they formed a channel for distributing salt, an important basis for revenue. In the interior districts they were willing to sell the salt at a price much lower than any ordinary merchant would.[8] These communities were, in fact, so important for this reason that they were given special protection by the administration in many cases.[9] So, when the question of confining these groups to restricted areas on the pattern of the North West Provinces came up, considerable foresight was shown in turning down the proposal. The extent to which there was official recognition of the salt trading role of these communities is evident in many government records and reports relating to salt revenue, discussed later.

In 1876 the Act was extended to certain parts of Bengal and in 1897 it was amended to enlarge the powers of the local government to notify communities and take action against a part of the 'gang' or community. Enhanced penalties for repetition of offences and breaches of rules were also added. The desirability of applying the provisions of a Criminal Tribes Act in Madras Presidency was considered again by the government at the end of the nineteenth century, but the conclusion drawn was that it was better to wait for the recommendations of the Police Commission on the subject.[10]

Thus itinerant communities in Madras escaped the provisions of the law that the North West Provinces had proposed. The relief lasted for 40 years, though individuals from these communities continued to be suspect. However, from the time the Indian government approached the Madras administration in the 1860s, these communities came to be described as 'wandering tribes', in the manner of those in the North West Provinces, with all the derogatory implications of the term.

II

Colonial economic policies during the nineteenth century destroyed the occupations of a number of communities. Specific policies of the administration severely affected itinerant communities involved in petty trading. The salt policy of the government, dictated by considerations of revenue, was instrumental in destroying the trade of Koravars, Yerukulas and Korachas, and even of Brinjaries and Lambadis who operated on a much larger scale across provinces.

The Korava community had been dealing in salt much before the East India Company assumed government functions in Northern Sircars, i.e. Vishakhapatnam, Ganjam, Krishna and Godavari. There are a number of references in nineteenth century documents relating to revenue from salt, and to the Korava community's traditional role as salt traders in these parts. The community is also described as traders in salt in the discussion on history of revenue collection under the Nawabs of the Carnatic and other rulers of Southern India.[11]

Though the Korava community shared trade with Brinjaries

and Lambadis, the areas of operation of these communities were almost entirely different. The latter communities were engaged in wholesale 'export' trade to other provinces.[12] On the other hand, in villages of the inland districts which were off the line of the high roads, the Koravas were acknowledged to be the chief means of distributing salt throughout the interior.[13]

It is possible to understand the Korava community's gradual loss of livelihood over a period of time only in the context of British colonial revenue policy. Changes in this policy affected the community in a direct manner, and these changes will be briefly described to show that by the last quarter of the nineteenth century, the community's salt trade had been destroyed to a large measure.

Before the assumption of office by the East India Company in the Northern Sircars, salt was produced and sold privately. From 1805 onwards, however, the government introduced a system under which traditional manufacturers were to sell salt exclusively to the government (at a low price fixed by the government), which was then resold at a higher price to petty salt traders like the Koravas. The Korava community had to now buy salt from the government stores for barter in the inland areas.

It is clear that revenue sought to be raised from salt was very substantial.[14] This policy was a great setback to the trading practices of the Korava community. Apart from the fact that they did not have the resources to buy salt from the government at such high prices in any but small quantities, the consumption of salt by the average peasant family fell drastically as a result of such high prices.[15] As the price of salt increased phenomenally, it rose even further in the interior, and the Korava community lost a steady stream of consumers.[16] It is interesting to note that the administration had been warned of the loss of livelihood by the Korava community when the monopoly price was going to be introduced for the first time.[17] These warnings, given essentially to safeguard an important channel of salt distribution, were ignored.

The most important reason responsible for the destruction of salt trade practised by the Korava community, however, was the introduction of the railways in the 1850s. By 1859, distribution of salt on the railways all over the Presidency was being carried on quite efficiently.[18] Opening of the railways, in addition, had given rise to a new section of wholesale 'railway traders'. To encourage them, several concessions were given by the government.[19] This process led to the inevitable concentration of the entire salt trade in the Presidency in the hands of a few large trading companies.[20] Prices of salt shot up as a result. The Korava community suffered because first, they had now to buy salt from the trading companies at a price they demanded, and second, because the railways were distributing salt upto a number of points in the Presidency.[21] The Koravas' area of operation was now only from these points upto a few interior villages, as opposed to the earlier route of coastal areas to the vast countryside. The only reason why the Korava community survived as traders was because of the fact that in the 1870s, there were still areas, both coastal and inland, which were not covered by railways and roads. The Korava community was now operating only in those areas where wheel traffic was not yet possible, or where the barter economy still persisted, and hence only to people of 'insignificant outlying villages'.[22]

The last and final blow to the salt trade of the community was dealt by a new government policy recommended by the Madras Salt Commission in 1876, called the excise system of manufacture. Private large scale trade by rail was to be supplemented with large scale private manufacture of salt. Large companies were now going to manufacture salt, and sell it through a new set of intermediaries 'whose sole object ... was to earn an undue profit for themselves'.[23] The monopolist manufacturer was in a position not only to create scarcity by reducing production; the new intermediary could demand his own price from traders like the Koravas.[24]

Thus as far as salt was concerned, the new systems and policies introduced over the nineteenth century culminated in trade mechanisms in which the Korava community had no place. The extent of destruction of traditional salt trading practises depended to some degree on the scale of operation as well. Koravars, Korachas and Yerukulas, predictably, were the first to be affected, as they operated on a smaller scale compared to the Brinjaries and Lambadis.

In addition to the salt policy, there were other factors which hastened the ousting of the Korava community as salt and grain traders. At the time of an expanding network of railways and roads, the 1876 famine led to loss of large numbers of heads of cattle owned by the Koravas, and the community was less able than ever to continue its trading practices; the cattle through whom the merchandise was transported were of critical importance. The forest policy prevented free grazing of the cattle owned by these groups and prevented them from collecting forest produce which they used to barter for salt.[25] Famines, managed under a policy of laissez faire, allowed grain merchants to hoard grain and sell at prices which could not be afforded by the majority of people.[26] Traders like Koravas who used grain as an important item of barter suffered a great setback.

It was undoubtedly the British administration's economic policies which were responsible for putting a decisive end to the trading practises of the Koravas.

III

There is no doubt that the official perception of these communities was changing as a result of the fact that they had lost their traditional means of livelihood. They had outgrown their usefulness as salt and grain carriers with the spread of a network of roads and railways. Around the last quarter of the nineteenth century, the increasing rate of unexplained and uncontrolled 'crime against property' in the countryside induced the administration to adopt the concept of the hereditary criminal.

It came to be asserted that the caste system, prevalent in India, explained the existence of hereditary criminals. Just as a family of carpenters would continue their trade for centuries, so would these special kind of criminals. Such a criminal is one 'from the beginning and will be so to the end, ...reform is impossible for it is his trade, his caste...almost his religion to commit crime'.[27] The trading communities who were for a brief period classified as 'wandering tribes' were now put into this new category, which was a precursor to their being formally classified later as criminal tribes.

The view of sections of Indian society as hereditary criminals allowed the British administration for a period to pin the problem down as one intrinsic to Indian society, and beyond their control. A significant change in official thinking came in the first decade of the twentieth century. There was a search for a more 'scientific' explanation of crime in India, and this time it was asserted that it was the loss of means of livelihood by large numbers of people during the nineteenth century which had led them to adopt the lives of criminals. Historical accounts to this effect, showing the famine of 1866 to be a turning point for many communities, were compiled by police officers. The new forest policy, competitive trade and spread of railways were also identified by the administration as having led to the loss of means of livelihood of some of them. These historical facts were used as evidence of the adoption of crime by *entire* communities and to make out a convincing case for their declaration as criminal tribes.[28]

While this was an advance on the earlier administrative view of some communities being hereditary criminals, in that external and not genetic or hereditary factors were considered the cause of criminal tendencies, as far as policy was concerned, this had disastrous consequences. In 1913, apart from the trading nomadic communities, a number of communities like Dasaris, Vaganur Parayas, Paidis, Rellis, Yenadis and many others were identified a having lost their legitimate means of livelihood during the nineteenth century and thus qualified as 'criminal tribes'. Brinjaries and Lambadis, still in possession of their trading activity, and still considered useful as exporters, were spared in the first list of notifications in 1913.

At the subjective level, there is an explanation for the association drawn by the administration between certain sections of society, and crime. British, and high caste Hindu police officers, held in contempt the life style of nomads and low caste communities. Unable to comprehend or sympathise with a way of life so far removed from their own, they regarded these communities as strange. Their 'peculiar' social practices, their consumption of alcohol and 'inferior' types of food, their so-called laziness and unwillingness to work were as influential in branding them criminal tribes, as any record of proven criminal activity. References were made to the 'immoral women' of these communities: the section on the Yerukulas in the Census of 1871 described the members of this community as 'somewhat loose in their sexual relationships'. Later accounts by police officers, too, spoke of their dirty habits, and slack moral code. An itinerant way of life, necessitated by earlier trading activities came to be described as vagrancy, or a lust for wandering.[29]

There was also a view amongst the British that the criminal tribes looked different from ordinary human beings. One author, as late as 1928, took it upon himself to assure his English readers that the physique of the criminal castes, when fed properly, differed very little from that of the other castes in South India. 'They do not have that flattened head with ears low down and long, which suggests a criminal.'[30]

The problem essentially seemed to be that many of these communities were not studied when they had legitimate means of livelihood. After all, sociological accounts of 'tribals', however colonial the undertones, were not uncommon in the late nineteenth and early twentieth centuries.[31] But many of these communities were 'studied' for the first time, purely from a law and order point of view, and these accounts emphasised their supposed criminal propensities rather than giving a comprehensive view of them as people.

A historical explanation of the phenomenon of the Criminal Tribes Act thus lies not only in the generalised fact of a number of communities losing their livelihood, and beginning to be considered criminal, but equally in the social prejudices of persons in authority towards them.

IV

According to the government's own account, the Criminal Tribes Act (CTA) 1911 had its origin in the report of the Indian Police Commission, 1902-1903.[32] The Commission laid down that the Indian police system should try and obtain knowledge about, and supervise control of a variety of criminals. Starting from this principle, the Commission declared that the police should have more powers to control the criminal tribes, and with that in view, recommended certain amendments to the CTA of 1871, then in force in certain parts of British India. The Government of India repealed the 1871 Act and substituted in its place the new CTA 1911 which put this recommendation into effect.

The new Act was more comprehensive than the old one. The primary task of the new Act, which was introduced after the 1909 political reforms, was to enlarge the powers of control of local governments. The new CTA, therefore, enabled them to declare any tribe, section or class of the people to be a criminal tribe; to order the registration of the criminal tribe members and the taking of their finger prints; to direct that such registered members should report themselves at fixed intervals to a police officer of the village; report to the police officer or the headman any changes of residence, and to restrict the movements of criminal tribe members to a particular area.[33]

A provision of the Act denied members of the CT normal rights under the common law; another specifically took away the jurisdiction of the courts to question the validity of notifications issued under the most crucial sections of the CTA by the Government. The registration of an individual or a community could no longer be questioned under this section, nor could their restriction of movements. It was not for any offence committed that all these punitive measures were employed, but only for 'preventive action' which was the professed purpose, albeit unofficially, of the Criminal Tribes Act. This could be done even though a CT member had no previous convictions, had never gone to prison, or even paid a fine. This was because all that was required for notification of a community as a CT was 'reason to believe' that the community was addicted to crime.

Another important feature of the Act was that local governments were authorised to establish industrial, agricultural or reformatory schools and settlements for the CT members. Under this scheme, employment was to be given to the CT members either on government agricultural land, or in a private enterprise. The members were not allowed to go out without a pass, which was issued at the discretion of the manager of the settlement.[34]

In substance, the Act enabled any local government to declare any section of the people which it had 'reason to believe to be addicted to the systematic commission of non-bailable offences' to be a criminal tribe (Section 3). After such a declaration (which could not be questioned in any court of law) had been made, the individual or group in question was outside the pale of ordinary law. If members of the group so notified did not appear for registration, or resisted it in any way, they could be imprisoned and fined (Section 21). The local government, albeit with the sanction of the Government of India, could not only restrict the movements of the CT members to any specified area, (Section 12) but also subject them to 'discipline', should they try to escape from such a settlement (Section 22). Hours of work in a settlement, rate of payment, disposal of surplus produce, all were to be decided by rules made by the local governments (Sections 20 and 22).

Thus under the terms 'settlements' and 'settled' were concealed the most unlimited powers.[35] Under the provisions of the Act the government could deport any number of persons any distance from the homes, could employ them in any form of labour, hire them out to employers, punish them with fine and imprisonment if they refused to work, bring them back if they attempted to escape, and subject them to additional disciplinary measures. These measures were not limited to persons against whom a conviction had been registered, or even to those who had no ostensible means of livelihood or who could not give a satisfactory account of themselves. They applied to all members of the group concerned—men, women and children.

Moreover, whereas a convict to be sent to jail had some limit to his sentence, and some hope of final release, a member of a criminal tribe under the CTA had almost none. Once he or she was 'settled', it could be for life. They could not go back to their villages or hope to escape from the work the government had considered it fit to get them.

The harsh provisions of the CTA would appear to be due to the fact that the bill regarding the CTs went through the Imperial legislative council practically without a debate. The Indian non-official members seemed completely indifferent to the fate of this section of the Indian population. It is interesting, however, that even as early as the 1910s the government had tried to include in the CTA provisions for 'combating secret societies (and) political preachers who might create unrest', and it was *this* provision of the Act that G.K. Gokhale successfully resisted, being politically active himself. Otherwise, 'nobody cared a pin' as to what was done with the CTs and the Bill was passed undiscussed and unopposed.[36]

Because of a debate about the provisions of the CTA within the administration, it was resolved that CT members would be settled only in 'extreme cases'. However, a crucial recommendation in spite of this debate was that this particular provision of the CTA should be applied 'to the worst characters and especially wandering tribes'.[37] Thus while the harshness of the CTA was recognised, it was still recommended that one of its most oppressive provisions should be applied, by definition, to the 'wandering' or itinerant communities. In this way, while a number of other communities escaped this provision of the CTA, according to policy the wandering tribes were now seen to be synonymous with the worst characters.

Notes

1. A draft bill submitted by the Inspector General of Police of NWP to the Government of India was also forwarded to the local governments for their consideration and views, before it was discussed in the Council. Government of India, *Abstract of the*

Proceedings of the Governor General of India in Council Assembled for the purpose of making laws and regulations (hereafter *Abstract*), vol. IX, 3.10.1870; Judl GO 1071 (Back Nos. 51-53), 10.8.1870. For a detailed discussion of the origins of the CTA, 1871 in north India, see Nigam (1990).

2. *Abstract*, vol IX, 3.10.1870.
3. Judl. GO 1071 (Back Nos. 51-53), 10.8.1870.
4. Kurnool 'considerably overrun by Lumbadi, Koravar and Yerukula gangs' and Nellore, virtually the home of the Yerukulas, and also visited by other wandering groups had a record of a total of 166 dacoities between the years 1864 to 1869. For the same period, in South Arcot, where all the dacoities were claimed to be the work of local offenders, the dacoities numbered 318. Judl. GO 1071 (Back No. 52), 10.8.1870. IGP's communication to Chief Secretary, Government of Madras.
5. Judl. GO 1071 (Back Nos. 51-53), 10.8.1870. Incidentally, only a few years earlier, in 1863, the first provincial IGP had successfully resisted the attempts of another police official from the North to extend the operations of the Central Thuggee and Dacoity Department to the Madras Presidency. He had argued that no special features like those in the north existed in Madras and the situation called for no special measures—that crime in the countryside could be contained by ordinary executive and judicial procedures. (Arnold 1979: 150).
6. Judl. GO 1071, (Back No. 52), 10.8.1870. IGP's letter to Chief Secretary to Government.
7. It has been recorded that at the beginning of the century, there was an almost complete absence of any roads in the Madras Presidency. As late as the 1850s, the roads were such that carts could move only in dry weather, and even then, only with light loads at a very slow pace and in very short stages. In the monsoon months, the roads were useless except for cattle or foot passengers. D.R. Gadgil, *The Industrial Evolution of India in Recent Times 1860- 1939*, Delhi, 1971, p. 4
8. Judl. 1071 (Back NO. 52), 10.8.1870. Letter by IG of Police to Chief Secretary to Government, Madras. A collector gave a reason for this low price of salt: the Koravars' means of transport cost them little as they bred their own cattle which subsisted 'chiefly if not wholly by the right of commonage'. Trichinopoly District Records,

Vol. No. 3653, p. 165-170. Collector of Tanjore to Board of Revenue (Hereafter B/R) 16.6.1813.

9. Madura District Records, Vol. No. 4680, pp. 326-330. Collector of Madura to B/R 18.11.1832; Advances were given to Brinjaries to the tune of Rs. 5,000 to enable them to sell salt at Hyderabad. Masulipatnam District Records, year 1813, Vol. No. 3079, pp. 338; Masulipatnam District Records, year 1800, Vol. No. 3075, pp. 612–15.
10. Judl. 725, 20.5.1903.
11. Government of Madras, *Nellore Manual,* Vol II, 1868, p. 489; 'The Brinjaries and Korchas, carriers of salt, were also said to be encouraged by Tippoo Sultan of Mysore and Nizam Ali Khan, Subhadar of the Dekkan.' Minute of Falconer addressed to Board of Revenue (B/R) dated 28.6.1804 in Government of India, *Report of the Commissioner appointed to enquire into and report upon the manufacture and sale and tax upon salt in British India, 1856,* (Hereafter *Report, 1856*).
12. 'Memorandum on the Supply of Salt for Presidency of Madras', prepared by B/R 17.6.1854; Correspondence between B/R and Collectors of Vishakhapatnam, Rajamundry, Ganjam, Masulipatnam, and Guntur. *Report, 1856:* 107, 222, 226, 208, 228, 237.
13. Settlement Report of the Fusli 1211 (1801) quoted in *Nellore Manual,* 1868, Vol II: 488; Jeyaraj 1984: 38; Collector of Tanjore to B/R, 16.6.1813, Trichinopoly District Records, Vol.3653: 165-170; Collectors of Nellore, Chinglepet, Madura and Madras to B/R, *Report, 1856*: 245, 253, 273, 298. Some of the exporters, however, occasionally acted as retailers within the Presidency. This was necessitated by the exporter's need for fodder for their cattle which they bartered for salt while passing through the village.
14. The crucial aspect of this policy was that while the actual manufacturing price was Rs. 3 or Rs. 4 per garce (and the price paid by the government to the manufacturer never exceeded Rs.10 per garce), salt was sold to the Korava all through the monopoly period for a price of Rs. 70 to Rs.120 per garce. (One garce equals 1265 pounds.)
15. It was revealed in 1856 that taking consumption of an average household at the then prevailing price of salt, it required one month's earnings to meet its requirement. of salt per annum. This happened not just in Madras, but all over British India, including other salt producing areas. In an estimate presented to the 1856 Salt

Commission, it was stated that an ordinary Bengali labourer with an average-sized family spent one sixth of the family's yearly earnings on the single article of salt. Conclusion of *Report 1856.*

16. *Report, 1856*: 99,109. In the interior, where the Korava community supplied salt, the price rose in proportion to the distance from the coast due to the cost of transit. For every mile, one rupee was added to the monopoly price. *Ibid.*: 108.
17. Collector of Trichinolopy to B/R 10.8.1803, Trichinopoly District Records, Vol. 3662; Collector, Tanjore to B/R 13.6.1805, Tanjore District Records, Vol. 3216.
18. Government of Madras, *Report of the Madras Salt Commission, 1876* (Hereafter *MSC, 1876),* p. 33.
19. *Report, 1856*: 77. Credit upto 6 months was given to those who opened accounts with the government for sums exceeding Rs. 5000. *MSC, 1876*: 37. The largeness of the sum shows the capacity of the new traders, and the scale of their operations.
20. *MSC, 1876*: 246.
21. As the Madras Salt Commission pointed out, 'no portion of Madras Presidency is more than 100 miles from the coast or from a railway station, and salt works or sale depots (of private companies) exist on the average of 18½ miles on the east coast. The communications are good, and being improved yearly'. By the 1870s, there were 17,186 miles of roads and 1269 miles of railways, besides many miles of water communication in the Presidency. *MSC, 1876*: 37,175. This was as opposed to 3,110 miles of roads in 1846 (Gadgil 1971: 4).
22. Collector of Salem, Collector of Tanjore. *MSC, 1876*: Appendix A.
23. *Report, 1856*: 355-56; Government of Madras, *Report of the Administration of the Department of Salt Revenue in the Madras Presidency and Orissa, Madras, 1894-95*, p. 6.
24. As pointed out, under the earlier system, there was little opportunity for extractions. The price at the government stores was fixed and known to all. The monopolist manufacturer, on the other hand, was likely to state his own price for possibly an inferior quality of salt. Collector of Guntur to B/R, *Report, 1856*: 339,356. This system was introduced in 1882 in a few districts and by 1887, 87 per cent of the salt consumed in the Presidency was manufactured under the new system. *Moral and Material Report 1886-87*, p. 73 quoted in *Monograph on Common Salt*, FICCI, Calcutta, 1930, p. 103.

25. Government of Madras, *Administration Report of the Forest Department* (Southern and Northern circles), Madras Presidency for 1889-90, Madras, p. 27. Revenue for grazing went up from Rs.40,138 in 1883-84 to Rs. 1,43,845 in 1889-90; Government of Madras, *Report of the Forest Committee*, Madras, 1912, Vol. II, p. 7 and p. 32.
26. Government of Madras, *A Memorandum on the Madras Famine of 1866*, Madras, 1867, Appdx viii, Government of India, *Report of the Indian Famine Commission, 1878*, Parts, I, II and III, Vol, I, p. 49. Also see, Sabyasachi Bhattacharya, 'Laissez Faire in India', *Indian Economic and Social History Review*, Vol. II, No. 1, January, 1965; S. Ambirajan, 'Laissez Faire in Madras', *Indian Economic and Social History Review*, Vol II, No. 3 July, 1966; S. Ambirajan, 'Political Economy and Indian Famines', *South Asian Studies*, No. 1, August 1971.
27. Quoted in V. Raghaviah, *The Problem of Criminal Tribes*, p. 6, See also Sanjay Nigam, 'Disciplining and Policing the "Criminals by Birth", Part I: The Making of a Colonial Stereotype—the Criminal Tribes and Castes of North India', *Indian Economic and Social History Review*. Vol. XXVII, No. 2, 1990.
28. Government of Madras, *Note showing the progress made in the settlement of Criminal Tribes in the Madras Presidency upto September, 1916*, (Hereafter *Note, 1916*), Madras, 1917.
29. David Arnold, 'Dacoity and Rural Crime in Madras, 1860-1940', *The Journal of Peasant Studies*, Vol. 6, No. 2, January, 1979, p. 153; George Macmunn, *The Underworld of India*, n.d.; M. Paupa Rao Naidu, *The Criminal Tribes of India*, No. II, Madras, 1905, p. 2; Mohammad Abdul Ghani, *Notes on the Criminal Tribes*, Provincial Police Training School, Vellore, 1915; W.J. Hatch, *The Land Pirates of India*, London, 1928, p. 21; According to David Arnold, the publication of Edgar Thurston's seven volume *Castes and Tribes of Southern India* in 1909 only served to give 'scholarly gloss' to official thinking. (Arnold 1979:150)
30. Hatch 1928: 30.
31. E.T. Dalton, *Tribal History of Eastern India*, Calcutta, 1872; C. Boden Kloss, *In the Andaman and Nicobars*, London, 1903; P.R.T. Gordon, *The Khasis*, 1907 (Reprinted Delhi, 1973).
32. Home (Judl) GO 523, 5.3.1917.
33. The Criminal Tribes Act, 1911. Government of India, *A Collection of the Acts passed by the Governor General of India in Council in the*

Year 1911, Calcutta, 1912. In its actual operation, it was always the socially vulnerable low caste communities who were its victims. There is no known instance of the CTA being applied to higher caste communities.

34. Home (Judl) GO 523, 5.3.1917.
35. Home (Judl) GO 2764, 23.11.1916, see IG of Prisons, A.G. Cardew in notes to the above.
36. *Ibid.*
37. Judl. GO 2764, 23.11.1916, see A.G. Cardew's comments.

CHAPTER 2

Notification and Surveillance

The CTA, 1871 did not allow communities to be notified and registered by the government unless they were first settled, and provided with a means of livelihood. This clause was later considered to be unnecessary, and the 1911 Act did away with it. Thus, a strict check on the number of notifications was now removed, and action under the CTA could be taken much more freely. Sections of the Korava community were declared CTs soon after the institution of the CTA, 1911.

Essentially, the administration had to identify the allegedly criminal community, notify it as a CT and instruct the police station or the headman of the village they lived in to make sure that proper surveillance was being carried out. For identifying the criminal community which needed such surveillance, it was necessary to show that there was sufficient 'reason to believe' that the community was a criminal one—that it was addicted to systematic commission of non-bailable offences. Registration of members of the CT was then to be done by a first class magistrate, if not by the concerned District Magistrate himself.

There were a number of intervening factors which made the actual working of the entire process an instrument of oppression for thousands of individuals. This chapter shows how this apparently simple procedure was used by vested interests—the landlords-cum-headmen and the junior police administration. It describes the ways in which the Act actually operated, and traces the reasons for the shift in the surveillance policy of the government.

I

One of the methods followed by the administration to confirm the alleged criminality of a group for initial notification was dependence on accounts by the so-called respectable people of a village. These invariably comprised of high caste headmen and landlords. By the time the Criminal Tribes Act came in force, the powers of the landlord had been increased due to the recommendations of the Indian Police Commission.[1] As the headman combined in his duties simultaneous functions of a village magistrate, police officer and revenue head, the headman system in Madras Presidency was considered by the Commission to be in a 'more efficient state' than in other parts of the country. The Commission felt that especially in Madras, the powers of the headman could safely be enlarged as far as disposing of petty criminal cases was concerned.

At the time of the Commission's enquiry, it was found that without help of the village headmen the regular police could accomplish little. Most of the reports of crime at police stations were received from village headmen in their capacity as village magistrates. The village headmen in Madras were found to relieve the general administrative machinery of the work of deciding petty disputes, both of a civil and criminal nature, to a far greater extent than in any other part of India. The Commission felt that the fact that the revenue officers all over India were also responsible for the discharge of village police duties was 'most satisfactory', as they were invariably men of influence and position.

In other words, considerable powers lay in the hands of the village headmen at the turn of the century, as far as police and judicial functions were concerned. The headman also happened to be the revenue officer. In spite of these quite substantial powers, the government decided that the position and influence of the headman should be strengthened, and the regular police be directed to look to the headmen for cooperation in their work.[2] The village headman was to be regarded as cooperating with, and not subordinate to the regular police.

The CTA required the system of surveillance of criminal tribe members to be extremely rigorous. As three CT settlements were situated in Guntur district, the surveillance procedure here was amongst the strictest in the Presidency. It was operationalised by directly linking the provisions of the CTA with the expanded powers of the headman.

Rules regarding surveillance under the CTA stipulated that a CT member could not leave the village either temporarily or permanently, unless he had first obtained a certificate from the headman. On arrival in another village, he was to present himself to the headman there, and show the certificate to prove his credentials. Failure to do so would qualify as another offence under the Act. The concerned individual could also be accused of having absconded in order to commit crime. The unlimited power in the hands of the headmen can thus be easily imagined, especially in the case of migrant communities who constantly needed to move from one village to another in order to practice what remained of their trade. They were required to notify their change of residence and report to headmen (or to the police) of each village through which they passed.[3]

It is important to emphasise here that not only were the headmen made responsible for surveillance of those notified under the new CTA, but were allowed to play a part in recommending initial notifications of CT members as well. It was generally in the interests of the landlords to have itinerant communities notified if they themselves were to be made responsible for the surveillance part. The registered members could then form a sedentary and pliable workforce in their fields, always held in check with the threat of prosecution on false charges of various kinds like failure to report at a particular time. Directing the registered CT members to report at fixed, short intervals at a specified place could very effectively restrict the movement of CT communities out of the village.[4] The shortness of the gap between any two rounds of reporting would ensure that the concerned individual could not leave a particular territory for more than a few hours. The headman, almost always a landlord, could in this way benefit by having in close proximity a number of CT members who were dependent on his patronage for finding work. Hence vouching for the criminality of the concerned group by landlord sections could be motivated by self-interest.

It came to be specifically alleged that a convenient method of getting agricultural workers by the landlords was to get the Act applied to socially vulnerable communities. 'If a landlord wants the services of agricultural labour, all that he has to do is to create some sort of disturbance and...to bring these people [Koravas] under the Criminal Tribes Act.' Several witnesses confirmed before a Madras Government Committee of Enquiry that free forced labour was extracted by the village headman from the registered members of criminal tribes who were stated to be always at his mercy.[5]

In addition, the Criminal Tribes Act could be used as an instrument of caste oppression. 'Suppose a Korava...refuses to comply with any desire of a high caste man of a village, a false charge is put up against him and with the connivance of the police, the unfortunate man is convicted for a month or so and therein he is brought under the Criminal Tribes Act.'[6]

Migrant communities like Koravars were also amongst those hired by feuding landlords like Kapus and Gounders to murder their rivals.[7] Declaring these communities as criminal would have certainly strengthened the hands of such landlords when these communities were defiant. Once these communities were declared criminal, the murders committed at the behest of these landlords would never be traced to the landlords.

The subordinate police also had a direct role in having more and more communities declared criminal. False charges were put up against groups with the connivance of the police, the accused were convicted for a month or so, and then brought under the Criminal Tribes Act.[8] This was because the low paid, subordinate police administration was well aware of the potential opportunities for extortion from the registered members in the course of surveillance. Apart from having actually to report at odd hours of the night (ostensibly to ensure that these communities did not commit a crime during the night), the CT members could never prove that they had actually reported to the police station. The attendance taken by the police at eleven in the night and three in the morning, might or might not result in it being recorded.[9]

These aspects of the working of the CTA assume further significance when it is recollected that as a result of the recommendations of the Indian Police Commission, both the regular and village police were under instructions from the headmen by the time the CTA came into effect in Madras Presidency. This led to a strengthening of the nexus between the subordinate police and the headman, leading to many more opportunities for oppression of the CT members under their charge.

II

As far as identification of the communities to be notified was concerned, it was simple in the case of settled communities; it could be done by naming the community living in a particular village. As far as the itinerant communities were concerned, this was obviously not possible.[10] This allowed the administration to justify the arbitrary criteria used to identify alleged criminal 'wandering tribes'.

The criteria that the administration came to apply to the communities to be notified were 1) blood relationship of individuals with those CT members who had convictions in their names and 2) blood relationships with those already notified. This led to innumerable cases of Korava communities being declared CTs. Since a large part of the community was still itinerant, they had many opportunities for forming kinship relations over a large geographical area.

Administratively speaking, the merit of instituting these criteria was that once one notification was done, it could be an automatic basis for a number of fresh notifications. A scrutiny of notifications under the CTA reveals that there were two categories evolved by the administration for this purpose. One identified a particular group by its relatively fixed camping place, and another by the group's current profession.

The category constituted according to camping place allowed ample scope for flexibility as far as itinerant communities were concerned. These communities were constantly moving from one part of the Presidency to another for large parts of the year. They would camp in a particular place, stay for some time, and move on in pursuit of their trade in coastal salt and other items. The camping period would naturally be affected by weather conditions—they could not sell salt at times of rain; the time of the year—the grain harvest was of crucial importance as they often bartered salt for grain; availability of casual work—they could work temporarily as agricultural workers, and also by other factors like availability of date-palm leaves and bamboo in a particular area, for the itinerant communities were invariably basket and mat makers. Difficulties posed by the terrain may have been another factor (the community used only asses and bullocks for transporting their merchandise), for sales were done primarily in the interior villages where trade through wheel traffic would not compete.

It is important here to point out that the 'wandering' or trading nomadic communities could not have been aimless, but the administration did not care to find out the logistics of their movements. They always had definite trade routes, depending on the demand for their wares and on the cycle of annual festivals and fairs. Their movements also depended on the salt manufacturing cycle, the most important item of their trade. Their routes and schedules of stopping and moving were thus fixed and cyclic.

At any rate, this category yielded administrative groupings like Salem Melurnad Koravas, Nawabpeta Korachas or Gandarvakottai Koravars. The flexibility of this category lay in the fact that any group of Koravas could be said to belong to a particular administrative grouping by merely asserting so. For a community that was itinerant, such assertions could not be questioned, especially if the group in question had ever been sighted, let alone camped in the place.[11] Applying it across districts stretched the flexibility of this category further.[12]

The true situation of itinerancy of these groups defied a single regional identification like 'Salem Melurnad Koravars' or 'Togamalai Koravars', as they camped in, or passed through a number of districts.

Professions practised by the Koravas defined the second category for the purpose of notifications chosen by the administration. Under this came communities like 'Uppu Koravas' (salt sellers), 'Dabbai Korachas' (makers of bamboo products), 'Inji Koravars' (ginger sellers), 'Kal Koravars' (stone breakers) and so on. The scope of this category could also be widened almost without limit by the fact that at any given point in time the itinerant communities could not rely on one single profession as the sole means of livelihood. 'Uppu Koravars', for instance, would be selling a variety of other items at different times of the year in a variety of places in the Presidency.

Such notifications thus allowed every Koravar, who at any point in time was engaged in these professions to be potentially notifiable.[13]

The most important point to be noted here is that the two categories—camping place and profession—could be made to interlock and serve each other by the overall criteria of blood relationship between any particular group and those already notified under the CTA. Hence, endlessly open in themselves, stretching across districts, the groupings under one category could be used to implicate in crime, grouping under another.[14] Further, blood relationship between any two groupings did not need to be proven; it merely had to be asserted to set off a chain of notifications.[15] There were cases where the criteria for blood relationship allowed the administration to use one notification not just across villages and districts, but different linguistic regions as well.[16]

III

Having framed the broad guideline for notifications, the administration still had the task of officially justifying them. After the identification of the groups to be notified, there remained the problem of proving the criminality of the members in order to bring them under surveillance. The process was in great part facilitated by considering the concerned group's blood relationship with convicted/notified members as evidence of their own criminality. In addition, there were several rules of thumb on which the British administration came to rely, as far as proving the criminality of a group under the CTA was concerned.

The fact of the 'wandering nature' of the community in itself could be considered to be proof of its criminality. Hence, while making out a case for the dangerousness of a community it would be emphasised that they 'do not lead a settled life' or that 'they always move from place to place for the ostensible purpose of their trade'.[17] The so-called Kal, Inji and Dabbai Koravars of Trichy were notified because not only were they related to a notified group, but because 'they wander from village to village and change their names'.[18] When the Yerukula community was being discussed within the administration prior to its notification, it was noted that Yerukulas had always been itinerant and hence were bound to be criminal. '...[All] the wandering gangs or tribes of Madras Presidency ... are criminal because they cannot make a living honestly.'[19]

Though, indeed, many members of notified communities were without regular work in the early decades of the twentieth century, this was only partly because of their losing their earlier means of subsistence. Much before the formal notification, a view of these communities as dangerous criminals was publicised by the administration with such success that it had another consequence: when members of these communities went to find work, they could not do so because new prejudices against them compounded the old. Declaring them Criminal Tribes officially only worsened the situation as far as finding work was concerned as they were feared and mistrusted by people, and 'haunted and hunted' by the police wherever they set up home. Villagers objected to their congregating together, and it was impossible for a member of a criminal tribe to make a living if other members of his community were already notified in the same village.[20]

At any rate, itinerant Yerukulas, ones who did not have settled work, could now be called Donga (thieving) Yerukulas. With this definition of a criminal, it was logical that a very large number of Yerukulas fell in the category of Donga Yerukulas. The definition, however, was to create an acute problem for the administration later.[21]

The nature of administrative criteria for assessing the criminality of a group can be judged by the fact that having implied that all wandering communities were criminal, the administration would also use the fact of their being settled as definite proof of their criminal propensities. The fact that the 'gang...had a permanent habitation...very much aggravates their criminality and should therefore be taken into account. It affords an additional justification to apply... CTA to them.'[22]

Another proof of criminality was held to be the actual number of convictions in the names of the individuals to be notified. Convictions which were considered were not just those under the Criminal Procedure Code, but those under security sections of the Indian Penal Code as well. About the security sections of the IPC, under which a Koravar or a Yerukula was so often charged, a district magistrate had this to say: 'Doubtless the [Koravars] are rogues and vagabonds; spasmodically the police put them under the security sections [as] there is never the slightest difficulty in showing that a Koravar has no ostensible means of livelihood and is presumably a robber. The order to furnish security is tantamount to a sentence of imprisonment; how can a Koravar furnish security? He goes to jail, wanders for a year or two till he meets a Sub Inspector anxious to show his zeal in working the security sections. Then he returns to jail.'[23] Thus the administration knew that convictions were easily acquired by certain communities under security sections, because of their indigent position, and were in no way proof of criminal tendencies.

The convictions in the name of a person could also be used even if they were decades old. Koravars who were notified and later sent to work in the Parrys' factory were deemed to have had a criminal record even though the convictions against their names dated back to 31 years. The concerned police officers after excavating such convictions urged the government that 'the rather old convictions should not be neglected in dealing with these people [as] Koravars are far worse criminals than appears from their mere recorded convictions'.[24]

The police, in fact, on many more occasions relied on the mere assertion that the Koravar was a more formidable criminal than was evident from the records, and effectively absolved themselves of producing concrete evidence of an individual's criminality. Groups of Koravars of North Arcot and Coimbatore were registered because they were suspected in cases of housebreaking, though the police could not produce evidence. Of another community of Koravars in Salem it was said that their 'criminality cannot be judged by convictions alone ... they are a dangerous sect always addicted to crime'. Sometimes, it would be cryptically stated that convictions would have been more numerous but for the kinds of crimes the Koravars committed. When convincing evidence was lacking, it would be claimed that evidence was insufficient as people did not report cases, and rhetoric instead of hard evidence was provided to prove the criminality of a tribe: 'The Korava is by training and tradition a criminal. According to his traditions, his God Subramanya being asked what trade the tribe should follow handed over a housebreaking implement!' This community was recommended by the District Superintendent of Police, Salem to be notified under the Act. Of a section of the Koravars in Salem it was asserted that 'they are thieves by tradition and inherent tendency' and application of the CTA was recommended as a matter of course. Of a group of Parayas it was similarly observed that 'the fact that the missions have failed to reclaim them shows their character, and there must be some means of keeping them in check'. The CTA was suggested as the remedy.[25]

Often, as evidence of the criminality of individuals, examples would be cited of their behaviour which stemmed from the traditional social practices of the community. Prevalence of the custom of brideprice led the administration to allege that these communities bought female children who were then married off to the boys. The administration often referred to the women of the community as 'so-called wives' and the system of polygamous relationships among men and women led to the charge of prostitution.[26] These instances of supposed criminal behaviour would be cited in all seriousness while making out cases for the criminality of a community.

Sometimes, the police administration would notify a group because of alleged insolence on the part of the concerned group. One police officer, while making out a case for the criminality of Koravars already vouched for by 'respectable' inhabitants, added that the criminality of this group could be proved by the fact that the members had adopted a system of ranking among themselves, clearly as a parody of the police administration. He was piqued by the fact that one was called inspector, another sub-inspector and so on. 'This alone shows what class of persons they are', he complained.[27]

These notifications had a particular legal sanctity because Section 3 of the CTA itself only required 'reason to believe', on the part of the local governments, that the community in question was criminal; the administration chose to ignore the second half of the requirement, viz., the notifiable community's *addiction* to *systematic* commission of *non-bailable* offences. Anyone who had a vested interest in notifying a particular group, and had influence with the authorities could now employ the CTA. Indiscriminate and wholesale application of the CTA was officially admitted in later years.[28]

One of the reasons for indiscriminate working of the CTA was also that the bulk of the registrations was done by the inspectors of police in spite of instructions from the government that these be done by first class magistrates, if not by the district magistrate himself. Even after the work was assigned to the sub-divisional magistrates, they registered each recommended case without questioning. The problem was exacerbated by the fact that administratively speaking, the middle level police were under pressure to produce results under the newly instituted CTA. It was confided to the government that '...there was departmental "boom" in the gang business at this time and each inspector vied with his fellow in sending in lists of *les miserables* to be added to the Superintendent's register'. Thus indiscriminate registrations of vulnerable communities were officially conceded. While recognising the injustice of the registrations, however, it was felt that 'it was no use crying over spilt milk' and cancellation of such registrations was actively resisted.[29]

It was, essentially, the confidence that the administration had in the landlord sections which was the key to the operation of the Act in the first decade after its institution. In a typical case, nine highly respectable inhabitants—landlords of the neighbouring villages—had confirmed the criminality of a group of settled Yerukulas: the respectability of the said inhabitants was provable by the fact that they were paying a substantial tax to administration.[30] In another representative case, a superintendent of police had asserted that he could personally vouch for the stories told to him by the respectable inhabitants of the concerned area. The gist of the stories was that the Koravars, who lived in two separate villages, were closely related by blood or marriage, and that they were clearly forming 'one organisation' for the purpose of crime. The interest that the respectable inhabitants—landlords of the area—had in such notifications was ignored by the administration.[31]

IV

After a decade or so of the operation of the CTA, the surveillance policy of the government was beginning to shift from dependence on the headmen to direct reliance on the police. Emphasis on the role of the police from the mid 1920s onwards seems to have been a result of the compulsions of the political developments in Madras Presidency. As the freedom movement escalated, the landlord sections began to be less reliable as allies.

In the 1920s, village officers had begun to organise to protest against government's plans to reduce their powers and village officer associations 'mushroomed'. During the non-cooperation movement, village officers had given in their resignations in large numbers, especially in Andhra districts. More worrying for the government was the fact that collection of land revenue during the movement became increasingly difficult because of the campaign for non-payment of taxes. It was found that for this most important operation, viz., collection of land revenue, police had to be deployed in some districts.[32]

The police, then, had played a very useful role for the administration in 1921-22. Its morale, however, had been seriously undermined during the period because of intensified demonstrations of hostility by the public. The government recognised this, and officially recognised the 'splendid loyalty' of the police. In the meanwhile, serious reappraisal of the role of the police was taking place within the administration during this period.[33]

In 1920, in accordance with the Government of India Act, 1919, the CTA had been amended so as to substantially delegate authority to local governments. This meant that the permission of the Governor General in Council was no longer required as far as the operations of crucial provisions of the CTA were concerned.[34] This strengthened the hands of the Madras administration in critical decisions regarding CTs. The powers that the local government now had allowed them to make the required changes in the surveillance policy. These changes were made in favour of giving more powers to the police administration in the 1920s. The wisdom of such a move was borne out later during the civil disobedience movement, when the headmen-cum-landlords were more firmly with the Congress. Also, '...the political imperatives of 1930-34 [had] forced from the government a new recognition of the importance of the police in preserving colonial rule in India.'[35]

The delegation of more powers to the police administration was, however, resisted within the administration. The police was, in fact, seen to be directly responsible for a serious administrative problem at that time which arose because of the way the Act was actually being operated: the number of people covered under the

Act was enormous. It was alleged within the administration that regarding Sections 3 and 10, there had been 'inadequate knowledge and enquiry by the police department which necessarily finds it much simpler to make proposals for wholesale registration for restrictions to an area for compulsory reporting... the police department offer passive resistance to any attempt at discrimination. The result is we have too many roped in, too few let out...' The IGP, it was claimed by the administration, continuously submitted proposals for bringing various communities under the CTA, which were accepted as a matter of course. As a result, it seemed that the administration would have 'a very perplexing administrative problem in connection with the CT Act before long'.[36]

The enthusiasm of the police was alleged to be such that lists of CT members for application of the CTA frequently contained the names of members physically incapable of committing crimes. It was also pointed out that the tendency of the secretariat so far had been to accept proposals by the Inspector General of Police without any scrutiny, and that if the Act was not worked discreetly it would, as already alleged by the public, become an instrument of oppression.[37] The administration had also become aware of the fact that the powers given to the headmen had led to a situation where its uses had attracted public notice. From the administrative point of view, the recommendations by the headmen for notifications surely should not have led to 'passive resistance to any attempt at discrimination', and some discretion by the police should have been exercised.

The policy of allowing the headmen to continue to wield power over a large number of CT members in any case would be a misguided one as they were clearly shifting their political allegiance. As far as the CTA was concerned, some rethinking about the role of the headmen as well as the police was required.

New rules under the CTA were devised in 1925. The Advocate General now declared illegal those rules which had hitherto allowed headmen to restrict the movements of a CT community by forcing its members to report at short, fixed intervals. Interestingly enough, this erosion in the authority of the headmen was resented by none other than the IGP himself who requested that the old practice continue both for settled and itinerant communities. He suggested that active criminals should be made to report more than once a week. The government permitted this.[38] This, however, was a dilution of the earlier authority of the headman. The IGP also requested that the government allow and encourage village magistrates (the headmen) to act as checking officers for the better working of the CTA. This was ignored.[39]

While shifting the surveillance powers to the police seemed to be the objective of the administration, in initial phases it was considered judicious to do so in a graduated way. The first step was to set into motion a process by which the police administration was made as responsible for surveillance of notified members as the landlords who were no longer the primary means of surveillance.

According to the new rules, a sub-inspector could inspect the residence of any member of a CT, and a (headman or) police officer could 'pay domiciliary visits' within their jurisdiction to registered members.[40] This sort of surveillance, incidentally, extended to the family members of the registered members. 'Sons were asked to account for their fathers' sins by being brought under the CT Act if their fathers had been subject to its provisions.[41] The women of the community were brought under surveillance if their husbands and fathers were registered members. This was done in the case of women who had absolutely no association with criminals, let alone a history of convictions.[42] While headmen still needed to be informed by CT members who changed their residence temporarily or permanently, the more crucial reporting of movements by CT members had now to be done at the police station or outpost. Only if such station or outpost did not exit was the headman to receive such reports.[43]

Simultaneously, as a way of giving patronage to favoured landlords (as opposed to the whole section), the administration instructed individual landlords to employ CT members as an 'ameliorative measure'.[44] This facility was not as institutionalised as it used to be under the CTA, and could be distributed with discretion by the district magistrate, depending on the political behaviour of the headman in question. The government, again to benefit an individual landlord, also instituted the 'patron system'. Under this, local influential individuals were to give employment to CT members and keep an eye on their conduct. They were, in fact, to act as probation officers of sorts and were to decide whether the concerned CT members were required to continue to report or not. This system gave a lot of power to such patrons. However, this system was not pursued with any determination by the administration and was claimed to be unsuccessful as 'supply of suitable patrons was totally inadequate'.[45] Essentially, this was a half-hearted attempt by the administration to win over the political support of the landlords, and the shortage of patrons was a result of shift in the political alliances of the landlord sections. Of necessity, the administration was forced to increasingly depend on the police for operation of the CTA.

Enhanced powers to the police led to widespread complaints of oppression. Apart from being given the authority to check the residences of the CT members, the notified people could be called to the police station even at midnight. A large number of CT members were required to report to the police at least once a day, frequently more often. Distance of reporting centres was deliberately made so long, that a CT member could be made to walk 14 miles a day in order to record his attendance. This meant that if he had to report more than once a day, he could not go home between the intervals at all. Sometimes, it was alleged, they had to walk many miles in the night to appear at the police station and wait there till daybreak.[46] This resulted in the community becoming more vulnerable to extortion by the police, apart from having to spend long hours at the police station in pitiful conditions.[47] Complaints against police oppression were more marked in the case of women members of the community, who became victims of sexual abuse by the police, as well.[48]

By the late 1930s, however, the political compulsions were such that the shift from landlord to police for surveillance of CT communities was complete. Now the most widely prevalent system was the 'system of abeyance'. The official rationale for instituting this system was the inability of the police force to keep a proper track of the large number of CT members. The system worked by holding a threat of prolonged period of reporting over the less tractable CT members. Newly registered members were given a dose of the rigours of reporting to teach them what to expect if they were 'difficult'. CT members who had already served a sentence in jail were also made to undergo a reporting period, after which their cases came up for review. At some point, under this system, the government was to exempt from the operation of the Act those CT members who gave evidence of good conduct. This system was to be supervised by the sub-inspectors of police, district superintendents of police and the district magistrates. A relatively subordinate police officer—the station house master—was put in day to day operation of this system; the role of the headman was conspicuous by its absence.[49]

V

It was found in 1938 that the shift of surveillance of CT members from landlords to the police had led to some 'unfortunate' results. The police officials at several rungs of the department had enormous powers at their disposal to inflict severe punishments on CT members without trial. It was admitted within the administration that those who were registered under the Act were now 'very much at the mercy of subordinate police officers.'[50] In fact, the excesses of the police were responsible for a fresh round of protests against the CTA.

There were a number of organised protests by the CT communities, against provisions of the CT Act and particularly against police oppression. The earliest recorded one as far as the itinerant communities were concerned was in 1927. Koravars of Madras city held two mass public meetings and they represented to the government that because of hardships the CTA inflicted on them, (and since they had a record of long and honest service in the Madras corporation) they should be exempted from the CTA. This issue went as far as the British House of Commons where two questions were asked on treatment of the community at the hands of the police. The House of Commons, however, decided to believe the Madras Government's version that there was 'misrepresentation engineered by others', and therefore no action was necessary in the matter.[51]

In the 1930s, there were three instances of protests from the Togamalai Koravars of Trichy district against the operation of the Act with special reference to women of the community. The women petitioners themselves wrote to the government describing the way the Act operated. These three petitions give a graphic account of the vulnerability of the communities who were notified. The general effect of the CTA seemed to be to make CT communities 'dance to the whims, fancies and dictates of the police'.[52]

Women CT members, like the men, had to present themselves at the police station at 11 pm and again at 3 am, which forced them to sleep at the police station itself. This put them in a vulnerable situation vis-a-vis the police. Of the 42 women who signed one of the petitions to the government, 34 were under the age of 35, some as young as 10-14 years old. Hence the younger women of the CT communities were the most severely affected by the requirement of reporting to the police or headmen. The women who petitioned were not exempted from the operations of the CTA by the concerned district magistrate, in whose hands lay the authority to do so. He ruled that since women 'harbour offenders and help them to evade arrest...', it was necessary to register them. Hence immense possibilities of police molestation of women CT members existed because women members were not exempted from reporting at fixed intervals. A provision *was* made in the revised rules of the CTA in 1926 to exempt women from reporting, but the final draft which was accepted after consideration by officials omitted this crucial provision.[53]

It was further alleged by the petitioners that as CT men and women had to go to their workplaces miles away from home and were often detained there by the employers, this fact was used by the police as grounds for entering their names in the CT register. The police were also accused of instigating employers to dismiss the CT members, or refuse employment to them on account of their supposed criminality. Amongst other charges was the fact that it was a herculean task, as the petition put it, to get passes. If reporting between 3-4 a.m. could not be done, due to some legitimate reason (like heavy rain), six months of imprisonment followed. There were a number of cases of registration on false charges of drunken brawling by CT members. As the petitioners reasonably asked: if this was the way the CTA was to be administered, how could reformation (the original and ostensible purpose of the Act) be achieved 'even in dreams'.[54] According to the rules, it was also pointed out, the names of CT men and women should be removed from the CT register if there was no offence by the concerned person for three years. In actual practice the names, once entered, were there for life.[55]

The petition, inspired by the nationalists, especially Gandhi, demanded exemption of women, young boys and old people from the CTA. It demanded educational facilities and land, and to emphasise the justness of the demands, quoted the public statements of the Minister for Prisons and Courts regarding reclamation of the CT members. The response of the District Magistrate while rejecting the petitions was that the police administration had got 47 of the 111 petitioners employment in Trichy mills in a nearby village—the implication was that this act showed that the police had the good of the CT members at heart and so no allegations against them could be taken seriously by the administration.[56]

Another instance of organised protest by the Korava community against the operation of the CTA came from Koravars of the Coimbatore district. This initially came in the form of the community forming itself into an organisation called Vedarkula Sangam, registered in 1931. This was done to disassociate the Sangam members from the rest of the community of Koravars. The Sangam later took up the cause, albeit unsuccessfully, of its members when they were threatened with registration under the CTA.[57]

Protests of this sort, though ineffective as far as the immediate outcome was concerned, did add to the general atmosphere of outrage against the CTA. This especially applied to wide sections of the nationalists, who influenced public articulation of such protests in the first place.

Notes

1. Christopher Baker, 'Madras Headmen' in, K.N. Chaudhary and Clive Dewey (eds.) *Economy and Society: Essays in Indian Economic and Social History*, Delhi, 1979, p. 35; Government of India, *Report of the Indian Police Commission, 1902-03*, paras 34- 51. This influence and position of the headmen was further strengthened by the Commission by recommending that headmen could be punished only under the orders of the District Officers or of 'carefully selected subdivisional magistrates'.
2. As early as 1816, the village police had been placed under village headmen who were invested with powers in certain criminal cases. The provisions of these regulations were in force at the time of the Commission's investigations.
3. Judl GO. 896, 8.5.1913; PWL GO 2303L, 10.9.1931. Once an itinerant community was notified and covered by Section 10, most of the convictions under the CTA would be under Section 22- failure to abide by the conditions of the pass given to registered members. These included visiting only those places which were mentioned in the pass and not exceeding the time limit for which the pass was granted. Home GO 7949, 8.12.1937. Such convictions would take place in the case of itinerant communities in large numbers because of the nature of their expeditions.
4. PWL GO 2008L, 21.12. 1926, PWL GO 1803L, 26.9.1927. This procedure was declared illegal by the Advocate General in 1925. The only legal way in which movements of a CT community could be restricted to a specific area was by formation of a CT settlement under one of the sections of the CTA. This required permission of the Government of India.

5. PWL GO 1806L, 16.7.1931, Budget Motion for 1931-32, Demand no.xxviii. An official document relating to Bombay Presidency had noted that 'if a police Patel wants people to bring fodder for their cattle, he registers a few young Dharalas (a community of Kaira district), who would become his servants. Report of the Criminal Tribes Act Enquiry Committee, 1939, p. 41 quoted in V. Raghaviah, *The Problem of Criminal Tribes*, BASS, n.d., p. 7.
6. PWL GO 1806L, 16.7.1931, Budget Motion for 1931-32, Demand no. xxviii. Regarding CTs of Bombay Presidency, it had been stated that 'if some Dharala goes about the village with a hukkah in his hand it is regarded as an impertinence and an insult to the Patel, who gets him registered. Government of Bombay *Report of the Criminal Tribes Act Enquiry Committee*, 1939, p. 41 in V.Raghaviah, p. 7.
7. David Arnold, 'Dacoity and Rural Crime in Madras, 1860-1940', *Journal of Peasant Studies*, Vol. 6, No. 2, January, 1979, p. 151
8. PWL GO 1806 L 16.7.1931, Budget Motion for 1931-32, Demand no. xxviii.
9. V. Raghaviah, *The Problem of Criminal Tribes*, Foreword by B. Pattabhi Sitaramayya. It had been also alleged by Sitaramayya that if a CT member failed to give 'a goat, a fowl or a couple of eggs, or some hard service' to the policeman, the next day he would be prosecuted for absence from home the previous night and for leaving the police station without leave, and sentenced in the first instance to one year, later to three years and finally to seven. He also charged that if there were no scavengers in the Madras jails, all that the Jail Superintendent had to do was to communicate this need to the police, and they would bring as many as required by applying the Criminal Tribes Act, after duly going thorough the motions of conviction.
10. In fact, even when the 1871 Act was being drafted, the potential problem of accurately identifying itinerant communities had been discussed in the administration. However, the police administration, when consulted, felt confident of being able to cope with the situation. Judl. GO 1071 (Back nos. 51-53), 10.8.1870.
11. Such groupings of course, sometimes led to considerable confusion within the administration, precisely because of the inbuilt openness of the category. When Salem Melurnad Koravars were notified in 1916, the sub divisional magistrate, Salem registered a large number of Koravars. The situation prevailing about category by residence

was apparent in this perplexed communication: 'There seems to be something wrong…all the (2800 persons registered so far) are Koravars but they are probably not all Koravars of the class originally intended.' DM, Salem in a letter to Inspector General of Police, Madras, 11.04. 1916 in Judl. GO 1205, 10.5.1916.

12. In all seriousness, the administration went about creating groupings like 'Korachas, Koravars or Yerukulas of Salem, Coimbatore, Madura, Tanjore, Trichinopoly and North Arcot known as Salem Melurnad Koravars', or 'Togamalai Koravars of Trichinopoly, South Arcot, Chinglepet, North Arcot, Salem and Cuddapah. Government of Madras, *Note, 1916*, p. 2.
13. Such a category allowed the administration to issue notifications of the following type: 'Uppu Koravars styled Kal Koravars, Kal Oddars, Kal-inji Koravars or Dabbai Koravars in Tanjore district (are) to be declared CTs'. Home GO 4932, 15.9.1939. Interestingly, the term 'Kal Odders' was also applied to this particular groups though (W)odders themselves were a separate stone-breaking community.
14. Thus, Kal Koravars, Inji Koravars and Dabbai Koravars of Trichinopoly could be notified as they were related to Salem Melurnad Koravars already notified. PWL GO 225L, 26.1.1929. Salem Melurnad Koravars were themselves notified as they were supposed to have notified relations in some taluks of Coimbatore. Judl. GO 1500, 30.6.1915.
15. Judl. GO 2010, 25.8.1915; Home (Judl.) GO 1834-35, 1.9.1917; PWL GO 119OL, 2.6.1932; PWL GO 1538L, 18.6.1928; PWL GO 2359L, 25.9.1928; PWL GO 2633, 16.9.1929; Judl. (Police) GO 646, 16.9.1929; PWL GO 1972-73L, 6.9.1927; Home GO 1349, 31.3.1937.
16. Thus Korachas and Koravars of the Telugu and Tamil speaking regions respectively, deemed to be interrelated, implicated each other. Judl. GO 1895, 13.8.1915. To one proposal, the response of an official of the normally zealous police administration was somewhat cautious: 'Five thousand people will have to be registered, a very large majority not criminals, as *I can at any time prove the blood relationship which exists between any two of them*. Emphasis added, Statement of DSP, Tinnevelly in Judl. GO 1890, 27.7.1916.
17. Home GO 4932, 15.9.1939; PWL GO 2633, 16.9.1929.
18. PWL GO 225L, 26.1.1929. The administration here chose to

neglect the fact that they did not change their names—those were given by the local administration—but changed their ***professions.***

19. Memo on Donga Yerukulas by Deputy IGP, Government of Madras, *Note, 1925.*
20. Booth Tucker to Governor of Madras in letter dated 31.10.1910, Judl. GO 2000-01, 3.12.1912; W.J. Hatch, *The Land Pirates of India*, 1928, p. 17. Conferences of London Mission, Minute adopted by South India District Committee, Judl. GO 1997, 15.9.1914.
21. Memo on Donga Yerukulas by Deputy IGP, Government of Madras, *Note, 1925.*
    There were as many as 3184 Yerukulas registered in Guntur district one year in a burst of enthusiasm for registrations, and the police administration was forced to raise the question with the District Magistrate of 'bringing the notification (under the CTA) more in accordance with the existing state of affairs'. This essentially meant that the DSP was asking for legitimation of a large number of earlier registrations. This was in direct response to the public outcry against indiscriminate application of the CTA. In response, a broader concept of a criminal was developed. A notification was issued to the effect that the CTA applied to Yerukulas who had not only been convicted of non-bailable offences, but were suspected of having committed them. The administration stipulated that the entire Yerukula community all over the Presidency could be classified as criminal or 'donga'—thieves. The term donga, it was urged, *need not be interpreted narrowly any more.* PWL GO 2864, 10.10.1929 (Emphasis added).
22. Note by Deputy IGP regarding Togamalai Koravars of Trichnololy Judl. GO 1193, 18.6.1913. The implication of the phrase 'permanent habitation' was consolidation of a life of crime, with insinuation of regular contact with criminals and so on.
23. Judl. GO 850, 15.4. 1914.
24. Judl. GO 2494, 12.10.1915.
25. PWL GO 2633, 16.9.29; Home GO 1349, 31.3.1937; Judl. (Police) GO 646, 10.12.1924; Home (Judl.) GO 1834-35, 1.9.1917; Government of Madras, *Note, 1916*, p. 8; Government of Madras, *Note, 1925*, p. 63.
26. Judl.GO 1890, 27.7.1916. It was, however, noted rather ruefully that 'though morality among themselves does not exist, no woman will yield to the temptation of an outsider' Judl.GO 1193,

18.6.1913, Note by Deputy IGP. When one such Korava community was being charged, the police administration decided not to take into account its economic status, which was otherwise supposed to denote respectability. In the case of this community which was referred to as buying female children and having no morality, its ownership of cattle worth Rs. 1600, and 182 acres of dry land, and admittedly being 'comparatively wealthy' did not prevent it from being declared a criminal tribe. *Ibid.*

27. District Superintendent of Police, Tinnevelly to Government, Judl. GO 2494, 12.10.1915.
28. Home GO 3113, 6.6.1939; PWL GO 2359L, 25.9.1928; PWL GO 2633, 16.9.1929; Judl. (Police) GO 646, 16.9.1929; Home GO 1349, 31.3.1937; PWL GO 1972-73L, 6.9.1927; Home GO 4932, 15.9.1939; PWL GO 2633, 16.9.1929; PWL GO 225L, 26.1.1929; Memo on Donga Yerukulas by Deputy IGP, Government of Madras, *Note, 1925.*
29. Home (J) GO 2194, 6.9.1916, Guntur DM's letter to Under Secretary to Government, Home (J) Dept.
30. Judl. GO 2494, 12.10.1915; Remarks of the Guntur DM in Review of the Administration Report of Police Department for 1916, Home (Judl.) GO 2130, 28.8.1916.

    Within the administration itself, it soon began to be admitted that too much reliance was being placed on mere gossip by people not in a position to know anything of the community. In Guntur, the DM admitted, for instance, that 'anyone and everyone' was prepared to swear that a Yerukula was a rogue. It was also recognised that in many cases of registration, there was very scanty or no evidence of an association with a criminal gang. Guntur DM's letter to under Secretary to Government, Home (J) GO 2194, 6.9.1916.
31. Judl. GO 2494, 12.10.1915. In the above cited case of Koravars who were to be notified and confined to the limited area of a village in Tinnevelly in order to work in Parrys' factory, it was definitely of advantage to the landlords to certify that they were criminals. They would have benefited from the confined movements of the notified members of the community. Though reporting in this case had to be done to the manager of the factory, the landlords benefited in terms of gaining potential agricultural workers forming a 'floating population' between the factory and the fields, when work at the factory was slack.

32. Baker 1979: 38-39; Government of Madras, *Fortnightly Reports*, 20.1.1922, 16.2.1922.
33. David Arnold, 'Bureaucratic Recruitment and Subordination in Colonial India: The Madras Constabulary, 1859-1947' in Ranajit Guha (ed.) *Subaltern Studies IV: Writings on South Asian History and Society*, Delhi, 1985, pp. 196, 202.
34. Judl. GO 451, 28.6.1926.
35. David Arnold 1985: 197; In Guntur, it was found that the 'bulk of the land-owning people...(the Kammas)... were completely and almost aggressively in sympathy with the movement'. Public General GO Ms 736 (S-17), 12.5.1932 (Guntur DM's report dated 3.5.1932). Guntur district, as mentioned, was one of the two districts where the landlords had a lot of powers earlier as far as surveillance of CT members was concerned.
36. Notes to PWL GO 2008, 21.12.1926; Home GO 4949, 12.10.1939, p. 319, Notes written in 1926.
37. PWL Order 2008L, 21.12.1926.
38. PWL GO 1054L, 12.5.1927. The senior police officials who depended on the village headmen for surveillance of the CT members wanted the continuation of the practice as it made the job of their own subordinates, as also the responsibility of the police administration, more limited.
39. PWL GO 2251L, 4.10.1927.
40. Rules 20 and 21, CTA Revised Rules, PWL order 2008L, 21.12.1926.
41. PWL GO 1806L, 16.7.1931, Budget Motion for 1931-32.
42. Petition from women of Edayapatti village, Trichy, PWL GO 1523L, 4.7.1935.
43. Home GO 4949, 12.10.1938.
44. *Ibid.*
45. PWL 404L, 10.2.1931.
46. PWL GO 1806L, 16.7.1931, Budget Motion for 1931-32.
47. PWL GO 404L, 10.2.1931; V. Raghaviah, *The Problem of Criminal Tribes*, Pattabhi Sitaramayya's foreword.
48. PWL GO 1523L, 4.7.1935; Home GO 4079, 24.8.1938, p. 319, Notes written in 1926; Notes to PWL GO 2008, 21.12.1926.
49. PWL GO 404L, 10.2.1931; Home GO 4999, 8.12.1937.
50. Home GO 4949, 12.10.1938.
51. PWL GO 1972L, 1973L, 6.9.1927
52. Petition from women of Edyapatti village, Trichy. PWL GO

1523L, 4.7.1935. 'Femalefolk are made to stand in a line in the street (to) receive the vulgar and filthy expressions of the police...which fill us with unbearable and inexpressible shame and any remonstration at them will bring us in the CT register and an eagle eye of the police.' Home GO 4079, 24.8.1938.

53. Rule 11 (ii), Draft Rules, CTA, PWL GO 2008, 21.12.1926.
54. Home GO 4079, 24.8.1938.
55. This fact was also alleged elsewhere. Budget Motion for 1931-32, Demand no. xxviii, PWL GO 1806L, 16.7.1931.
56. Home GO 4079, 24.8.1938.
57. PWL GO 2098L, 25.9.1935

CHAPTER 3

The Concept and Policy of Criminal Tribe Settlements

In the initial phases of the operation of the CTA, notifications/registrations were often done with definite ideas and plans for the majority of those thus notified or registered. A number of Koravars and Yerukulas were notified and registered so that they could be confined to settlements already in existence, or already conceived of by the administration. This practice was in absolute violation of the principle laid down by the CTA that settlements were to be formed for 'extreme cases' among those notified and registered, and were for those found to be 'incorrigible', i.e. those on whom the effect of reporting to the authorities over a period had not been a deterrent as far as commission of crime was concerned. This chapter looks into the concept of CT settlements, the role of the Salvation Army in refining the concept, and the official policy regarding these settlements.

I

The idea of CT settlements was first mooted in 1868 when the CTA, 1871, was being considered. They were conceived on the same lines as those attempted by the Thuggee and Dacoity Department in the 1830s in the north.[1] When the new CTA was being considered by the British administration, there was not much enthusiasm shown about the existing settlements.

Settlements in the north were perceived to have been a failure, as their success seemed to depend on the degree of commitment of individual officers.[2] It seemed that the government might not include the provisions about CT settlements in the proposed CTA.

Deemed to be relatively more successful were settlements run by missionary organisations, with some government assistance. Settlements managed by the London Mission in Madras Presidency,[3] and by the Salvation Army (SA) in the north were among these. The existence of these settlements influenced to some extent government's policy towards settlements for CTs.

The SA had been functioning in India since 1882. Its work seems to have been intensified in the years preceding the institution of the CTA, 1911. In 1908, three years before the new CTA came into operation, the SA was entrusted with work among the Doms, numbering thousands, in Gorakhpur in the United Provinces.[4] In the column called 'Interesting Items' in the Salvation Army newspaper, the following news item appeared in 1909, showing that forced labour was the key to reformation of criminals:

> One man in our settlement (in Gorakhpur) had been flogged 15 times, another 6 times. They are now both happily at work in our Salvation Army factory.[5]

The Punjab government followed the example of the United Provinces in inviting the SA to 'undertake another experiment in Criminocurology,' with a thousand young men of the Borstal Prison in Lahore, which essentially meant that work would be found for the settlers in a factory or a mill. This experiment was apparently a success.[6]

It appears certain that the SA was instrumental in the inclusion of the provision regarding CT settlements in the CTA, 1911. William Booth of the SA had written to the Governor -General in Council, in 1910, *before* the CTA was formulated, where he made out a case for the establishment of settlements for the criminal population of India. He pointed out that operating against 3 to 4 million of the hereditary criminals were

150,000 police and 700,000 village watchmen. While he 'would not advocate any relaxation of the vigilance of the present system of suppression, [he] would strongly urge that side by side with repression and punishment a system of reformation and employment should be introduced.'[7] He urged the establishment of industrial settlements, where employment of suitable and remunerative nature would be provided. While pointing out with confidence to the success of settlements already run by the SA in the northern provinces, he set out some of the terms on which the settlements under the CTA would be run.[8] The success of the SA with Doms in Gorakhpur clinched the issue, in spite of lingering scepticism, as far as the policy makers were concerned.

The Governor General in Council was directly approached by Booth Tucker of the SA with proposals for the establishment of industrial settlements for released prisoners and CTs in India. Booth Tucker in a letter to the government now formulated a definite scheme for CT settlements, before the CTA was passed.[9] One of the officials of the SA was to look back with some satisfaction upon this role much later:

> We will not enter into the details of legislative enactments that were necessary to legalise [our] work, nor of the great influence of the [Salvation] Army in framing them. The writer recalls with pleasure a large and influential conference called together by the Government of India... Representatives of all the provincial governments and of many native states attended the conference. The army representatives were the only non officials present, and the deference paid to our views...was most gratifying.[10]

William Booth had already written an influential book, *In Darkest England and the Way Out: A Study of Poverty and Vice in England and a Scheme by the Salvation Army for Reclamation of Criminals and Prevention of Crime* in 1890, laying out his scheme to work with the poor of England. When Booth wrote this controversial work, he laid out in detail programmes to salvage what he called the 'submerged tenth' of the English population—the three million destitute and unemployed. A scrutiny of this work reveals that he decided to ignore the industrial workers, whose economic situation was no better, and concentrated on 'thieves, harlots, paupers, drunkards, prodigals…'[11] The large majority of these people were Irish. William Booth's plan was to convert them to Salvationism and employ them in a variety of enterprises supervised by the SA. In the Indian case, similar plans were aimed at the criminal tribe communities.

This book had, for all practical intents and purposes, also laid out important principles of the SA's work in colonies like India. A comparison of the programmes of the SA in India and England reveals that what the SA adopted in India was a slightly modified version of the original scheme. In fact, it was the other way round too, in that the scheme in England was shaped partly by the work the SA had already been doing in India and elsewhere.[12]

The plan in *Darkest England* suggested the establishing of farm colonies (colonial models for agricultural settlements) based on diligent use of wasteland, and city colonies with labour yards (later models for industrial settlements) where 'work will be extracted rigorously'. Work with prisoners in Britain, where the SA was to 'seek from the authorities the privilege of supervising and reporting upon those who are discharged … so as to free [the prisoner] of reporting at police stations', was the basis on which Prisoners' Homes were established in India. The Industrial Schools for children in Britain, where young people were trained in various skills were also established in India, and were a vital part of the scheme to separate children from allegedly criminal parents and to bring them up in a wholesome atmosphere.[13] In several other details there were a number of parallels in the scheme envisaged for the poor of England, and schemes run for CT members in India. The city colonies run by the SA in England (where, incidentally, it was charged with sweating the workers), were, in particular, a mirror image of industrial settlements in India where CT workers would make mats, rear silkworms or weave carpets. Weaving and winding would be justified by the administration on the basis that the lightness of touch of the consummate thief could be used in a productive manner.[14]

General Booth had envisaged for the English poor what he called city *colonies* and farm *colonies*. For the Indian criminal, however, he decided on *settlements*. Of course, in this case, this imperial term took on a new meaning—the itinerant communities were to be 'settled', as opposed to being allowed to wander. In keeping with its emigration schemes, conceptualised on the basis of providing workers to areas facing a shortage of workforce across countries, the SA tried to send CT members to Mesopotamia for military service or to Assam as plantation workers. Given the geographical expanse of British India, however, the great exchange of labour between countries envisaged by *In Darkest England* could take place within India itself through the medium of CT settlements.[15]

On the eve of the finalisation of the CTA, settlements in the vicinity of, and in the service of factory managements already existed, helping the government to crystallise its new concept of CT settlements. The government could rely on the SA's assurance that the organisation already had considerable experience in dealing with factory officials in connection with the employment of settlers in industrial settlements. Work on waste land to make it cultivable could be the basis of the agricultural settlements, and here also the SA had shown itself capable of making settlers work on such land.[16]

II

By the time the SA came to work in Madras Presidency, the architect of its programmes, William Booth had been able to establish in England and in 55 countries all over the world, emigration bureaux, labour colonies, a banking business, huge trading concerns, 'and what not'.[17] Booth had been described by one of his associates as an

> evangelist... company promoter, assurance director, banker, farmer, printer, publisher and bookseller, tea merchant, commission agent for lamps, bicycles, pianos and drapery, financier...(and) politician...[18]

It is of interest to note the kind of prestige and power which the SA enjoyed at the turn of the century. When a journalist interviewed 20 odd eminent personalities in 1907-1908, William Booth was in the company of Asquith, Edward VII, the Kaiser, Curzon and the Bishop of London. The author stated somewhat in awe:

> You went in to meet a saint and a visionary. You come out having met the astutest businessman in the city. You feel that if [this] tradesman's son of Nottingham had applied himself to winning wealth instead of to winning souls, he would have been the Rockefeller of England.[19]

The same author noted, several times during the article, Booth's acute business sense.

Yet, equally, the SA and the methods it employed were critiqued. A study of Salvationism in the early twentieth century alleged that the SA had been collecting large sums of money from the public, ostensibly for its social schemes, but was actually involved in an 'emigration scandal' which was to operationalise the great exchange of labour visualised in *Darkest England*:

> ...the SA not only collects large sums in connection with its emigration schemes, but charters steamers for its emigrants, (charging ordinary fares), earns commissions from shipping companies, receives capitation grants, and is able to do business more cheaply than other agencies. Every year it receives thousands of pounds on account of passage money, commissions, fees and grants.[20]

The same writer accused the SA of earning money by finding work for the unemployed, in its own factories and works. On the pretext of the workers being damaged labour, the SA underpaid them, so that the products could be sold very cheap.

> On the scandalous instance of salvationist sweating in the joinery works...the United Workers' Anti Sweating Committee publishes a damaging exposure...[the conclusion reached by the Committee was that] the value of men's labour is enormously higher than the payment...given to them...and the Army...appropriates the surplus.[21]

The SA officials had something to say in self-defence.[22] Moreover, in reply, the founder of the SA had made it publicly clear that 'paying the starving workers as much as capable workmen is stark, staring lunacy.' Under the title 'Damaged goods: On the old libel of sweating', Booth wrote:

> It is equivalent to maintaining that damaged goods or second-hand goods should be sold at the market price of new goods in first class condition...Damaged labour is like damaged goods...it is the most difficult thing in the world to find a market for it. I make a market.[23]

This conviction was legislated into the provisions of the CTA, where the managing agency in charge of a settlement could fix the wages of settler-workers.

There were other critics of the SA. While discussing his play *Major Barbara*, Bernard Shaw had warned that SA was building up a business organisation whose future would be in the hands of staff who were likely to be unscrupulous men of business. He felt this was because of the economic deadlock in which the SA found itself.[24]

What led to such assessments of the SA by contemporaries were both the SA's current practices in Britain, as also its plans for the future. The SA was born in the decades succeeding widespread industrial unrest. With its special concentration on the pauperised sections, it had the potential to constitute a reliable groundswell of future strikebreakers and blackleg workers, for which the Irish had already become notorious.[25] If this could be achieved in a systematic way, then it would also prevent any threat of solidarity among the urban unemployed poor and workers in their struggles.[26] In the Indian case as well, the CT workers were turned into blackleg workers to break strikes in a variety of enterprises, including the plantations.[27]

The SA needed financial support in order to grow and expand its operations.

> The millionaires were not slow to see the value of the Army, and General Booth was not slow to see the value of the millionaire... *In Darkest England* was not only a cry for help, but also a threat.

> The rich found themselves faced with the trouble of Salvage or the terrors of socialism...hence the plutocratic support of the SA.[28]

In his discussion of the SA, Shaw also noted that

> [these] religious bodies, as the almoners of the rich, become a sort of auxiliary police...taking off the insurrectionary edge of poverty.[29]

For similar reasons, the SA received funds from a wide section of the public: the pauperised population posed a 'law and order' threat of an immense magnitude to the propertied.[30]

This perception of the usefulness of the SA extended to India as well. The Indian industrialist Ratan Tata contributed 6000 guineas as his personal contribution as the 'nucleus' of the SA fund in India.[31] There is an explicit indication of the success of this kind of investment. A Salvation Army official mentions approvingly

> [the] 'partnership between the [United Provinces] Government and the Salvation Army—we supply the workers and control them, enjoying generally great freedom of action, the government meets the cost...[32]

Such an organisation would however also recieve the active support of both the district administration and the police. The services of a Deputy Inspector General of Police were to be used for the general supervision of the settlements, but day-to-day affairs were to be left entirely to the managing agency. A more systematically worked out partnership between the industrialists, the British Indian administration and the SA would manifest itself in the conception of industrial CT settlements.

Harold Stuart, later member of the Governor's Council, Madras was instrumental in bringing the SA to the Presidency. The SA claimed that it was the success of its work in the United Provinces and the Punjab which impressed Stuart, who invited it to start operations in Madras. In 1910, under the supervision of the SA, the first settlement of the Presidency was opened for Yerukula prisoners. What was to be later one of the largest CT settlements of British India—Stuartpuram—was an extension of this informal settlement.

III

Once the provision for CT settlements was incorporated into the CTA, the general official statement about criminal tribe settlements in Madras Presidency was made public. The objective of a settlement was stated to be the reformation of CT members, not merely their segregation or confinement. For this reason, it was professed, the management of the settlement was to fall as little as possible in the hands of the police (recognised to be a directly coercive branch of the administration) who had no training for this work, and who would inspire further distrust in the CT members. A religious or philanthropic body, it was asserted, was needed to run these settlements. The Salvation Army was an important contender for this task; others like the American Baptist Mission had less experience in India.

The official reason given for preferring missionaries was that, unlike government officials who were frequently transferred, these organisations were expected to provide continuity in the work of reclamation. An important consideration was economy, as the government were convinced that they could not get more skilled and devoted personnel for the remuneration paid to such agencies. Moreover, it was claimed by the government, that a non-official manager of a settlement would be more independent of the administration and likely to have enough confidence to run a settlement without needing the help of the police to maintain discipline. He would also not need to refer every minor matter to the higher authorities for decisions he could well take himself. Such an agency would be more effective in this work—the work would be treated as a mission, whereas government servants were likely to view it as just another post in their careers. The government argued that for these reasons missionary organisations were ideal.[33]

An official press communiqué set out the objectives of the CT settlements very clearly: A CT settlement was to reform its inmates by inducing them to lead a settled life,

'to break them of their idle, vicious and restless habits by regular discipline, by removing the temptation... to drink, and by holding out hopes of an independent life as farmer or artificer'.[34]

Tact and pressure were to be used with those who were allegedly lazy, inefficient and unwilling to make them work. Penal settlements were to be considered for those not amenable to tact and pressure. As would be noticed here, 'restless habits' was a special reference to the itinerant nature of the trading communities. As mentioned earlier, the settlements were meant for 'worst characters, especially wandering gangs'. Hence, by policy, itinerant communities were singled out for settling.[35]

In spirit, the graduated scheme of the CTA was notification, registration, reporting and restriction of movements. Only as a last and most drastic step was settling to be done. However, as pointed out earlier, once the first step was taken, all steps were sought to be applied.[36] Once the CTA became operational, the provision about settling the itinerant community of Koravas was used simultaneously with notifications and registrations. In fact, in the late 1920s, of the 61 official settlements with a total of 31,000 inmates, the population of the three all-Yerukula settlements itself was 6,495—nearly one fifth of the entire settled CT population of British India.[37]

The Salvation Army revealed that operations under the CTA fell in two categories: i) action against the itinerant communities through the SA, ii) action against settled communities through the police.[38] The initiative to form the settlements for itinerant communities was thus left in the hands of the SA:

> [The] Salvation Army will invite the assistance of the district authorities... to induce members of CTs ...to enter the settlement but if persuasion [by the SA] fails, the government are quite prepared to apply the provisions of the CTA.[39]

In 1910, Sitanagaram settlement was opened with a few Yerukula women whose husbands or other male relations were in jail.[40] Stuartpuram settlement was opened as an 'overflow' settlement soon after the decision by the government to use the provisions of the CTA. Essentially, the increase in the number of interned Yerukulas far exceeded the capacity of Sitanagaram to hold them.[41]

In other words, though persuasive measures did fail, the settlements had grown quickly. This was for a number of reasons. Firstly, there were members of the itinerant communities who entered the settlements purely to avoid police harassment. For instance, a large group of Yerukulas of Guntur district who carried grain for the ryots of Ongole, Bapatla and Tenali taluks used to camp near the Stuartpuram settlement site. In 1913, when the police became more active as a result of the new CTA, they 'took shelter' under the SA and were put into Stuartpuram settlement.[42] Further, under the security sections of the Indian Penal Code, an individual could be sent to jail if he failed to furnish security. This happened frequently in the case of members of the itinerant communities who, faced with the choice of either going to a settlement or to prison, preferred to go to a settlement.[43] Sometimes, the communities were tricked into coming to a settlement.[44] At any rate, there was a lot of coercion needed to populate the settlements:

> The first settlers we received [in Stuartpuram] early in 1913 were a grim looking trio, brought in by six armed police, handcuffed, with their legs in irons.[45]

The District Magistrate of Guntur, in which as many as three criminal tribe settlements were located, admitted that in Guntur, indiscriminate registration and internment of Yerukulas did take place. Any member of CT community would be interned in a settlement if he were reported to be a 'bad character'. Settlements grew for still another reason. According to the official definition of a CT, persons who were associates of criminals were anyway to be put into settlements; unofficially, so were persons related to them. This meant that the whole family was put into the settlement, if one member—always a male—was alleged to be a criminal.[46]

The point to be noted here is that the men at least had convictions in their names even if there was doubt about their actual guilt: the women were ordinary members of their families with no record of crime. The question of confining the children of settlers to these settlements had been considered by the administration, and the CTA allowed the local governments to separate them from their parents, and bring them up in a 'more wholesome atmosphere'.[47] The question of women's confinement was taken for granted, and there is no evidence of any controversy on this matter. This happened invariably in the case of all the settlements of Madras Presidency, and possibly of British India. This policy was a result of the perception that a criminal was more effectively reformed in the company of his family. In fact, when a settler was sent to a 'penal' settlement, it was officially recommended that his wife and small children accompany him.[48] (The conditions at a penal settlement were especially harsh since the so-called incorrigible CT members were brought here. Their families were also subjected to the same conditions.)

It was precisely because of these measures that a settlement like Sitanagaram which existed in a small way before the Act came into operation, could now provide the SA with a large number of charges under their control. As Booth Tucker said:

> Our work in Madras was started [late], but has quickly forged ahead of other Presidencies and provinces. Nowhere in India have the provisions of the CTA been so effectively taken advantage of as in Madras.[49]

The SA had, in fact, been surprised by the large number of Yerukulas who were suddenly brought to them as settlers:

> Indeed so admirable have been the arrangements of the Madras district authorities, and the police, for bringing [the Yerukulas] in, that we have been somewhat embarrassed with the rain of riches.[50]

IV

The settlement policy, however, had a troubled career. There were accusations from the public, and from within the administration that settlements were novel kinds of jails where the CT members could be detained for indefinite periods.[51] The

Government seemed aware that settlers could easily become 'the most useful and handy men about the settlement, and the managers had every reason to try and keep them there.'[52]

The CT settlements were, in fact, managed like jails and 'discipline' within the settlements was rigorously imposed. The need for such discipline arose out of the interest of the managing agencies to make sure that the settlers once interned did not escape. Not only would the managing agency then have fewer workers, the agency could be held responsible for an increase in crime in the neighbourhood.[53] Watching and monitoring movements of settlers thus became very important parts of the day to day running of a settlement.

The problem was complicated by the fact that it was on the subordinate police administration that the managing agency had to depend for routine surveillance of settlers.[54] This section, like the landlords, welcomed the provision regarding CT settlements but was opposed to their actual establishment. The Indian Jails Committee had noted that it was within the power of the police to recommend that any individual member of a criminal tribe be selected, for an unlimited period, for detainment within a settlement. Thus, as the Committee pointed out, the power of blackmail in the hands of the subordinate officials was almost without limit. Any police subordinate could go to a CT member living in village and threaten him with removal unless a sufficient payment was made. Similarly, anybody could bribe the police to make a report that a particular CT member should be deported and placed in a criminal settlement.[55] The subordinate police, did not, however, want the CT members to be interned—they merely wished to use the *threat* of internment for extortion, because once a CT member was interned, there was no possibility of further extortion. That the settlers used to bribe the subordinate police to escape internment is mentioned by SA sources explicitly.[56] If the settlers managed to escape from a settlement, they had to bribe the police again in order to stay out.[57] The relationship between a managing agency and the subordinate police, for these reasons, was bound to be a difficult one.[58]

Given the situation, the bulk of the supervision of a settlement had to be undertaken by the managing agency itself. The SA, in fact, tried to lay down the principles on which settlements could be physically located: the plan was to settle small communities contiguous to each other, thus greatly facilitating their supervision as in the case of native American Indians.[59]

The manager of Parrys' factory, which was declared a CT settlement, had solved the problem of supervision in another way:

> The whole of the settlement was fenced in with a stout barbed wire fence on steel rail posts and reinforced with a thorn hedge, the exit being under control of a watchman the whole of the day and night. Besides this, the lines where the settlers lived were illuminated by electricity—50 candlepower, 210 volt lamps... This arrangement has made the work of supervising the settlers very much more easy and has in fact been a great factor in counteracting many a vicious tendency to which the Koravar is addicted.[60]

Generally, the guard at the settlements was extensive. Settlers were checked four times from sunset to sunrise. Settlers whom the manager considered really troublesome and desperate were confined to 'enclosures' within the settlement. In fact, as late as 1946, one of the settlements reminded a member of the provincial enquiry committee of Nazi concentration camps.[61] When escapes lessened as a result of ruthless vigilance, it would be described as a growing 'fondness for settlement life.'[62]

An aspect of such closely monitored settlements was that access to CT settlements was restricted. Even decades after their establishment, if attempts were made by some organisations to visit the settlements, permission was refused 'in the interest of discipline in the settlement.'[63] The managements of industrial settlements also went to great lengths to prevent workers from mixing with surrounding population, as also with other non-criminal tribe workers or non-settler members of the same community.[64] As a result, the settlements tended to be insulated and isolated from the public.

If the settlers tried to escape from the settlements, they risked being convicted under the CTA which made such 'absconding' an offence.[65] The high incidence of escapes, themselves a result of harsh discipline, only served to tighten the surveillance. At one point, the problem of escapes from the settlement was so severe that in despair a manager of a factory (which had been declared a CT settlement) actually recommended to the administration that the punishment for absconding should be greater than that for robberies.[66] In any case, good behaviour on the part of the settlers came to be identified as much with not absconding as with not committing dacoities. In this way, a settler easily acquired a criminal record with the settlement authorities, given the strictness and arbitrariness of the rules governing discipline.[67]

The settlements were sufficiently like jails for a proposal to come up within the administration to transfer control of CT settlements from the Commissioner of Labour to the IG of prisons.[68] The IG of Prisons, interestingly, objected to the proposal on the basis that it was wrong to place *possible offenders and unconvicted persons* under the control of the jail department. He thus confirmed that settlers might not have had any convictions at all, and also that the inmates were potential, not actual criminals. It was explicitly admitted elsewhere within the administration that settlers with no convictions were detained in settlements much longer than they would be in jails.[69]

The managing agencies were given powers not only for internment of the settlers but also for discharges. There were, predictably, virtually no releases. Once interned, CT members proved to be 'most useful and handy men around the settlements,' and the managing agency had every reason to try and keep them in the settlement.[70] When a District Magistrate, realising the extent of illegal confinements tried to release some Yerukula settlers, the Salvation Army protested strongly on the grounds of the erosion of their authority. This incident led to the vesting of powers in the hands of the managers as a policy.[71]

V

In 1931, the Government of India wrote to the Government of Madras drawing its attention to certain extracts from the draft convention concerning forced, compulsory labour adopted by the International Labour Conference in the previous year. The problem for the administration seemed to be that ratification of this convention would have serious implications for the functioning of the criminal tribe settlements.[72] The Government of India was aware that the work extracted from CT members in settlements could not be described as voluntary, and that ratification of the convention would involve discontinuance of such labour. There was an apprehension on the part of the government that it might be faced with a demand from the nationalist sections of the public for ratification of the Convention, and wanted the Madras administration to furnish information on the conditions of work and payment in settlements in the Presidency.

The situation was far from ambiguous. In fact, the true spirit behind the CTA had by now begun to make itself felt; having drawn a relationship between lack of means of livelihood and criminality, it was now repeatedly claimed within the Madras administration that more work—forced or otherwise—would mean more reformation. With this end in view, the Factories Act had been relaxed in at least one factory where CT settlers were made to work, so that there was no check any more on the number of hours of work in a working day or per working week. Nor was it necessary any more to conform to the stipulation regarding rest periods during the day, or a day of rest during the week.[73] The strict control and coercion in CT settlements made the workers abscond, rather than work voluntarily for a wage. One factory agent in his report to the Madras government stated repeatedly that all the convictions in the name of the workers were for running away from settlement work, not for any other crime.[74] Combined with the fact that CT members were forced to work in settlements, pitifully low wages were the norm.[75]

The nature of work in CT settlements in general was, in fact, clear to the administration even in the early days of the operation of the Act. One of the Council members in an effort to stop further excesses on CT members had rhetorically asked another council member: 'I shall be glad if my honourable colleague would indicate in what essential particulars the conditions authorised by the CT Act differ from slavery.' He had explicitly alleged that CT members were farmed out for compulsory labour in settlements.[76] One of the earliest public objections to the CT settlements in Madras in particular had been that free labour was being converted into indentured labour.[77]

The government itself had stipulated that in all agricultural settlements, the manager could fix the hours for which inmates were obliged to work apart from having the power to decide the 'terms of remuneration'. In industrial settlements, any settlers who disobeyed the manager, or refused to obey 'any reasonable order' given by the manager could be subjected to additional or more arduous work with loss of wages, cancellation of leave, restriction of movements to any particular area within the settlement, a fine, or even prosecution.[78]

The government also knew that there were 'arrival enclosures' for those who refused to work initially. Regarding work on land in the Aziznagar settlement in Madras Presidency, a settlement directly under government supervision, the manager himself had recorded that

> As a preliminary measure I had recourse to a stick.
> I was glad because it brought the desired result quick.[79]

While considering proposals for allowing the Parrys' factory to employ Koravars, even before it was declared a CT settlement, it was recognised within the Madras administration that the government might be accused of 'supplying forced labour for a brutal English commercial.'[80] In fact, in this case, the government did not initially declare the factory a settlement fearing that the British administration might be portrayed as 'handing over of Indians—in a state of quasi-servitude—to a European firm.'[81]

In other words, the administration at all levels seemed aware of the situation in CT settlements all over India. However, the official reply sent by the Government of Madras to the Government of India, ostensibly after consultations with the IG of Police, the Commissioner of Labour and the SA officials did not reflect any scepticism. It was claimed that conditions of work in settlements were hardly different to that outside. While on the one hand it was claimed by the Madras administration that the work was done by settlers as a result of moral persuasion by SA officials, and the measure of compulsion was very small, it was argued on the other that if the powers to enforce work were taken away, there could be no hope of success of reclamation of settlers. (In fact, it was emphatically stated that the SA had a group of people in the settlements who was very *grateful* to the government for restricting them to the settlement.) The response by the government of Madras concluded with the warning that in case the activities of the SA ceased as a result of ratification, the effect would be disastrous as far as work to 'bring up the rising generation with better ideas' was concerned. In any case, it was pointed out, the CTA was not a punitive Act. It was framed only to restrain, and to deal with conditions which most ILO members would anyway not be aware of.[82]

This was around the time when nationalist sentiment was at its most articulate and several questions were being raised about the Criminal Tribes Act and the administration of the CT settlements. Protests were voiced in the Madras Legislative Council about the Act and the way it caused unimaginable hardship to the CT members concerned.[83] Nationalists in the Central Legislative Assembly now brought up the specific question of the ratification of the ILO draft convention on slavery. The argument that they put forward was that if, as claimed by the Government, there was no forced labour in the settlements, then why the hesitation and delay in ratifying the convention.[84] (Interestingly, the ratification was not supported by some Indian landlord members of the Legislative Assembly, one of whom managed to see a parallel between slavery and tenancy.[85])

Finally, the issue was discussed in the Council and it was noted with regret that the draft convention contained no exemptions which could cover the administration of CT settlements, and that for this reason it was not possible for the Government of Madras to accept ratification.[86] The concerned draft convention, then, could not be ratified unless it was modified so as to exclude labour extracted under the CTA and similar legislation in force in India.[87]

The general argument that the government was to put forward to the public for some years to come was that

> it is a complete mistake to imagine that all those who are now in settlements are straining at the leash for freedom and the right to live in nomadic poverty.[88]

Essentially, the general attitude of the administration to the CT members was such that it was unlikely that it could be moved as a body to support ratification of the UN draft convention. This attitude is summed up by a remark of a British official to one of the missionary agencies: 'I don't know how you live and work among them. To us they are cattle, just cattle.'[89]

Notes

1. Judl. GO 1071 (Back nos. 51-53), 10.8.1870.
2. Government of India, *Report of the Indian Police Commission, 1902-03*, para 137.
3. Judl. GO 1997, 15.9.1914.
4. Bernard Watson, *A Hundred Years' War*, London, 1964, pp. 142,147.
5. Salvation Army, *The War Cry*, February, 1909, XV, No. 1, p. 15
6. Salvation Army, *Social Problems in Solution*, (Papers read by SA officials at the International Social Council, London), 1921, p. 130, 131.
7. William Booth, London, letter to Governor General in Council dt. 2.8.1910 in Judl. GO 2000, 3.12.1912.

8. He advised, for instance, that the settlers should leave it to the SA to sell their produce—one of the important ground rules on which it was worth the SA's while to undertake such work. These rules were later to be formalised in the form of sweeping powers to the managers of the settlements.
9. Communication by Stuart, Acting Chief Secretary, Government of Madras to Secretary, Government of India, Home Department, 1.4.1911 in Judl. GO 2000, 3.12.1912.
10. Commr. Baugh, *The CT Work in India: an Economic Experiment* (Written for the *Staff Review*, October 1930).
11. William Booth, *In Darkest England and the Way Out*, Salvation Army, London, 1890, p. 93.
12. *Ibid.*, p. 174.
13. *Ibid.*, pp. 107, 124-7, 113, 196, 203.
14. Judl. GO 1193, 18.6.1913.
15. William Booth, *In Darkest England*, p. 113.
16. F. Booth Tucker, *Mukti Fauj or Forty years with the Salvation Army in India and Ceylon*, n.d., p. 224. From 1908 onwards, a chain of agricultural settlements had been established by the government all over north India and these had been managed by the SA. Bernard Watson, *A Hundred Years' War*, London, 1964, p. 142.
17. Staff Captain E. Kirk, *Unveiled—A Study of the Salvation Army from Within*, London, 1915, p. 12; James Gilchrist Lawson, *Deeper Experiences of Famous Christians*, New York, 1911/1970, p. 252.
18. Quoted in Conrad Noel, *Byways of Belief*, London, 1912, p. 196.
19. A.G. Gardiner, *Prophets and Kings*, London, 1914, p. 186.
20. Noel 1912: 191.
21. *Ibid.* In fact, SA's factories would provoke protests from merchants and workers alike. In 1905, it was alleged that as a result of the sweating practises of the SA, not only were thousands of workers thrown out of the legitimate factories, but such 'unfair and mischievous competition (led) to lower prices and wages'. *Ibid.*, p. 190.
22. '[On] Sweaters and sweated: Our business differs from that of an ordinary manufacturer in that he considers his output to be what his factory produces as a finished article from the raw material supplied to it. But we have more than the industrial product in view. Our chief product is the man. Our output includes humanity as well as merchandise.' *Some Aspects of Salvation Army Social Work*, paper read at the International Social Council, London conducted

by the Founder, 1911, The Salvation Army Printing Works, 1917, p. 95.

23. Salvation Army, *All the World*, no 5, May 1908, Vol. xxix.
24. In this play, a distiller and arms manufacturer offers a conscientious SA worker money. When the play led to a controversy among the critics about the appropriateness of the offer, the reply of the SA itself, according to Shaw, was prompt and conclusive. As one of the officers said, they would take money from the devil himself. Bernard Shaw, Preface to 'Major Barbara', *The Complete Prefaces of Bernard Shaw*, London, 1965, p. 124.
25. The Irish would be assaulted regularly for playing this role as those who were unemployed 'proved useful fodder for masters intent on wage reductions'. David Jones, *Crime, Protest, Community and Police in Nineteenth Century Britain*, London, 1982, p. 101.
26. Incidentally, Salvationism was considered to be the latest phase in Methodism, itself accepted by historians as having prevented revolution in England in the 1790s. Halevy quoted in E.P. Thompson, *The Making of the English Working Class*, Harmondsworth, 1963, p. 45.
27. Meena Radhakrishna, 'From Itinerant Communities to Wage Workers—The Criminal Tribes of Madras Presidency, 1910-1947'. Paper presented at the first annual conference of Association of Indian Labour Historians, March 1998, p. 37; Judl. GO 2991, 13.12.1916; Home (J) GO 2650, 12.11.1916.
28. Noel 1912: 184-185.
29. *The Complete Prefaces of Bernard Shaw*, p. 132.
30. For a discussion of the perception of potential of crime by the dispossessed in Victorian England, see David Jones (1982), Chapter 1.
31. Solveig Smith, *By Love Compelled*, London, 1981, p. 102.
32. Commissioner Baugh, *The CT Work in India: An Economic Experiment* (Written for the *Staff, Review* October 1930 in SA archives). A leading raja also approached the SA for help in order to 'reform his crims': *Social Problems in Solution*, p. 137. By the early twentieth century in India, a weakening of the relations between the agricultural workers and the landed sections was taking place. The SA with its reputation of wielding an iron hand for extracting work seemed an attractive medium through which to work.
33. *Note, 1925*.

34. Rev. GO 559, 8.3.1920.
35. Recommendations of Delhi Conference on CTs. Home (J) Go 3000, 3.12.1920; Judl. GO 2764, 23.11.1916.
36. PWL GO 2008L, 21.12.1926.
37. PWL GO 2011L, 24.9.1932. Home Secretary in Council of States Debates, Vol. II, No. 9, p. 208; Government of Madras, *Administration Report of the Labour Department, 1925-26*, Madras. There were settlements which were unofficial in the sense that they were not officially declared CT settlements. But for all practical purposes, once CT members were employed in an enterprise, it would be treated as a CT settlement. There were a number of such settlements. For instance, Salem Melurnad Koravars were settled at Krishnaroyapuram, Coimbatore, to work in spinning and weaving mills. PWL GO 574L, 20.2.1929. Togamalai Koravars were also employed in the mills in the area. Home GO 4079, 24.8.1938.
38. *The War Cry*, London, June 1913.
39. Judl. GO 2000, 3.12.1912.
40. It may be noted that it was not even claimed that these women were criminals. The men were to be released before their terms as a part of a reform experiment by SA. The Yerukula prisoners, who had still got six months to two years' sentence to serve, were put into the settlement and given remunerative work. This was, ostensibly, to take away the stigma of earlier imprisonment and allow them a period to reform themselves under the SA's guidance. F. Booth Tucker, *Mukti Fauj*, p. 226; Note on the Sitanagaram Settlement, *Note, 1925*.
41. In spite of the opening of Stuartpuram, Sitanagaram had to be divided into two, for the same reason. They were called the Sainyapuram and Kondapet settlements, and each had a SA officer.
42. PWL GO 711L, 5.7.1926.
43. 'The men generally preferred to go to a settlement when given a choice between that and jail under security sections'. Demi official letter from DM, Tinnevelly to Judl. Dept., Judl. GO 850, 15.4.1914. In a typical case, Yerukulas who were condemned under the security sections of the Criminal Procedure Act, volunteered to go to Kalichedu settlement to escape its enforcement. To avoid going to Kalichedu in turn, they took shelter under the American Baptist Mission in Kavali settlement. Most of these Yerukulas were finally confined to Stuartpuram settlement. Judl. GO 850

15.4.1914. IGP to DM, Tinnevelly. Note on Kavali Settlement, *Note, 1916*; *Note, 1925*, p. 47.

44. This was true of settlements elsewhere as well. Of the Hewettpur settlement at Aligarh, the Salvation Army Manager Mabe had this to say: 'First settlers... arrived under the walls of the fort, crossed the first bridge and caught sight of the water in the moat. In front they saw a second bridge and beyond that the huge gate and frowning walls surmounted by a dozen gun emplacements. Frightened, they halted and despite the urgings of their escort, beat a hasty retreat until well outside, where they set up such a howling as you can scarcely have heard. With unseemly gesticulations they declared the Government had tricked them, who had promised to take them to a home but had brought them to a prison. It was impossible to comfort them.' W. Bramwell Baird, *The Call of the Jackals*, Salvation Army archives, n.d., p.-72.
45. *Ibid.* p. 125.
46. In fact, it was repeated again and again by the police that women were not criminal as far as the Yerukula community was concerned. The women, as late as 1913, did not have a single case of criminal conviction in their names, and also 'did not teach their children to steal'. Memo on Donga Yerukulas by Deputy IGP, *Note, 1925*.
47. Home (J) 523 dt. 5.3.1917. This subject, however, did raise some controversy. The Indian Jails Committee (1919-20) observed that they had a 'humanising and civilising' effect on the parents and should be allowed to stay with them.
48. Government of India, *Report of the Indian Jail Committee*, 1919-20, Vol. I, Chapter XXII.
49. F. Booth Tucker, *Criminocurology or the Indian Crim and What to do with Him—A Report of the Released Prisoners in India*, n.d., p. 58.
50. To explain the use of the word 'riches' for criminals, the SA officials said: 'To others they may hardly appear in the light of riches, but to us each one bears the image and supersubscription of the Divine Mint.' Address to be presented to the Governor at the Stuartpuram settlement, Judl. GO 3219 (Mis.), 21.12.1015.
51. *Report of the Indian Jails Committee, 1919-20,* Chapter XXII.
52. Home (Judl.) GO 2194, 6.9.1916. District Magistrate, Guntur to Undersecretary.
53. Opposition to the settlements for other reasons invariably took the form of this particular allegation. Note on Stuartpuram settlement. *Note, 1925*.

54. To watch 150-200 settlers, one sub inspector, two head constables and 25 constables were needed. PWL GO 7112, 3.7.1926.
55. *Report of the Indian Jails Committee, 1919-20*, Chapter XXII.
56. F. Booth Tucker, *Mukti Fauj*, p. 218. Booth Tucker mentions '[a] long and trying struggle with some subordinate police' about a settlement in Gorakhpur. The police, according to him, had vowed that they would wreck the settlement as their regular supply of income was suddenly cut off. *Social Problems in Solution*, p. 127.
57. 'If any of them absconded—as they frequently did—when captured by the police, their captor received a reward of Rs. 5. This led to a system on the part of the subordinate police of leading some of them out into the country and bringing them back as captives in order to claim the reward. It was a common saying among the Doms that no one need be captured provided he had in his possession Rs. 6—one more than the reward—to offer the policeman as a peace offering.' F. Booth Tucker, *Mukti Fauj*, p. 207 quoted in W. Bramwell Baird, *The Call of the Jackals*, p. 281.
58. It was only by the mid-1920s that the Salvation Army could, with relief, claim a 'very happy relationship between the management and police', PWL GO 697, 1.7.1926. By this time, the powers of surveillance over CT members had been shifted from the headmen to relatively senior police officials.
59. Judl. GO 1605, 24.7.1914. Booth Tucker, who suggested this surveillance method patterned on the settling of native American Indians, had wanted another settlement close to Sitanagaram and Stuartpuram for this reason, but was restrained from doing so. (As a member of the Council put it, 'Booth Tucker is apt, in the elegant American phrase, to bite off more than he can chew.' Cardew in notes to the above GO.
60. Law (G) GO 1896, 13.6.1925.
61. A. Aiyappan, *Report on the Socio-economic Conditions of Aboriginal Tribes of the Province of Madras* quoted in Arnold 1985: 144.
62. Home (Judl.) GO 1059, 6.5.1918.
63. Home GO 918, 24.2.1940. A representative of the All India CT Association, Nellore had wanted to go and confirm whether the Stuartpuram settlers' complaints about several issues were legitimate. Among others was the charge that even private meetings within the settlement were not allowed. He was not allowed into the settlement.

64. To prevent the settler workers from going to the village, Parrys' management, for instance, established a cooperative store within the factory where rice was sold 'at a loss to the firm'. Here it is worth noting that the quantity sold to the workers at that store at a concessional rate was governed by the wages earned by the workers. The more the wages earned, the greater the quantity allowed at concessional rates. Since the wages themselves were earned by the piece rate, this was another ingenious way of increasing the output of the workers by holding out the attraction of cheaper rice. This was in addition to the original and more important purpose of segregating the workers. Within the settlement, a dispensary was built and even a toddy shop opened by the management so as 'not to give [the Koravars] the excuse of loitering about in the village'. This segregation was carried out not only as far as the mixing of Koravars with the villagers was concerned. Once the factory was declared a CT settlement, there was objection to the workers interacting with unregistered members of the same community in the district who came to visit them or live with them. It was recommended to the government through the police administration that the registered settlers should live in a separate block, fenced all round. Access to their quarters by others should be by permission by the manager. If the unregistered members of the same community insisted on visiting the settlers, they should subject themselves to registration, as the manager could otherwise 'exercise no disciplinary authority over them'. Instead of being the medium through which outside influence could be brought into the settlements, the visitors *were* finally registered and made to join the segregated lot of workers. Interestingly enough, it was the IGP who protested, albeit weakly, that the Koravars in question were not really addicted to systematic commission of non bailable offences—a requirement for their notification as CTs. Home (J) 1798, 9.8.1919; Law (G) 2137, 1.9.1922.
65. About 80-90 per cent of the convictions under the CTA in Stuartpuram resulted from absconding. In the case of Parrys' factory, all the convictions were stated to be for absconding.
66. Parrys' manager's suggestions in Government of Madras, *Administration Report of the Stuartpuram Settlement, 1918-1919*, Madras.
67. The problem of absconding was directly related to the insistence on the settlers settling down to the plough, or to factory work. The

settlers would be deliberately made to do ill paid and very hard quarry work with the objective of instilling in them 'discipline and industry' as was done in the case of Sitanagaram settlement. The initial explanation given by the SA for large numbers escaping from Stuartpuram was the Yerukulas' unwillingness to work hard. Slowly the SA accepted that it was also the lack of irrigation facilities in the settlement which was leading to the escapes, dependent as the Yerukulas were on cultivation for their sustenance. Thus the problem of an itinerant community being forced to cultivate would be aggravated by the lack of irrigation facilities. (This was evident from the fact that the number of escapes lessened whenever the crops were successfully cultivated, and conversely, lack of rain in a particular year would lead to an increase in the number of CT members escaping). A further reason for the rise in escapes would be the decline in the living conditions—an outbreak of an epidemic, for instance, in the absence of adequate medical facilities. Government of Madras, *Administration Reports of the Stuartpuram Settlement*, 1915-28, Madras.

68. PWL GO 370L, 12.2.1932.
69. PWL GO 711L, 3.7.1926.
70. Remarks of Guntur DM, Home (J) GO 2194, 6.9.1916.
71. Home (J) GO 2194. 6.9.1916.
72. The term 'forced or compulsory labour' was defined as 'all work or service which is extracted from any person under the menace of any penalty and for which the said person has not offered himself voluntarily.' PWL 1791, 13.7.1931.
73. See Chapter 5 regarding work in the ILTD factory by settlers from Stuartpuram settlement. Devt. GO 1315, 27.10.1933; PWL GO 2671L, 6.12.1934.
74. Law (G) GO 2677, 23.9.1924. A young boy had been taught sense by being forced to do 14 days of undefined 'dirty work' in punishment for running away, and the agent expected that he would not do so again. Law (G) GO 1910, 3.8.1923.
75. When a settler complained to a visiting non-official visitor about low wages, the flippant response was: '...but then we might all complain on that score...more wages will doubtless mean more toddy.' Law (G), GO 1910, 3.8.1923.
76. Cardew to Stuart, Judl. GO 2764, 23.11.1916.
77. Memorial from Bapatla residents to Governor-General in Council, Judl. GO 2509, 14.10.1915.

78. Judl. GO 2308, 22.9.1916.
79. M.C. Tiruvenkata Achariar, *History of the Aziznagar Settlement*, Viriddhachalam, 1926, p. 16.
80. Judl. GO 850, 15.4.1914.
81. Home (J) GO 2113, 14.9.1918.
82. PWL GO 1791L, 13.7.1931. Secretary to Government of India, Home Dept., 13.7.1931.
83. PWL GO 1806L, 16.7.1931. Budget Motion for 1931-32.
84. Legislative Assembly Debates, 3.10. 1931, Vol. VI, No. 9. pp. 1509-25. Speech by Gaya Prasad Singh.
85. 'If a tenant has to work on landlord's land on the penalty of losing his land, it cannot be called forced labour [as this condition was] incidental to his tenancy.' Speech by B. Sitaramaraju, p. 9. It is worth noting here that quite apart from other ways of forcing the settlers to work, tenancy was also used for extracting work from them on land.
86. PWL GO 2011L, 24.9.1932. Home Secretary's speech in Council of States Debates, 5.10.1931, Vol. II, No. 9.
87. Good Conduct Prisoners' Probational Release Act was another such piece of legislation.
88. Secretary's Notes, Home GO 4999, 8.12.1937.
89. Bernard Watson, *A Hundred Years' War*, London, 1964, p. 141.

CHAPTER 4

Land Reclamation, Industrial Recruitment and Settlements

We see how by the first decade of the twentieth century, a more rational sounding view of the itinerant communities was emerging, in turn, paving the way towards their declaration as CTs. This view held that over a period of time, entire communities became criminal because of their loss of traditional means of livelihood. A corollary of this view was that if members of such communities were given work, they would give up their criminal activities, and their reformation would be achieved. The advance made by the administration on the earlier view of these communities as being hereditary criminals was thus coincident with the government's new wish to reform them. The earlier view of them as 'hereditary, habitual and incorrigible' criminals could not coexist with such an aspiration, as it implied unchangeability of character.

In reaching the conclusion that the Criminal Tribes had to be set to work, the government was assisted by the Salvation Army. The organisation managed to convince the government that if a means of livelihood was given to criminals, a majority of them would be only too glad to settle down to a steady and respectable life. 'Wandering gangs' were to be singled out for such settling.[1] Work which was found for such people was in the planned agricultural or industrial settlements.

This chapter discusses the government's land reclamation policy which guided the agricultural settlements and describes the reasons for failure of these settlements. It also looks into the more successful phenomenon of industrial settlements—finding work for CT members in private enterprises—which became official policy in 1916.

I

One of the overall objectives of the government was land reclamation and this consideration also dictated the day-to-day administration of the earlier CT settlements. In fact, the entire set of decisions about the so-called agricultural settlements was based on the government's plans to increase revenue by turning large tracts of wasteland into cultivable land. This could be done by parcelling out land to missionary agencies that would get the settlers to work on it for a living. (Land was also given to members of the depressed castes with the same objective.) Over a period of time, once continuous work on the land had made it productive, the government could start collecting land revenue on it either by making the cultivators owners, or by leasing the land out to them. Thus, the twin objectives of reclamation, reformation and rehabilitation of certain sections of society on the one hand, and an increase in the revenue of the government on the other, could be achieved simultaneously.

The public rationale, which knit together these two objectives, based itself on the assertion that agriculture was the 'natural profession' of all Indians. It was hoped that 'by getting the (itinerant communities) to adopt a pastoral and agricultural life, their nomadic habits...[would]...be broken'. The SA, on its part, agreed and expressed its desire to 'bring up little boys bubbling with crime...in an atmosphere of agriculture.'[2]

As far as the proclaimed policy regarding agricultural settlements was concerned, small plots of land were to be parcelled out to settlers who were to be tenants of the managing agency. A rent would be charged, which was to be used for covering the expenses of the settlement. The land itself was to be given free of assessment by the government to the agency in charge, the operational owner of all such land. It was to be so distributed to the settlers that each family got a piece of both wet and dry land, and was held responsible for the cultivation of both. If any family was found to be neglecting either, it was to be put on hard labour, such as breaking stones and digging earth and the land was to be given away to another deserving family. While land was not to be made over to a family immediately, lest it be alienated, in due course of time a *patta* (title deed) was to be given to the family who had proved by its good conduct and continuous hard work its fitness to own the land. This desirable end, the government reasoned, would ensure an honest means of livelihood for the settlers, and the task of the criminals' reformation would then be complete. The government was the final judge of when that appropriate time had come, in what share the pattas were to be given, and to which settlers.[3]

A confidential document for government's own use and reference, however, reveals government's actual concerns as far as agricultural settlements were concerned. It was repeatedly noted with some anxiety that the work of 'opening up the lands was not pushed on with, and no regular work on the land was insisted on.' It was noted of a particular settlement that 'there had been too much loafing allowed and the progress made in reclaiming the land had been very slow.' Generally, the progress of the settlement itself was identified with progress in land reclamation and it was hoped that the Salvation Army officials would reclaim the lands granted expeditiously.[4]

Under one of the rules of the CTA, settlers in agricultural settlements were to carry out all tasks for improvement of the land or growing crops as might be ordered by the manager.[5] In places where the settlers rebelled, the 'Gospel of Compulsion' could be used by the agency in charge.[6] (The Salvation Army genuinely believed that they were divinely ordained to force civilising habits on born criminals.) There was also a specific policy regarding settlers who owned small pieces of land outside the settlement, and who agitated to be given leave to go and look after them. Forcible selling off of such land by the authorities and refusal to give leave to the settlers helped the settlers to concentrate on settlement land instead.[7] (Here the administration was dealing with sections of the so-called wandering tribes who were already 'pastoralists'. The irony of first making them landless, and then of settling them on government land to make them respectable cultivators seems to have escaped those zealously involved in their reclamation.)

Land could be reclaimed by the government in several ways. In a typical instance, a group of Koravars with families was made to surrender by police harassment and made to complete some unfinished tank work. After the tank work was completed, the entire group was notified as a CT, and moved to a CT settlement. Here they were given swamp land to reclaim.[8] While making out proposals for reclamation of CTs, land reclamation would be posed as an important incentive for the administration to spend money on settling them. While trying to convince the government of the viability of an ambitious Korava Reclamation Scheme, the District Magistrate, Salem assured the government that 'by making 10,000 odd Koravars of this district... respectable and hardworking, the expenditure (on digging wells and developing the land) will be returned to government in the shape of increased receipts [taxes] from land.'[9]

II

Many of the schemes to settle CT members on land, however, failed. A plan to settle Gandarvakottai Koravars was a typical one. When they were given land 'some fair, and some very poor', the land was not cultivated. The community that had been declared CTs for the scheme had to be sent back to their villages.[10]

The plan to reclaim land and run agricultural settlements failed for a number of reasons. The settlers were not from peasant backgrounds; the tools were too primitive, and the quality of land too poor:[11]

> The Salvation Army found it very tedious.
> To convert them into good cultivators industrious.
> To work on land they were forced and could not be induced.
> Though driven like a flock of sheep the first crop failed...

No crowbars no proper spade and no physical strength.
So work turned out did not reach the desired length.[12]

These reasons substantially contributed to the failure of the schemes. More importantly, the hitherto itinerant communities resented being forcibly settled on land. Nor did they share the government view that 'ownership of land was a means of acquiring self respect.'[13] Apart from this, the wages given in the agricultural settlements to settlers for cultivating land owned by the managing agency were less than they got as agricultural workers outside. Those settlers who were tenants of the managing agency had to also pay a substantial rent.[14] In addition, the settlers in agricultural settlements would often be made to grow only commercial crops instead of food crops.[15] If settlers had to buy rice for their consumption from the open market, proper wages and a reasonable rent were crucial:

The wages distributed never reached per day even annas four
What could they do? as to live they wanted much more.[16]

The most crucial reason for the failure of the agricultural settlements, however, was active opposition by the landlords to the whole scheme of settling the landless on land. There were a number of protests when the settlements were being planned, and large tracts of land were being granted to the settlement authorities, mostly missionary agencies.

When the SA was given assessment-free land to run Stuartpuram settlement in Guntur district, it sparked off an agitation by landholders in the surrounding areas. The proposal to make CT communities into tenants and eventually patta owners was not acceptable to the landlords of the neighbourhood. The paddy land in particular was greatly in demand, and when suitably irrigated, was very valuable.[17] Numerous petitions flooded the government, protesting against the proposal. One of the inspirers of the settlement policies, Harold Stuart, after whom the Stuartpuram settlement was named, personally visited the district to meet the petitioners. He took a strong position, and reprimanded the (high caste) landlord agitators for 'being opposed to their own scriptures' in not giving the itinerant communities a chance to reform.[18]

The real reasons for the protest, however, soon became clear to the administration. When the vociferous protest by landlords against the Yerukula settlement was being discussed within the administration, it was remarked that the

> monied folk of [Guntur had] counted...on buying the swamp land at cheap rates and rack renting the actual cultivator whenever a crop could be raised.[19]

This, in fact, was precisely what some other individuals and missionary organisations were planning to do, and sections of the administration were not at all averse to the idea. This is exactly what the protest was about and there were at least two plans that such protests foiled.

A failed plan, which the landlords never got to hear about, was one that Stuart had felt the government should 'gladly accept'. It was put forward by an individual entrepreneur who wanted to purchase land in an auction, which he admitted would cost him so little as to become his 'for nothing'. This he would convert into a CT settlement with all the powers under the CTA to drive the workers. He would begin to pay a rent to the government after he had reclaimed the land. This plan had to be dropped because of some internal differences within the administration about other uses to which the land in question could be put.[20]

The above proposal was kept confidential, but when a similar proposal was being actively considered by the government, the news reached the landlord sections and there was an uproar. The subject of their attack was the person who was going to start a settlement for the Yenadi community. It was alleged by the landlords in the petition they submitted that he had used influence with the local officials to acquire forest reserves and a tract of 1500 acres of land was being dug with irrigation channels.[21] It was alleged that the person, Thommsen, was encouraged by the fact that the Salvation Army was given 2000 acres: he saw that 'settlement of CTs was the hobby of the hour...and with all the resources of a pushful personality' had applied for land himself in the name of the Church Panchayat.[22] This person, the petition went on, was involved in 'trade in labourers', sending Indians overseas for work, and it was argued that such a person was unfit for being in charge of settlers. The proposal to give land to the Church Panchayat had to be dropped.

Another settlement was proposed by the American Baptist Mission in the form of a suggestion to form a cooperative. The Mission was to be put in charge of a CT settlement 'with an objective to demonstrate that cooperation in agriculture, manufacture, banking and trade produces wealth and benefits the community.'[23] The Mission put forward an estimate of the extent and value of land they would need to run the proposed CT settlement. The government informed the applicants that the public spirit which prompted the offers was much appreciated. However, it was regretted that the administration would not be able to accept the offers as there were already three CT settlements existing in Guntur.[24]

Apart from the objection by high caste landed sections to 'wandering tribes' becoming patta holders, the protest by the landlords was in a large measure due to the fear of losing the services of the CT members as agricultural workers on their own land.[25] Essentially, village headmen and landlords were beginning to take for granted the possibility of extracting free forced labour from CT members under their surveillance: the formation of settlements would take away such opportunities. The memorandum by the landlords had explicitly demanded from the government that the number of settlers in Stuartpuram be reduced. The freedom of the settlers was crucial for the landlords as agricultural operations on their land suffered if too many settlements were formed in the area.[26] This was about the time when emigration to Ceylon was also affecting agricultural work in the presidency as a whole.[27] It is important to note here the difference in approach by the landlords to the declaration of communities as CTs, as opposed to their confinement to settlements—the landlords could use the provisions regarding notification and surveillance for their own purposes, but establishment of settlements was not welcomed by them.

Opposition to agricultural settlements run by missionaries was often posed on religious grounds. High caste Hindus, frequently landlords, objected to the reclamation work being entirely entrusted to Christian missionaries, who were inclined to look upon conversion as an important factor in the process of reclamation.[28] The landlords had experienced in the past, and this was also noted by the administration, that lower caste Hindus thus converted ceased to be amenable to earlier pressures. This had happened in the case of Malas and Madigas.[29]

There was a general awareness growing within the administration that there was a certain amount of ill feeling between the 'adjoining ryots and settlers.'[30] The result was an accompanying decline in enthusiasm about agricultural settlements, and a recognition of the need for a policy about CT settlements which would not alienate the landlords, important allies of the British during this period.

III

Immediately after the institution of the CTA, while the government was settling CTs on land, another parallel process was taking place by which CT members were being employed in private enterprises with the help of the senior police administration.

It was in 1913 that employment of CT members in private enterprises on a fairly large scale was proposed in Madras Presidency. A series of notes was submitted by police officers, urging the government to apply the provisions of the Act to various communities, and suggesting means of employment for them.[31] This was because under Section 11 of the Act, it was necessary when recommending the restriction of movements of a community, to propose some area to which their movements were to be restricted, and to show in what manner they would be able to earn their living within such an area. This area could then be called a CT settlement.

The provision regarding CT settlements came as a boon to the police administration, which had hitherto been at a loss to explain the ever-increasing rates of crime in the Presidency. The high rates of organised and grave crime were now explained as being due to CTs not settled as yet, or due to absconders from the settlements.[32] Within the administration itself, however, it soon began to be alleged that the whole policy of the Act and the establishing of settlements had been done in the interests of the police, and without sufficient regard for the happiness and well being of the concerned people.[33]

The Criminal Tribes Act was used by the police administration for confining a number of CT members to various private enterprises. The procedure was as follows: A senior police officer would make out a case that the members of a particular community were dangerously and desperately criminal and should be notified and restricted to an area. Sometimes facts and figures would be produced to support the case made out for notification. When convincing evidence was lacking, which was often the case, other ways were found to prove the criminality of the concerned group.[34]

At the time of a proposal for the notification, suggestions would be given about possible employers. In the case of Dasaris, mica mines owned by Brandt and Company in Nellore were deemed to be a suitable area for providing means of livelihood. In the case of Kilagudi Kallas, Harvey's cotton mills at Madura were recommended as a place where a settlement could be formed. The agent of the Company was proposed as the manager of the settlement. For another community of Kondadoras the manganese mines owned by Vizianagaram Mining Company was recommended as a settlement. A community of Koravas was to be given work at the Magnesite Syndicate Ltd; the Nakkalas were to be settled at Kodur mines and their movements restricted to the area owned by the Company; a branch of Koravas was to be settled with a local fund contractor in quarries near Tanjore and another section of Koravas at the Parry's sugar factory in Tinnevelly, and so on.[35] The Inspector General of Police had also entertained a demand for workers from the United Planters' Association of South India (UPASI). Over 2000 workers were required for different estates in the Annamalais, and the Nilgiris. According to the list sent by the Association, these workers were to be spread over 18 estates.[36] Giving employment to criminal tribes for their reformation, in this case at least, was obviously not the aim. The workers were needed only for two months, and no individual worker was to be employed for more than a month.

Sometimes, individuals from vulnerable communities would be invited to work in an enterprise on a 'voluntary' basis. At the same time, the administration explicitly stated that the provisions of the Criminal Tribes Act could be employed if the voluntary scheme did not work satisfactorily. The general policy of the government was that 'either persuasion or force' should be used. If persuasion failed (which was invariably the case), the force required could be sufficiently provided by the Criminal Tribes Act.[37]

Such forced work was, however, posed by the administration as a favour by the employers to the concerned CT workers. A CT settlement was formed for Brandt and Company to provide workers for the mica mines, but the settlers were said to be subsisting on the charity of the employers. That this charity was unsolicited by the settlers was clear from the fact that the Superintendent of Police had to keep a strong police guard at hand. Similarly, a Mudaliar quarry owner was to take a 'close and fatherly interest in the Koravars ... with the help of a head constable and a few constables in the village...'[38]

In contravention of the rules or logic of the CTA, an enterprise's need for workers was identified first, and notifications done accordingly of the communities who were to work in it. This happened in a dramatic way in the case of the mica mines owned by Brandt and Co. When the Kathiars refused to work voluntarily in the mines, not only did the government declare this community a CT, but also the Dasaris of Kurnool and Guntur, Pachappas of Godavari and Kistna, and Dommars of Nellore. In this way a total of 1500 settlers were collected to work in the mines.[39] Similarly, when there was a request for workers from the Wolfram mines in Burma, it was discovered that even this total of 1500 was not enough, as planters from Annamalais also wanted 1000 workers. It was then decided that a Telugu branch of Koravas should also be registered for the purpose.[40]

The provisions of the CTA allowed special powers to deal with CT workers in case the company authorities wanted to take disciplinary measures against them. This was done by *declaring an ordinary factory to be a settlement* established under the Criminal Tribes Act, and by appointing the manager of the factory as the manager of the settlement, with all the powers of control. This could be done even if the conduct of the workers was 'good' and even if none of them was guilty of even petty theft.[41]

The case of Parrys' factory was typical. In 1914, two years before the factory was actually set up, an official from Parrys' wrote to the Government, asking to be provided with members of the 'wandering tribes' as workers. The scheme did not profess to be a philanthropic one—the management openly confessed that the factory was short of workers.[42] Once established, the manager of Parrys' was in due course given all the powers under the CTA. When the government initially hesitated to do so, continuing instead to make the police responsible for the surveillance of the workers, the following bitter words of the Company agent clinched the issue:

> Their [the Koravars'] general behaviour...is also getting worse, such as abusing of writers, *refusing to carry out work assigned to them and running away from work*. All this proves the Koravars are getting out of hand. I have no legal power whatsoever to restrict or nip in the bud any criminal tendency or enforce discipline necessary for the control of labour. At the beginning when the proposal was posed [to the Government], it was to be a criminal settlement [and] the firm took up the matter as a business proposal...[43]

The government, after consultations with the Inspector General of Police, did declare the factory a settlement. It was recognised that the manager was not in a position to sack the captive workers; if he did so, the whole economic rationale of the enterprise would collapse, as would the entire logic behind industrial settlements. The workers *had* to be controlled and made more pliant through the provisions of the CTA, both from the point of view of the factory management and the government.

As evident from the Parrys' case, leave to CT workers was

granted sparely, and only on the recommendation of the manager. The factory supervisors were entrusted with the task of reporting, to the local police, workers' movements in the settlement during the day. They also had the powers to check the attendance at the settlement at different times of night and report their findings to the police.[44] The Annual Report submitted by the factory manager to the Government on the working of the Parrys' settlement noted with satisfaction that the 'thieving propensities' of the wandering tribe in question were nowhere in evidence:

> Considering that the tribe was leading since generations a roving life, I consider that they settled down to their present mode of life better then expected.[45]

Once strict rules to govern an industrial CT settlement were formulated to meet the specific needs of a particular employer, they could then act as a precedent and as a model for other settlements.[46] As described earlier, certain communities would be initially registered because workers were required for work in a particular private enterprise. If for any reason the enterprise closed down, the members of the community remained registered. Thus Koravar workers of the Parry's factory were instructed to report to the police or the headman of their village after the factory closed down.[47] Similarly, Koravars of Bellary were registered for the specific purpose of working in the Magnesite Syndicate, but when the company decided to suspend its operations, the members were transferred to a criminal tribe settlement.[48] This also happened to the 1500 workers acquired for the mica mines in Nellore. When work was stopped in the mines, the registered CT members were sent to work in the plantations.[49]

Sometimes, those already at agricultural settlements would be tempted away to private enterprises on a 'voluntary' basis. Many settlers had entered the agricultural settlements under the illusion that they were more tolerable than prisons;[50] some now volunteered to work in private enterprises when the conditions in these settlements were found to be intolerable. Promises of factory work outside these agricultural settlements seemed attractive in relative terms.[51] What the settlers did not know was that the manager of each enterprise (where they were going to be employed) was, for all practical purposes, given the powers of the manager of a CT settlement. This was inevitable as the bargaining position of employers (who took settlers for work in their enterprises) vis-a-vis the administration was strong: the government was all too eager to relieve congestion at the agricultural settlements.[52] The settlers who worked in these enterprises were entirely in the hands of their employers, whose potential position was admitted to be 'even more despotic than that of a slave owner'.[53] The SA confirmed that

> while the European directors and proprietors were usually affable and reasonable, many of their foremen were perfect slave drivers, and the tendency in all was to extract exceedingly long hours and heavy tasks from the [CT] employees.[54]

What has been described above is the way in which a particular provision of the CTA was used by the police administration to serve the interests of private entrepreneurs. The factory form of employment for CT members was not a part of government policy yet and in principle 'agricultural' settlements were still preferred by the government.

IV

The official policy about the CTA being used to provide workers for private enterprises developed in the context of increasing opposition by the landlords to the agricultural settlements, as also hostility towards missionaries in charge of such settlements. The administration initially calculated that if missionaries were to be put in charge of CT settlements located within the private enterprises, the mission would stand to gain so much financially that it would be under 'a very considerable pecuniary obligation to government'.[55] However, the way the policy of the industrial settlements unfolded, missionary agencies like the Salvation Army were seldom put in charge. This was because the administration sought to give almost absolute powers of control over the workers to the employers themselves.[56] It is worth looking into the reasons for this.

As far as official policy regarding the Criminal Tribes settlements was concerned, there was a significant development in 1916. A conference was held at Ootacamund to discuss questions raised by the government of Bombay Presidency relating to the working of the Act. At this conference, representatives of different provinces and states in Southern India were present.[57] Of particular interest in this conference was the 'Bombay method' of establishing industrial settlements, and providing the settlers with employment. Here Starte, Settlement Officer for CTs, Bijapur, explained his novel method of settling communities in the vicinity of the textile mills. The advantages of this were described to be two-fold: the settlers were able to make more money by this than by any other means of employment and secondly, they were employed regularly.[58]

According to Starte, the chief advantage of mill work for CT members was self-evident:

> There is such a shortage of labour in the mills, that they [the employers] are ready to take anyone, no matter what his previous character or training may have been.

This was reported to be true of most seasons of the year. He pointed out that in normal years, work in the mills was sustainable for just a few months during the rainy season; full strength work was possible only during the famine years. The mill authorities, he confided, liked CT workers. Having once trained them, there was a good prospect of retaining them sufficiently long to recover training expenses. A further advantage of factory employment was that it afforded employment for men, women and children alike.

In a pamphlet, 'An Experiment in the Reformation of CTs' Starte had testified that all the mill owners employing the CTs were willing to accept more. This, he explained, was due to the difficulty they experienced throughout India in finding workers. The experiment of settling CTs in the vicinity of factories was seen to be valuable as then 'a new source for recruiting labour will be opened up'.[59]

The need to find *workers* for enterprises, then, was projected as the primary rationale for industrial settlements. This was put together with another rationale—that regular employment was necessary for reforming criminal tribes. In this way, the package could be made acceptable to sceptical elements both within the administration, and the general public.

Significantly, this development was not seen with much concern by the Indian press. The press was, in fact, quite appreciative:

> A large and efficient addition has been made to the mill labour supply of the Presidency, out of material which consisted of...professional coiners, cattle lifters, thieves and petty pilferers... The results hitherto obtained should prove of special interest to mill authorities of the [Madras] Presidency in view of the ever increasing difficulty experienced by them in finding sufficient workers for their mills.[60]

Another nationalist newspaper spoke appreciatively of the 'unqualified success' of the experiments by Starte and the fact that nearly half the labour required for the mills in Bijapur and other mills in the Belgaum district came from the CTs.[61]

Thus the refrain about 'shortage of labour' runs through the arguments of all those who supported the settling of Criminal Tribes in this way. 'In Bombay, they are moving CTS from place to place as the demand for their labour in mills requires,' Harold Stuart had to admonish the Inspector General of Prisons, who had protested against the shifting of a particular CT to the Assam estates from Madras Presidency.[62] Also, as the Settlement Officer pointed out, captive workers would have to be employed in the mills if the employers were to recover the expenses of training: the mill workers from CTs lived, in most cases, in houses surrounded by a wall and guarded at night by a police guard. The normal worker, it appeared, was not willing to come for 13 hours a day, on a continuous basis as it was 'very trying to the health of any person'. Many of the mill workers would go to their villages for a month or so in connection with their agricultural work. The CTA was to the advantage of the employer here as the government could legitimately prevent the CT employees from 'wandering about on a holiday' as it would be dangerous to let them loose on the general public.[63] With this rationale, a CT member could be employed throughout the year, without a break. As was recognised within the administration itself, in another context,

> [a]ll the advantages from docile and regular labour will go to the company...which has a marked advantage over a company bidding for labour in the open market.[64]

Moreover, once in the factory, CT workers could be prevented from defying the management in any way.[65] Apart from absconding, which was punishable with imprisonment upto a year and a half, fines could be imposed on the settlers for the following offences—being late for work, leaving the work spot, being absent from work, sleeping on duty, loafing and *being impertinent.*[66] For this reason, it was important to have not just CT labour which could be made to work regularly, but also the manager of the enterprise had to be given the powers of the manager of a CT settlement.

From the administration's point of view, an important advantage, agreed to by the conference participants in 1916, was that factory work formed the cheapest mode of settlement tried up to then by the authorities: it meant little or no investment by the government.[67] Housing was provided by the factory owners, with a rent charged to the settlers. In the meanwhile, agitations by landlords against agricultural settlements helped make up the administration's mind.

The Madras police administration already had some experience of the success of this experiment in the case of mines, quarries, factories, and tea and coffee estates from 1913 onwards. By the end of 1916, a proposal to run industrial settlements for CTs 'on the lines followed so successfully by Mr Starte' was officially accepted by the Government of Madras. The DIG of Police was requested to consider the formation of a few such settlements in Madras

Presidency.[68] Under the provisions of the Act, in combination with this new scheme, the CT members could be employed not only within the Presidency in private enterprises, but were actually sent out to Ceylon and the Penang Peninsula.[69]

It was generally felt by 1920 that the most successful CT settlements in India were those where settlers were employed in private enterprises.[70] The only fear was that some agitators might take up the cause.[71] In fact, the government would sometimes hold back in handing to the manager of an industrial enterprise the powers under the CTA. The reason was the fear that 'Mr Wadia and Kesava Pillai and other protectors of the poor would take up the case of the powers of both the factory manager and the settlement manager being vested in one individual.'[72] Non-official visitors to the settlement were to be appointed as a safeguard against malpractice by employers. These visitors, however, were to be chosen only in consultation with the managing agency.[73]

V

The British Indian government had, from the beginning of European private enterprise in India, helped the employers if not to find workers, then at least to keep them.[74] Use of the provisions of the CTA was another way of achieving the same or better results: while asking the administration for CT workers explicitly, the employers mentioned their aim to acquire a *permanent* workforce.[75] It is important to emphasise here the difference between a 'regular' workforce, which implied uninterrupted attendance or work throughout the year (to enable a factory to recover training expense on workers), and a 'permanent' workforce, which implied stabilisation of the same community of workers over generations. The second kind of request was evident only in those cases where workers were difficult to find, let alone keep—an aspect of those enterprises which were geographically isolated and needed an assured supply of workers over some years.

Two such cases are discussed briefly—the plantations in

Annamalai, and the sugar factory owned by Parrys' in Tinnevelly. In both cases, CTA was sought to be used to achieve this ambitious end.

In the case of Parrys, when the management wanted to set up a sugar factory in Tinnevelly, the area was found to be sparsely inhabited—mainly by palmyrah tappers—and workers were not easy to find. As the Agent of the company candidly stated:

> ...we were in want of permanent labour we could depend upon and government wanted to settle down a CT. In order to acquire permanent labour we were prepared to undergo trouble and expense...[76]

That the factory management aimed at acquiring a regular and permanent workforce is also evident from the interest taken in the education and training of the children.[77]

Parry's partial success lay in its being able to combine in a single community of workers, virtually all the operations carried out in the factory. Even younger Koravar children were incorporated into the manufacturing process in different ways. Girls and boys too young to be employed on the operations of the factory proper, for instance, were employed on 'Mrs Weth's casuarina plantation'.[78] Mrs Weth was the wife of the manager of the factory, and though her work was posed as a harmless gardening activity, it was in fact an integral part of the factory's fuel raising projects: 'Fuel was lacking in the area...casuarina was planted to meet this shortage.'[79] The incorporation of the family into various work processes at the factory is evident from a study of the factory records.

The more instructive case, however, is that of the plantations in the hills where CT workers were specially sought after. Soon after the institution of the CTA, a planter member of the Legislative Council was approached by H.A.Stuart, member of the Governor's Council, with the suggestion that settlers of an overcrowded CT settlement be sent to the plantations to work. It was mooted that as in Assam, the workers would be encouraged to settle down in the Annamalais on small plots of land and form a *local* supply of permanent workforce. Moral improvement of the settlers was also likely to be greater in fresh surroundings and open air.[80] Stuart suggested that each estate be made into a CT settlement and the Superintendent of each estate appointed manager of the settlement. A police officer was put on special duty as an intermediary between the government and the estate owners.

This arrangement was in response to the several proposals made by the planters to the administration. The District Magistrate of Nellore had received repeated requests from planters, including those from Assam, to allow Yerukula inmates of a CT settlement to be recruited, and had in fact allowed European estate superintendents to visit the settlement and address the settlers with this proposal. The District Superintendent of Police, Salem, was in correspondence on his own with the Yercaud Planters' Association about employment of CT members on plantations. The government, to make the procedure more regular and official instructed him to correspond, as far as recruitment was concerned, through the labour department of United Planters Association of South India (UPASI). The director of UPASI was also in touch with the Inspector General of Police for recruitment of CT workers for Annamalai, Nilgiris and Wynaad.[81] A year later, the planters wished to acknowledge the government's role in these recruitments:

> We have to thank... the Government for being allowed to take a hand in the reclamation of the [CT] settlers. We do not expect to reap great advantages from [CT] employment at first, *but we feel that as the younger generation grows up, we shall secure a valuable labour force.*[82]

The planters were clear about the kind of workers (and their families) they wanted for work on the plantations in order to achieve this end. While the isolated location of an enterprise necessitated a permanent workforce, it was also important to ensure that the workers themselves were those who effectively had no other homes and no ties other than those on the estates. The administration and the planters had in mind a case of hundreds of Uppu Koravars, who after their release from a jail in Trichinopoly, were approached directly by a planter to work in his estates. As they had no homes any more, and the bullocks they used to possess to transport their merchandise had died while they were in jail, they accepted the proposal.[83] This 'authentic instance of a successful effort to reclaim criminals by a planter on own initiative' was quoted as an encouraging pointer to the fact that CT members could work in plantations, provided they had lost all contact with their original homes in the villages from which they came.

Though the SA officials were eager to work in the estates, the planters wished to be in direct charge of the workers. The SA scheme contained a crucial provision of separating children from the parents in order to ensure complete reformation of the new generation. This was looked upon with displeasure by UPASI.

> From the planters' point of view, the brightness and intelligence of the children and *the chance of their ultimately forming a settled labour force is the most attractive part of the whole thing...*[84]

Hence, the planters decided to manage the settlements without assistance from the SA.

The provisions of the CTA thus promised to assist the planters in gaining a permanent workforce. Booth Tucker of the Salvation Army in his interview to a newspaper, speaking about the advantages of transporting CT workers to Assam, said:

> This scheme has the enormous advantage that these people [CT members] when once ordered into a settlement cannot leave it without a pass which, of course, is what the tea gardens want. There could be no talk of bolting coolies, of defaulting coolies, because if a man tried to escape or to go elsewhere, he would at once be arrested, brought before a magistrate and sent to prison.[85]

Initially, when the Yerukula settlers at Kavali were approached, they refused to go to the plantations. The reason why the settlers were finally forced into 'voluntary' emigration to the inhospitable hills was lack of employment opportunities at the settlement and the harshness of the disciplinary methods employed by the administrators of the settlement. It was officially admitted that at this settlement, wages were low and paid according to the piece rate. Since work itself was very scarce, the actual wages received by the settlers were not just low, but also erratic and irregular.

The 'irksomeness of discipline' at Kavali, among other things, meant that children were separated from parents and not allowed to sleep or eat with them.[86] The logic of the planters, on the other hand, was to keep families together in order to acquire a regular work force. This coincided with the desire of the settlers to keep their children with them, and was a very important consideration which finally made them decide to go to the estates. In other words, the impetus for working in the estates came not in the form of incentives, but because of the serious disincentives that the CT settlement in question imposed.[87] Such Yerukulas who were transported to the hills had no idea that they were being transported effectively to another settlement.

It is not surprising that this community was so attractive to the plantation owners. The specifications laid down by the United Planters Association of South India for an ideal workforce absolutely coincided with the kind of communities held imprisoned in the CT settlement. The UPASI director had sent 'ideal gang' specifications to the government, which were essentially composed of extended families of both the husband and the wife. It is worth reproducing here what the UPASI director considered an 'ideal gang':

1. An elderly man capable of working
2. His wife
3. His grown up son
4. Wife of 3
5. Children of working age of 3 and 4
6. Infants of 3 and 4
7. Grown up daughter of 1 and 2
8. Husband of 7
9. Children of working age of 7 and 8
10. Infants of 7 and 8
11. Brothers or sisters of 4
12. Wives or husbands of 11
13. Progeny of working age of 11 and 12

14. Infants of 11and 12
15. Brothers and sisters of 8 and their progeny and so on.

The ideal being seldom attainable, the nearest thing to it should be aimed at.[88]

Under the circumstances, the desire of the Yerukulas to keep their children and the shreds of their community life together worked completely in favour of the plantation owners. Once at the plantations, the Yerukulas found the picture stark but initially, except on one estate, they made neither any attempt to leave, nor to strike work. The reason for this reluctance lay in the original cause of their acceptance of the proposal to work in the estates—harsh living conditions at the CT settlement from which they were initially drawn, and the separation of their children from the families. A few wanted to leave saying they 'preferred to be killed rather than work in the plantations', but they were caught at the foot of the hills, and sent back to the plantations through the application of the Criminal Tribes Act.[89]

Criminal Tribe workers joined other striking workers only sporadically, and had the reputation with the management of being extremely reliable workers.[90] This they earned by appeasing the management in order to survive the tough working and living conditions on the hills as well as at the plantations. They tried to please the management in various ways and ended up becoming blackleg workers during strike actions by CT and non-CT workers alike. Meanwhile, the settlement from which they were initially enticed away to the plantations had generally become the recruiting ground for strikebreakers.[91] Once on the estates, the settlers were found 'more amenable to reason...and well reported as workers'. The administration had made it clear that any recalcitrant settlers would have to go back to settlements 'where there is stricter discipline.'[92]

Thus CT settlements at one point promised to become a recruiting ground for not just workers on the estates, but blacklegs too, as a result of the combined efforts of the planters and the administration to form a reliable pool of workers. However, the 'permanent labour scheme' did not entirely work to the satisfaction of the plantation owners, and had to be wound up.[93]

Notes

1. Judl. GO 2000-01 (Press), 23.12. 1912, letter from F. Booth Tucker to Governor of Madras, 31.10.1910; Judl. GO 2764, 23.11.1916; Home (J) GO 3000, 3.12.1920.
2. Judl. GO 2205, 10.10.1914. 'Carrying out of ordinary rough farm labour is an essential part of training of the boys...and will help to leaven the general lump of dirt and criminality which the Koravars represent'. PWL GO 618L, 10.3.1932; Government of Madras, *Administration Report of Stuartpuram Settlement*, 1917, Madras.
3. *Note, 1925*.
4. Home (Judl.) 525, 5.3.1917.
5. Rule 37 (CTA, 1911), PWL GO 2008L, 21.12.1926.
6. Report on Madanpalli settlement, *The War Cry*, June, 1913.
7. Judl. GO 629, 8.3.1916.
8. DM, Chittoor to government, in reference to Nawabpeta Korachas, Judl. GO 520, 2.3.1914; Judl. GO 1405, 12.7.1913.
9. Parenthesis added. PWL GO 1072L, 27.3.1929.
10. The DSP could now say triumphantly that the scheme was bound to fail as it had been started by an earlier DSP at a time 'when settlements were in fashion'. Home GO 2357, 14.11.1917; Law (General) GO 1846, 7.11.1921.
11. Home GO 3953, 20.7.1939; Law (General) GO 2030, 17.6.1926; Judl. GO 1533, 14.7.1914.
12. M.C. Tiruvenkata Achariar, *History of the Aziznagar Settlement*, 1926, p. 2,13. It was revealed by the author, who was the manager of the settlement, that to cultivate 700 acres of land, only 40 pairs of bulls were available (p. 15).
13. When the Registrar of Cooperative Societies was approached to form a cooperative society among Koravars, he declined to do so. He pointed out that the waste land assigned to them had very little value, and in any case land was not even registered in the names of the Koravars. Moreover, the collection of loans would be done with active police supervision. '...[that] is not cooperation,' he concluded. PWL GO 1099L, 3.4.1930.
14. 'The Commandant has a fat rent roll...' it was reported of a

settlement managed by the SA in the north. *The Times of India*, 9.12.1921 quoted in F. Booth Tucker, *Mukti Fauj*, n.d., p. 219.

15. Home GO 1486, 24.6.1918. Incidentally, this was probably a major reason why the SA wanted legal powers to be given charge of the produce of the settlement.
16. M.C. Tiruvenkata Achariar, *History of the Aziznagar Settlement*, 1926, pp. 12-13.
17. According to the SA, it was Rs. 1000 per acre. F. Booth Tucker, *Mukti Fauj*, p. 232.
18. F. Booth Tucker, *Mukti Fauj*, p. 233; The road from the settlement to Bapatla, a distance of five miles, was full of placards hanging from the trees, claiming there was no land to spare, and demanding immediate removal of the settlement from the neighbourhood. *The Hindu*, Madras, 2.8.1915.
19. Demi-official letter from Guntur Collector to Stuart, Member of Council, 20.3.1915 in Judl. GO 2509, 15.10.1915.
20. Home (Judl.) GO 2028, 28.9.1917.
21. To add to the outrage, he was selling timber to the local people.
22. Memorial (sic) from residents of Bapatla under the leadership of President of Taluk Association, Bapatla to Governor General in Council, 2.2.1915 In Judl. GO 2509, 14.10.1915.
23. Judl. GO 155, 22.1.1914.
24. *Ibid.* 'In short, the Christian Missionaries became unpopular for ...getting profits from the land,labour and capital of the settlements and as a result the situation of the settlers became just like that of the Hawaian who said to a Christian Missionary, "When the white man came you had the Bible, and we owned the land; now we have the Bible and you have the land".' Sher Singh 'Sher', *The Sansis of Punjab: A Gypsy and Denotified Tribe of Rajput Origin*, Delhi, 1965, p. 253.
25. Notes to Judl. GO 2509, 14.10.1915. Comments by IGP. Opposition to establishment of agricultural settlements continued. 'Counter-efforts' were also organised at a later stage by landlords when the Yenadi Reclamation Scheme was being put into action by the administration in Chittoor district. This, it was pointed out, was due to the landlords' fear of losing cheap Yanadi labour. Government of Madras, *Administration Report for Criminal Tribe Settlements and Kallar, Koravar and Yenadi Reclamation for 1940*; *The Hindu*, Madras, 26.3.1965; Judl. GO 2509, 14.10.1915. Representation to DM, Guntur.
26. Judl. GO 2509, 14.10.1915. Many CT members were not only

employed as agricultural workers by the landlords, but also used to carry the grain from the fields to the landlords' homes, using their own animals for the purpose.

The objection of the landlords to the settlements could be for another reason. Itinerant communities like Koravars were heavily indebted to the landlord sections. PWL GO 1072L, 27.3.1929; Judl. GO 1605, 24.7.1914. Once settled, such people were out of reach of the landlords.

27. 'Labour is becoming scarce by reason of emigration...this question of emigration most vitally affects agricultural labour.' And again, '...the mirasidars are louder and louder in their complaint that labour is becoming scarce by reason of emigration. Indentured emigration under Emigration Act in 1911-12 show that 34 per cent of the number is from Madras...constant stream of agricultural labour going out of the country is a serious handicap to us.' C.P. Ramaswami Aiyar's speech at Tanjore District Conference on 23.9.1916. *District Problems*, Home Rule Series NO.17, Madras, 1916. p. 30.
28. PWL 1072 L, 27.3.1929. Protests over conversions, forced subscriptions towards missionary funds, and similar allegations were frequent, and were to continue. PWL GO 1184L, 12.4.1929; PWL GO 380L, 7.2.1929; PWL GO 1390L, 4.5.1929; Home GO 918, 24.2.1940.
29. Notes to Judl. GO 2509, 14.10.1915. Comments by Inspector General of Police. In fact, the hostility of the landlords towards agricultural settlements sometimes took the form of physical assaults on missionary officials. F. Booth Tucker,, *Mufti Fauj*, p. 231.
30. PWL 268 L, Dt. 5.2.1927. The pipes which brought water to the settlements, for instance, would be found blocked with stones and straw in an attempt to thwart cultivation by the settlers.
31. *Note, 1916.*
32. Remarks of Superintendent of Police, Guntur, Judl. GO 2205, 10.10.1914: 'When the existing settlements are put on a satisfactory footing, and discipline perfected in them, and when remaining CTs still at large are also settled, the Presidency will see a very marked and gratifying reduction in organised and grave crime.' *Note, 1916*, p. 18.
33. Home (J) GO 2764, 23.11.1916, notes by A.G. Cardew.
34. See Chapter 2, especially Section III.
35. *Note, 1916.*

36. Judl. GO 1569, 17.6.1916. Director of the Labour Dept. of United Planters' Association of Southern India to IGP, 22.3.1916.
37. *Note, 1925*, p. 47.
38. *Note, 1925*, p. 47 and p. 70.
39. *Note, 1916*, p. 8.
40. Judl. GO 526, 25.2.1916.
41. *Note, 1925*. p. 25; Home (Judl.)GO 1965, 17.9.1912.
42. Judl. GO 850, 15.4.1914. DO (Demi Official) from DM, Tinnevelly to Judl. Dept.
43. Home (J) GO 1712, 25.7.1919 (emphasis added).
44. Home (J) GO 758, 5.4.1917.
45. *Ibid.*
46. For instance, in the case of a settlement located at mica mines in Nellore, the rules formulated for its management were to serve as a model for the settlement in Parry's sugar factory in Tinnevelly years later. Judl. 1560, 4.8.1913.
47. PWL GO 2088L, 26.7.1929.
48. Judl. GO 1205, 10.5.1916; Home (J) GO 2460, 17.10.1916.
49. *Note, 1916*, pp. 8-9.
50. 'The men generally preferred to go to a settlement when given a choice between that and jail under security sections.' Demi official letter from DM, Tinnevelly to Judl. Dept., Judl. GO 850, 15.4.1914.
51. Plantation workers in Annamallai were partly from the Kavali settlement, which was proving to be a difficult administrative problem because of overcrowding. Because of the active application of the CTA, the settlements were generally so congested that there was rampant disease, as also lack of employment opportunities for all. Judl. GO 1016, 10.5.1915; Judl. GO 451, 28.6.1926.
52. In the case of the plantations, for instance, the costs both of transporting the CT workers and of their accommodation was to be borne by the government. Judl. 1569, 17.6.1916.
53. Judl. GO 1997, 15.9.1914.
54. F. Booth Tucker, *Mukti Fauj*, p. 224.
55. Collector of Salem to Government, Judl. GO 1997, 15.9.1914.
56. The reasons for the private employers' resistance to missionaries are discussed a little later.
57. Judl. GO 1911, 31.7.1916.
58. Starte began this work in 1909. By 1916, he reported to the Government that 1650 settlers were working in spinning and

weaving mills in Sholapur, Dharwar and Belgaum. In other words, even before the institution of the CTA, members of supposedly criminal communities were being employed in the so-called industrial settlements.

59. Judl. GO 629, 8.3.1916.
60. *Indian Patriot*, Madras, 18.2.1916.
61. *The Hindu*, Madras, 29.4.1916.
62. Judl. GO 2764, 23.11.1916.
63. Home (Judl.) GO 2671, 14.11.1916. Letter from Starte to Secretary to Government, Judicial Department, Bombay.
64. Judl. GO 1997, 15.9.1914. Letter from Collector of Salem to Deputy Secretary to Government dt. 17.8.1914. In fact, when the private enterprises were located outside urban areas, the employers especially welcomed members of itinerant CT communities. The hordes of cattle owned by them could be used for carting the material for the management. This happened both in the case of Koravars employed in Parry's factory, and Yerukulas employed in the ILTD Co. Members of such communities made even cheaper work force when compared with other CT members. 2000 heads of cattle belonging to Yerukula settlers of Sitanagaram were all used to carry stones from the quarries. Government of Madras, *Note, 1925*. p. 61. Mats and baskets, which itinerant communities invariably made, could also be incorporated into the manufacturing process.
65. In an enterprise which was not a CT settlement yet, the manager had observed 'a striking instance of flouting of authority'. A group of workers had gone to a village festival together when the manager had instructed them to go in batches of two or three. Another group of workers had broken out of a cholera segregation camp. Home (Judl) GO 2099, 8.10.1917; Home (J) GO 1965, 17.9.1917.
66. Law (G) GO 2677, 23.9.1924. These measures were said to have led to 'enormous improvement in the work of the Koravars' in the case of Parrys' factory. So as not to appear to be fining the Koravars for only non-performance of work, the list of offences included quarelling in residential quarters, and stealing money from fellow Koravars.
67. Home (Judl.) GO 2671, 14.11.1916. Next to a settlement of this kind, in order of preference, came the settlement where trades of different kinds like carpentry, weaving etc. could be taught. Next was an agricultural settlement, where land was given to the settlers to till. This last form of settlement, though considered 'suitable under Indian conditions', was the most expensive in the short term.

68. *Ibid.*
69. W.J. Hatch, *The Land Pirates of India*, 1929, p. 60; PWL GO 1072, 23.7.1929, Letter from DSP, Salem to District Magistrate, Salem 29.5.1928; *Report of the Ceylon Labour Commissioner for 1914-15*, p. 38; There was a proposal by the Salvation Army to send CT workers to Mesopotamia for 'military service' but it was judged to be 'entirely mistaken' by the government, and did not materialise. *Report of the Indian Jails Committee, 1919-20*, Chapter XXII.
70. *Report of the Indian Jails Committee, 1919-20*. Chapter XXII.
71. Judl. GO 850, 15.4.1917.
72. Home (J) GO 2113, 14.9.1918. This happened in the case of the Parrys' factory. Earlier in the year, B.P. Wadia had founded the Madras Labour Union.
73. Home. (J) GO 1712, 25.7.1919.
74. The Workmen's Breach of Contract Act, 1859, for example, was instituted for this purpose.
75. Home (J) GO 1712, 25.7.1919 in the case of Parry's and Judl. GO 1027, 25.4.1916 in the case of estate owners.
76. Emphasis added. Home (J) GO 1712, 25.7.1919. The trouble and expense mentioned, however, was not for the welfare of the workers, but for their segregation from the villagers, and virtual imprisonment. Law(G) 1876, 13.6.1925.
77. Boys from the settlement were trained in workshops and made to learn 'tinkering' and carpentry; they were to be later employed on contract in various departments of the factory. Government of Madras, *Note, 1925*, p. 28.
78. Law (G) GO 1910, 3.8.1923.
79. N.S. Ramaswami and S. Muthiah, *Parrys 200*, p. 111. At a later stage Koravar men did the work of felling trees, splitting them, and stocking the fuel. Law (G) GO 2677, 23.9.1924.
80. Nellore DM on the subject, Judl GO 1016, 10.5.1915. The workers were to be sent to Annamallai's as opposed to Assam, as 'our own planters have the first claim upon us'. H. A. Stuart, Member of Council, *ibid.*
81. Judl. GO 1862, 11.8.1915; Judl. GO 1569, 17.6.1916.
82. Emphasis added. Para deleted from the draft of speech to be delivered by Chairman of the Planters' Association to the Governor during his visit to Annamallai. 'His Excellency decided that no reference should be made to this subject on any public occasion.' Home (J) GO 2558, 1.11.1916.

83. Judl. GO 1027, 25.4.1916.
84. Emphasis added. *Ibid*. Notes by Martin, Director of UPSAI.
85. *The Madras Mail*, Madras, 20.11.1915.
86. Judl. GO 1016, 10.5.1915; Judl. GO 451, 28.6.1926.
87. The acute employment problem at this settlement itself, as admitted later by official reports, was due to mismanagement of the settlement —a far too rapid increase in the strength of the settlement took place as in the case of other settlements. The unrealistic plans by the American Baptist Mission to turn the settlement into an agricultural one had resulted in an acute crisis regarding employment of the settlers. Judl. GO 451, 28.6.1926.
88. Letter from Martin, Director of UPASI to Gadsden, officer on special duty, through IGP. Judl. GO 2565, 25.10.1915.
89. The owners flogged them for breaches of work norms, their rations were cut down to the minimum, they were not given warm clothing in the hills to which they were totally unaccustomed, their babies died of exposure at an alarming rate. The death rate at the estates was 'a most serious 55 per mille and among infants 470 per mille'. Home (J) GO 2650, 12.11.1916. This itself was reported to be due to the mothers carrying their babies on their backs while at work and the infants being constantly wet as a result. There was so much sickness that it was observed that half the workers who had left the plantations should have been in a hospital. *Ibid.*
90. Home (J) GO 2650, 12.11.1916.
91. *Ibid*; Judl. GO 2991, 13.12.1916.
92. Home (J) GO 2650, 12.11.1916. Notings; Judl. GO 1016, 10.5.1915.
93. For one, the CT workers in many cases were prevailed upon finally by other workers to join the strikes. There was a suspicion among the administrators that two factors may have influenced the encouragement of the Yerukulas to either strike work, or to leave the plantations. Firstly, the police deputed to watch the settlers disliked service on the hills. They had a direct interest in termination of the scheme, and may have worked actively towards this end. Secondly, petty officials at CT settlements from where the workers were drawn were also interested in ending the exodus of the settlers from the settlements, as they were worried about loss of their jobs if all the settlers left for the hills. Home (J) GO 2650, 12.11.1916.

CHAPTER 5

From Itinerant Community to Industrial Wageworkers: Stuartpuram Settlement

Yerukulas, the Telugu branch of the Korava community were declared a Criminal Tribe in 1911. Soon after this, a large number was sedentarised in Stuartpuram settlement in Guntur, under the charge of the Salvation Army. It is here that about six thousand Yerukulas lived for several decades from 1913 onwards. Subsequently, a section of this itinerant community developed into a militant organised trade union in the short span of about twenty-five years. This process had a trajectory, which makes for both instructive and poignant study. This chapter is an attempt to understand this process.

I

Stuartpuram settlement was meant to be a settlement for well-behaved, reformed and non-criminal members drawn from another criminal settlement for Yerukulas, Sitanagaram, also located in Guntur.[1] However, when the Salvation Army was given land in Guntur to set up this settlement, there were immediate charges from the surrounding landlords that CT members escaped at night from the settlement and committed crimes. Thus, this settlement was also declared to be a criminal settlement, and a substantial increase in the police force was sanctioned in the area, to intensify patrolling.[2]

Spread over 1500 acres of swamp and sandy land, Stuartpuram was initially set up in 1913 as an agricultural settlement. Very quickly, with the help of the police, and with efficient application of the Criminal Tribes Act, it had forcefully settled between three to four thousand men, women and children. Whole families were put into the settlement, even if only men were admitted to have been criminal, as the families were deemed to have a humanising effect on the offenders. As a result, Stuartpuram became a large settlement in terms of numbers as whole communities—not individuals—were put in at a time; after all, the Criminal Tribes Act was meant to work with the concept of whole 'Tribes'. The settlement was named after Harold Stuart, who was the moving force behind the idea of such settlements in general, and a senior government official, in charge of the police at that time. The spirit behind the settlement, thus, can be imagined to be punitive, rather than reformative, contrary to the claims by the administration. This settlement became the literal 'site' where the British administration and the Salvation Army together decided to conduct what they called an 'experiment in criminocurology'. Being a large settlement, Stuartpuram needed extensive police presence outside to prevent escapes, and inside, the Salvation Army took attendance upto five times in 24 hours.[3] There was strict punctuality and discipline for both children and adults and a system of fines and corporal punishment to deter disorderly behaviour.[4]

Land given to the SA was to be so distributed that each family got a small plot and was held responsible for its cultivation, or else punishment followed. Theoretically, the settler families were supposed to be tenants of the SA, and at some future date, when their reformation was complete, were to become patta holders.[5] In actual practice, settlers were given a wage for cultivating their small plots instead. There is very little indication in the records as to why the SA chose this particular mode of agricultural work for the settlers. The SA had, after all, all the necessary administrative powers to develop a community of wageworkers on a large farm rather than breaking up land into small plots.[6] One possible reason could be that a well-knit community, which initially entered the settlement, was more likely to offer resistance, whereas families settled separately and made responsible for cultivation of small plots of land could be isolated from one another. Working collectively on a large farm and having identical interests, the community would potentially be less manageable.

An equally important reason for family units to be created around small plots of land could be that a social process had to be set in motion which would be more conducive to Christianity and to imbibing the appropriate ethical norms and gender roles. The family as a concept fitted this requirement better than the community.

The plan to make Stuartpuram into an agricultural settlement failed for a number of reasons.[7] Essentially, the land was of very poor quality, and the implements of agriculture primitive. Moreover, the Yerukulas did not want to till the land, and made unenthusiastic agriculturists. However, as mentioned earlier, what decided the administrative mind against further agricultural settlements was fierce opposition to the Stuartpuram settlement from landlords in the area. This was an era when landlords were important political allies of the British administration and on balance, the administration decided not to alienate the landlord/headmen sections any further. Irrigation facilities—plans to make available water from the Krishna river to Stuartpuram settlement—were withheld, and alternative means of supporting the settlement had to be now seriously considered.

It was at this juncture, that the Indian Leaf Tobacco Development Company (ILTD), began to be discussed within the administration and the Salvation Army circles, as possible alternative employers.[8] The Company's initial contact with the Stuartpuram settlers seems to have been through the mats made by the Yerukula women which were an essential part of the manufacturing process at the factory. The Salvation Army was the medium through which the sales had been taking place to the ILTD, and thus its officials were in regular touch with the factory.

By 1925, the factory was said to have employed half the total adult population of the settlement. Slowly, almost the entire female population came to be employed in the factory as regular wageworkers; the men continued to work fruitlessly on land. The situation, in a way, was forced upon the settlers. According to government policy, once the government had provided infrastructure for the settlement, the settlements were meant to be self-supporting. When income from land was found to be inadequate, the settlement gradually became very dependent on the factory for the employment of the settlers, as the Salvation Army had no other means of finding employment for their charges.[9] The financial situation of the settlement had now become quite stable and the ILTD management, the Salvation Army and the administration seemed optimistic about the future progress of the settlement.

II

Given that an entire section of the community had been interned into the Stuartpuram settlement, some reorganising of the community's social and cultural priorities was needed. Drastic transformation in the lives of the Yerukulas followed.

Most important, of course, was the fact that the itinerant mode of existence was suddenly replaced by a forced settled life. The Salvation Army further set about its task of making the Yerukulas successful cultivators by breaking up the community into families, and making them into new social and economic units. Removing the children to another part of the settlement, however, broke up the family. The Salvation Army felt that the 'rising generation' should be kept away from their wicked parents, and brought up in a more wholesome atmosphere. Separate schools and dormitories were established for these children, and they were allowed to meet their parents only on Sundays during church activities. The two components of criminals' reformation were moral education and work. The Salvation Army concentrated on the children for moral education, and on the adults for work.

Once the community had been divided into families, a new division of labour within the new unit was devised and appropriate gender roles defined. Women were initially trained in feminine virtues and were expected to sew, embroider and cook for their families. In fact, mat-making, which was a traditional activity of both men and women of the Yerukula community, was now handed over exclusively to women, to be combined with other indoor activities.[10] Men now ploughed and tilled the wasteland, albeit unsuccessfully.

There were a myriad ways in which 'true' women were fashioned out of what the Salvation Army called 'thievish raw material'. For instance, they were taught to pay attention to their appearance. The Salvation Army even held periodic parades of the 'most neatly dressed women' (and gave the winners a prize of one rupee each).[11] The women would also not be allowed to go outside the settlement on a pass if they looked like 'so many vagrants'. The 'before' and 'after' photographs of women in the Salvation Army records show the 'after' version with a completely changed Hinduised appearance, complete with neatly tied saris, oiled hair with flowers and vermillion marks on their foreheads.

After more than a decade of such remoulding, these newly domesticated women were required to work outside their homes for a wage in the ILTD factory as the land was found to be unable to support the families. As already mentioned earlier, the government expected the Salvation Army to make the settlements under their care completely self-supporting once the initial infrastructure had been paid for. Now that there was a severe financial crisis, these women were persuaded or forced in hundreds to go and work in the newly established tobacco factory several miles away.

It is important to emphasise here that this was a totally unforeseen development as far as the SA was concerned. The SA did not normally prepare women for wage work in any of its settlements—their work at the ILTD factory was more of an aberration than policy. This was true not just of the Salvation Army in India—recent work on Africa also shows that missions in general expected women to remain in domestic surroundings, and men to earn a wage outside. In fact, from the mid-nineteenth century onwards, a general mission slogan regarding women was 'Improve the wives of the poor and [in the process] servants of the rich,'[12] meaning that if at all women must work outside, they must again be in a domestic environment and continue to engage in child-minding or home-making activities. However, because of a specific set of circumstances, the Salvation Army found itself supporting wage work for the Stuartpuram settlement women in a harsh factory environment, which made them neglect their homes and babies in a theoretically unacceptable way.

The Salvation Army had so far been systematically inculcating in the women an indoor culture of housekeeping and child-rearing. Now they were expected to walk a distance of seven miles every day, and spend a total of 12 hours outside their homes, earning a wage. Interestingly, the Salvation Army even asked the government to provide crèches for the infants and toddlers in the settlement, so that young mothers could also work in the factory. For the next 10-12 years, the women alone earned as much as 80 per cent of the entire settlement income.[13]

Ironically, while women were the principal earners in their families, the Salvation Army consolidated the new moral code for them. Unable any more to scrutinise their outdoor activities, unable also to adhere to the notion of them as dependent wives, the Salvation Army began to take on a more active role in their personal, marital affairs. This was done partly in order to continue to have authority over the women, and partly to make sure that economic independence did not confound gender identities, as it had gender roles.

Women used to have the freedom to choose their spouses—the Salvation Army now granted permissions for marrying. The Salvation Army officials had always been votaries of proper matchmaking in the settlements, now they became urgently active on the issue. They wrote to the government wanting 'a voice in the choice of spouses'[14] and got it. They were finding to their alarm that bride price, something they had been trying to suppress as it meant 'mere selling of females', now rose steeply (sometimes as much as Rs. 500).[15] The Salvation Army substituted it with dowry, which the mission itself financed. It always consisted of saris and vessels for the bride—true symbols of lost domesticity. (Incidentally, in other settlements in the north, the Salvation Army used to insist that the man be able to support his wife before letting them marry—it had to give up that condition here, which it did quite willingly.) It also forbade completely what it called 'desertions' by women of their husbands. So ironically, the women lost their autonomy in marital affairs at a time when they were the principal contributors to the family income.

It is worth mentioning here that the ILTD Company supported the Salvation Army on the severe discipline in the settlement, and its active role in the women's family affairs. In fact, at a later point in time, the ILTD management became quite active on its own on both these issues. The discipline—strict punctuality, orderly behaviour and a system of harsh punishments—resonated well with factory life.

The Salvation Army's insistence on an irrevocable form of marriage worked in the company's favour as well. The ILTD had an interest in keeping families together at the settlement. Apart from stemming from a patriarchal, Victorian attitude to the concept of marriage, this attitude had a strong economic basis: a family wage paid at the ILTD was much lower than a combined one of an individual man and woman.

In the records, there were at least three petitions by Yerukula men in the company records, where the management was requested to intervene and help them in getting their deserting wives to come back to them. The ILTD obliged in all three cases by threatening the women with loss of their jobs in case they divorced their husbands. Interestingly, there were no similar petitions by women on record. On the whole, the ILTD management, with the help of SA and the CTA, made sure that these workers were 'less troublesome' than others, and much more pliable.[16]

III

In the late 1920s, a process set itself in motion, which changed the balance of forces explicitly in further favour of the ILTD and the Salvation Army. This was in the form of availability of men workers from the settlement for factory work, and more powers of control for the Salvation Army on settlement land. Given below is a brief account of the direction that the settlement followed in the period 1928-35. It was an important seven-year period which would change the character of the settlement, and the destiny of the settlers for generations to come.

What happened was that in 1928 'natural flow' (fresh water) was discovered under the sandy soil. This water was not brackish as had been believed all along, and was found to be suitable for rice cultivation. This revived the interest of the settlers in cultivation.[17] In the same year, the settlers petitioned the government for permanent pattas as had been promised to them.[18]

The Salvation Army was firmly opposed to the plan of transferring land to the settlers, and wrote to the officials to this effect.[19] In the interim period, the land had risen enormously in price and 'the place prospered so much that it had its own railway station and villages sprang up like a wild west town after a gold strike.'[20]

The petition by the settlers had been pending for five years before it was turned down on a number of administrative grounds. The most important official argument, was that the concept of permanent pattas was inconsistent with the running of the place as a reformatory settlement—settlers were supposed to leave the settlement after their reformation had been achieved, to make place for new criminals.[21]

Essentially, there had been ominous signs shown by the settlers. There was an indication that the settlers had been found to be not totally without resistance to the policies of the

Salvation Army, and had in fact organised themselves into a cooperative society.[22] Members of this society were now preparing to invest their own funds in digging an irrigation channel to improve the land, so that the fruit of the land would then legitimately be theirs, and not be appropriated by the Salvation Army.[23]

The response of the Salvation Army was to discharge a large number of settlers from the provisions of the Criminal Tribes Act, and thus from the settlement itself, and transfer them to a new area called the New Colony near the ILTD factory premises in Chirala. There was the official requirement of ensuring a means of livelihood before a settler could be discharged from the settlement; this was met by finding the settlers employment in this factory.

This plan was fully supported and, in fact, financed by the government. Building a new colony involved digging wells, building huts, and providing other infrastructure. This was done in great hurry just before the start of the tobacco processing season in 1935, so that the discharged settlers could immediately be employed in the factory. Taking advantage of the situation at this juncture, the ILTD management decided to expand its operations at Chirala. There had been a strike by the 3000 seasonal workers in 1932, and the ILTD had since then been looking out for a more pliable workforce.[24] The Yerukulas made popular workers, as the threat of the CTA could be used to keep them pliable.

This is how able-bodied men from the Stuartpuram agricultural settlement joined their womenfolk as regular factory workers at the ILTD Company.

IV

The problem of men, hitherto tenants of the Salvation Army, however, had yet to be sorted out: these men had to be found work in a factory where work processes had been designed to employ mainly women. The manager of the settlement now wrote to the ILTD management urging that the provisions of the Act should be relaxed to enable the men settlers to work as long hours as possible. The 'concession', according to him, if granted, would benefit the administration of the settlement and indirectly make the task of control of criminal tribe settlers easier and cheaper for the government. In 1933, the manager of the ILTD, Chirala, also wrote to the Chief Inspector of Factories, requesting him to exempt the workers in the factory from the provisions of the Factories Act, as the factory needed to work for 12 hours a day, and 66 hours a week. The case made out was on the basis of the nature of the processes themselves.

The fact which convinced the administration in favour of the exemption of ILTD from crucial sections of the Factories Act, however, was that 'machine room operatives were drawn mostly from Stuartpuram settlement,...maintained by public funds'.[25] Soon after this, a large number of settlers were discharged and transferred to the new colony near the factory on the grounds that 'to walk 3½ miles in the morning for work is not conducive to efficiency' and that the workers needed to live near the factory.[26]

The exemption from the Factories Act, which the ILTD wanted, was for Section 21 (rest periods in factories), Section 22 (weekly holidays), Section 27 (limiting of working hours per week), and Section 28 (limiting of working hours per day). The exemption, which was granted, was from Sections 27 and 28. It applied to all machine operatives in all tobacco handling and redrying factories.[27] In this way, Yerukulas were used as an instrument in a major modification of the law, which would now cover not just machine room workers from this community in the ILTD factory, but *all* machine room workers in *all* tobacco factories in the Presidency.

By the beginning of 1935, every available man and woman from Stuartpuram was employed at ILTD, which as a result of the new exemptions, was now working double shifts, from 5 am to 1 am the next morning, except on Sundays.[28] The number of hours that the Yerukula settlers worked in the machine room in a working day is not clear. What is known is that firstly, Yerukulas were to be especially considered for employment for 'as long hours as possible' on the request of the SA. Secondly, the ILTD believed in employing a set of workers in the machine room regularly, and on long shifts. According to the manager, shorter shifts caused dissatisfaction among the workers on account of proportionately lower wages.[29] The factory manager was reported to have given the government very good accounts of the Yerukula workers. On the whole, these workers were found to be thoroughly satisfactory by the ILTD.[30] They found regular work in the factory for ten months in a year—a pattern that was to continue for years.

A point worth mentioning here is the presence and intervention of the SA as a 'go-between' as far as settler workers and the management were concerned. This seems to have provided a very important balancing mechanism between the workers and the management so that the slave driving that the supervisors would normally do could be restrained and checked. The SA officials, of course, were potentially perfect slave drivers themselves but they wanted the CT settlement to survive as a self-supporting economic entity. This was the only condition on which the government had given them charge of thousands of men, women and children, and granted them subsidies of all kinds. The ILTD work as a means of livelihood was too crucial for the survival of the settlement for the SA to jeopardise it by allowing blatant exploitation of the Yerukula workforce, and incite either rebellion or absconding. (Incidentally, fear of the nationalists played a similar restraining role in the minds of the company management vis-à-vis the Yerukula workers to some extent.)

V

Upto a certain point in the life of the union at the ILTD factory, CT and non-CT workers, clerical employees and factory floor operatives, men and women had worked together in the ILTD Workers' Union to press for their demands. Group consciousness systematically nurtured by the union had led to militant action on a family basis. There were a number of ways in which the unity of the workers was sought to be broken up by the management.

The company first took steps to divide the family within the factory, and to restructure it in a hierarchical fashion by pitching different generations against each other. It is interesting to note that it was the older generation of Yerukulas who joined the Christian Association floated at the factory as a parallel organisation by the management.[31] The younger workers, both men and women, resisted this attempt to break the ILTD Workers' Union under Yerukula leadership, and stayed with this union. The Christian Association not only isolated the older generation of workers from the younger ones within the family, it also managed to partly beak up the union on religious grounds by dividing the workforce into CTs and non-CTs.[32] There were also some Christian workers, who were not CTs, who joined the new association.

Within the same community of Yerukulas, a further break was engineered by dividing men and women in the family. This was partly achieved by creating categories of skilled and unskilled workers within the factory. The management, through a specific interpretation of an industrial tribunal's decision, managed to define the machine room workers, all men, as 'technical staff', and these Yerukula men were now assigned to the more highly paid, skilled category. From 1947 onwards, the management also promoted a Staff Association, comprising of clerical and more highly paid supervisory staff, again, all men.[33] Men workers from the machine room were incorporated into the Staff Association while it remained another irony that in point of fact their working conditions remained much worse than those of the women, who continued to belong to the low paid unskilled category. The Staff Association came to be controlled by the Congress, while the ILTD Workers' Union continued to be under the guidance of the Communists, leading to additional fissures.[34]

Break-up within the family and the union, then, could take place not only along the lines of age and gender, but also educated and non-educated; skilled and unskilled; Christians and non-Christians; Congress supporters of management versus those in the Communist-led union. This was apart from the division encouraged between CT and non-CT workers.

Having enumerated multiple manoeuvres by the management, however, it is worth dwelling at length on the fact that qualitatively, Yerukulas made very different kind of workers from the non-CT ones—this fact would manifest itself in their struggles against such manoeuvres.

VI

Once at the factory, there was constant negotiation the Yerukulas had to manage in their relationship with other workers as well as with the management. It is interesting to study the complex and quite subtle ways in which these workers from a criminal tribe learnt to overcome some of their situation's disabilities over the years.

From the inception of the settlement, rigorous discipline had been the watchword of the SA officials. A new generation of settlers had grown up, systematically put through the discipline of schooling and an unrelenting daily schedule. The Salvation Army had taken over entirely the tasks of surveillance and education, as also inculcation of ethical values like obedience to authority. It was this new generation of young settlers, brought up separately from the influence of their parents, who found work at the ILTD factory in the initial phases. The ILTD management on several occasions expressed its satisfaction with the young women workers from the settlement, compared to those drawn from the surrounding areas.[35] This generation of workers was punctual and regular, used as the young women were to a harsh daily regime in terms of rigorous and oppressive discipline at the settlement, and were also accustomed to punitive relations with the authorities.

The work processes in the factory were organised in such a way that a majority of the workers were unskilled women. However, the settlement women made satisfactory workers as there was less of a turnover because of the regularity of their attendance, and over a period of time they became skilled and adept at their work. These young women had attended the SA schools in the settlement, and their families had got used to their being away from home at school. Thus no particular contradiction was felt within the family at their working long hours in the factory.

Moreover, SA itself had not had the opportunity to mould them into housewives and mothers. There was a certain contradiction there, as the mould that the SA had visualised for them after they left school was at best as teachers in the settlement itself; or making a new generation of good wives and mothers; or as reliable, educated servants for the SA or ILTD staff families. Now, because the settlement did not succeed as an agricultural settlement, these women formed the bulk of the factory workers at ILTD and were supporting the entire settlement with their income.[36]

The processes that unfolded in the transition of these women first from young mothers to reliable workers at ILTD, and then to principal earners at the settlement is a study in irony. As described earlier, contradictions triggered off by women's wage work within the family had to be consciously negotiated by the SA. But yet another set of processes came into play when whole families began to work in the ILTD factory which proved to be beyond the control or manipulation of both the ILTD management, and the SA.

The settlement had been a place where settlers were not allowed to have any meetings of more than four people at any given point in time. Factory work, though coerced, gave them the breathing space and an environment where they could meet and exchange views. The ILTD Workers' Union was born within a couple of years of whole families' employment at the factory. Moreover, the repressive conditions of the settlement, in themselves designed to isolate the settlers from influences from outside, became a cause for nationalist enquiry committees to scrutinise settlements more vigorously. This led to regular contact of the settlers with nationalists. In fact, repeal of the CTA became a very important election issue in the 1938 elections, and a number of questions were asked in the Legislative Assembly about the conditions in CT settlements in general, and Stuartpuram settlement in particular.[37]

Organisation of women workers within the ILTD factory, which had its beginnings in the early 1930s, began to develop rapidly.[38] Relaxation of the Factories Act for Stuartpuram settlers forced men settlers to work long hours in the machine room of the factory and this influx of men workers helped to consolidate the existing union. Substantial success was achieved in building union membership and improvement in working conditions. There was a prolonged strike in 1938, ending with firing on the workers, which attracted the notice of the entire nation and was widely used as a political issue in nationalist propaganda. (The management, predictably, used the workers' criminal tribe antecedents to justify the firing.) The women and men of the community worked together for the success of the strike and subsequently, the management conceded special demands like maternity benefits, facilities during monthly periods, presence of a woman doctor and more crèches.[39] Essentially, women by now had been unionised long enough to be assertive about their specific needs within the factory, even though at home the SA was trying hard, and succeeding in reversing this tide.

Children who were taken away from their parents made a completely autonomous and radical body of workers once they grew up as far as their views on politics, or their notion about their rights were concerned. They were always more active in the union than the older generation who were also gradually absorbed by the factory.

There were other ironies. The machine room workers, who had been put in charge of a dangerous task forcedly, were managing the most important operation—drying of the tobacco leaf, on which the entire processing operation depended. In case they did not dry the leaf within a stipulated time or follow the required procedures, the factory could not function. The Yerukula workers used this advantage to paralyse the factory during strikes. The CT machine room workers had also become very skilled and productive compared to the few non-CT workers in this department. This was a technical job in any case, and the educated Yerukulas were more suitable compared to illiterate workers on the same job. In addition, because of the powers available to the management under the CTA, they were forced to work on the same operation for a number of years at a stretch inspite of the unbearable working conditions. As a result, there was almost no CT worker turnover in this department. The CT workers turned this handicap into a strength, and used their superior work experience to increase their bargaining power during strikes. The management found that it could not sack these workers even after repeated strike actions by them as they had become close to indispensable; 'free' non-CT workers would work in the machine room for a few days and leave. Over a period of time, it had become clear as much to the Yerukulas as the management, that it was extremely difficult to recruit and retain workers in this department.

Further, under the CTA, it was the whole community which had been defined as the criminal tribe, the individual counted for nothing—it was this handicap that the union used to consolidate itself. In the course of struggles, the revival of community solidarity by the union leadership served as another means of mobilisation. Interestingly, this solidarity had been commented upon at least a decade earlier by an author who wrote that the Yerukulas as a community were

> trade unionists of the most thorough-going kind and united action was a necessity in [their] tribal existence...[They practised] group thinking and believed in group action...they formed themselves into a close brotherhood and would on no account betray their fellow clansmen...they were freemasons and helped each other to the end...[40]

The management invoked the CTA during strike actions to prejudice public and administrative opinion against the ILTD workers. The workers were posed as members of a CT indulging in criminal pastimes rather than legitimate union activities. However, quite unexpectedly for the management, the strikes inspired some other oppressed CT communities like Malas and

Madigas in the area close to the factory to rally around the workers and build what the administration called in exasperation a 'confederacy of criminals'. During the crucial 1938 strike, these communities supported and sheltered strikers during police action and firing on the workers. Thus an artificially created category of CTs attracted real unity among similarly persecuted communities.

It is, then, obvious that their 'criminal tribe' antecedents would in a large measure determine the way the Yerukulas would handle some of the onslaughts by the management, sometimes successfully, sometimes not.

Notes

1. The Salvation Army called Sitanagaram a sieve through which the criminals had to pass and be tested, and 'only those who responded to the treatment could find their Canaan in Stuartpuram'. Judl. GO 3219 (Mis), 21.12.1915.
2. Note on Stuartpuram settlement, *Note, 1925.*
3. Meena Radhakrishna (1992).
4. There were virtually no outsiders allowed into the settlement for scrutiny, and enquiry committees could enter it only in the 1940s, when the nationalists took up this issue seriously.
5. Government of Madras, *Note, 1925*; Judl. GO 2308, 22.9.1916.
6. Memorial from Bapatla residents to Governor-General in Council, Judl. GO 2509, 14.10.1915. Judl. GO 2308, 22.9.1916.
7. See Chapter 4, Section II.
8. The ILTD had existed in Guntur district since 1908 in order to procure local tobacco as the leaf wing of British American Tobacco Company and Peninsular Company. It was later to become a branch of the Indian Tobacco Company (ITC).
9. Government of Madras, *Administration Report of the Labour Department, 1925-26*, Madras; PWL GO 2394L, 23.8.1929; PWL GO 2338L, 19.8.1930; PWL GO 1313L, 17.6.1932.
10. The notion that this was primarily a woman's job seems to have not been confined to the Salvation Army. It is interesting to note that Yerukulas under a Roman Catholic priest underwent a similar division of labour. Home (Judl.) GO 1534, 14.6.1916.
11. F. Booth Tucker, *Mukti Fauj*, p. 234.

12. Deborah Gaitskell, 'At Home with Hegemony?' in Dagmar Engels and Shula Marks (ed.) *Contesting Colonial Hegemony—State and Society in Africa and India*, London, 1994, p. 121.
13. PWD GO 1313L, 17.6.1932.
14. Home Judl. GO 1759, 5.8.1918, Booth Tucker to Member of Council, 12.7.1918.
15. *Ibid.* As the Salvation Army official put it, girls who had been straightened out and cured of drinking habits were sold to the highest bidder.
16. PWL GO 1654 L, 6.7.1928.
17. The acreage under paddy almost doubled in 1928. Government of Madras, *Administration Report of the Labour Department, 1928-29*, Madras.
18. PWL GO 1147L, 26.5.1933.
19. Salvation Army records at Stuartpuram settlement, Bapatla. Letter from Manager to Deputy Tahsildar, Chirala dated 26.8.1930. The policy so far had been that the tenancy of the family was taken away if its members were found to be resorting to crime. This could not be done if the family owned the land.
20. Bernard Watson, *A Hundred Years' War*, London, 1964, p. 145.
21. PWL GO 1147, 26.5.1933.
22. This society, called the Stuartpuram Yerukula and Staff Tenants' Cooperative Society came into existence in 1926 and was free of patronage, unlike other such societies, of the Labour Department, or Christian organisations.
23. Government of Madras, *Administration report of the Labour Department, 1934-35*, Madras.
24. Government of Madras, *Administration Report of the Labour Department, 1932-33*, Madras.
25. Devt. GO 1315, 27.10.1933. Communication from Commissioner of Labour to Secretary, Government of Madras, Devt. Dept. dt 1.10.1933, enclosing letter from the ILTD manager to Chief Inspector of Factories dt 22.7.1933.
26. PWL GO 2671L, 6.12.1934.
27. Devt. GO 1315, 27.10.1933.
28. PWL GO 2726L, 17.12.1935.
29. Devt. GO 1315, 27.10.1933. In reality, however, efficiency would be the reason why the ILTD management was keen on the same machine room workers working long shifts rather than employing fresh workers in shorter shifts. The existing workers were

experienced at their work, and the machines could work continuously for 20 hours, except for one break for rest. More shifts would have required more breaks, affecting the productivity of machines.

30. Government of Madras, *Administration Report of the Labour Department for 1934-35*, Madras.
31. Devt. GO 1689, 22.7.1940.
32. The CT workers were mostly those converted to Christianity by the missions.
33. Devt. GO 242, 19.1.1948, letter from ILTD CO. Staff Association to Commissioner of Labour, dt. 11.11.1949.
34. Devt. Go 92, 6.1.1949. ILTD Workers' Union with a membership of 2230 and ILTD Co. Staff Association with a membership of 750 were affiliated to the AITUC and INTUC respectively.
35. PWL GO 1654L, 6.7.1928.
36. PWD GO 1313L, 17.6.1932. As much as 81 per cent of the settlement income was earned by the ILTD women workers.
37. Home GO 18.10.1938; Home GO 1544, 20.3.1939.
38. A congressman, Yagananarayana, helped in charting out the formal demands of the Union in 1937. The ILTD Workers' Union was registered in 1938 with him as president. Public (General) GO 448, 21.2.1938, Labour Strikes and Lockouts for the Week ending 29.10.1937.
39. The union membership within a year of formation rose to 3347 in 1939. Devt. GO 47, 6.1.1939. By 1939, there was a 'modern' creche, a full time qualified nurse and a new building for tiffin time. This was at a time when the conditions of the workers in other tobacco factories were deplorable.
40. W.J. Hatch, *The Land Pirates of India*, London, 1928, p. 67.

CHAPTER 6

Historic Memory

The foregoing chapters have dealt with the colonial construction of the Yerukulas' criminality, and also some of the ways in which their daily lives were actually lived. It is within this dual context that I will now try and locate this community's current perception of its own past history.

About ten years ago, I met the descendants of the Yerukulas in question, still living in Stuartpuram settlement and working in the very same tobacco factory, the ILTD. When I met them, they were about to be retrenched in thousands, because the factory was going to have a mechanised plant to do the work that these workers had been doing manually. At this time, Stuartpuram was officially not called a Criminal Tribes Settlement, and the community, Yerukulas, were not considered 'criminal tribes' anymore—after independence, the Criminal Tribes Act, under which they had been notified by the colonial administration, had been repealed. The Salvation Army, now a much depleted organisation both as far as its authority and the number of personnel were concerned, was however still operating in Stuartpuram, with a hospital, a school and other welfare activities.

I spent a long time with the community. Both men and women talked eloquently and at length about their work in the tobacco factory, the various strikes they had conducted to protest against the mechanisation and so on. The workers were very articulate, and talked a great deal about their experience with ILTD and were quite emphatic about the unfavourable, partisan role of the Salvation Army in their struggle with the Company. They also freely expressed their displeasure at the factory management's mechanisation plans which would now make them redundant.

During my stay at the settlement, I noticed that in their leisure time the children and the adults would sing. Sometimes after the day's work, they would gather together and tell each other long tales with much enthusiasm. Slowly I learnt that the stories they related so often were different sagas of how their forefathers were dangerous criminals; how the Salvation Army had worked tirelessly and selflessly for them for decades; how the tobacco factory had weaned their forefathers away from an earlier life of crime, by giving them employment. Their songs, I found, were those taught by the Salvation Army in praise of Christ.

I wondered how this had happened. When they were so clear about their present destiny, and relationship vis-a-vis the Salvation Army and the ILTD, why were their narratives and songs in such a different tone as far as their past was concerned? I knew by then from official records that this community had been an itinerant one for generations before they were interned in this settlement—in fact, the village community around the settlement remembered their salt and grain trade, and other activities. However, there were no traces of this relatively recent past etched on their memories in any form. There were no songs or folklore, which in any way reflected links with their earlier itinerant life, or their earlier work. Their stout denial of an itinerant past intrigued me as much as their assertions of an earlier dangerous criminality—and I could not understand this phenomenon until quite recently, when I stumbled upon some official publications of the Salvation Army.

Since I am discussing a community here which was unlettered, and has not left behind any written records, its own folklore (as also folklore about it) becomes an extremely important source of data to understand a whole range of issues. It also becomes very crucial to pose some of the following questions: whether the components of this folklore originated from inside the community, by and large, or from outside. If the latter, then was it an involuntary, 'natural' and gradual assimilation of versions of their past into their oral culture, or were some of these consciously or 'artificially' introduced; whether the folklore of the community, in however small a way, is a positive reading of its own past, or does the new version/s undermine its confidence or resources to fight its disabilities of the present; have stories or tales about a community, which pass off as its history with outsiders, become a part of that community's own historic memory? And equally, whether subsequent generations of that community keep these narratives alive by making such versions a part of their own oral tradition.

Reproduced here is a poem, which appeared in the Salvation Army newspaper, *The War Cry*. It was called 'The Crim as we Find Him in the Telegu (sic) Country'.[1] It appeared in 1916, a few years after Stuartpuram settlement had been established. It stands by itself, has no explanation or prose narrative to go with it, and is written by a Major Anandham, a non-Indian Salvation Army officer. (The Salvation Army officials always adopted local names, but never from the 'criminal' communities with which they worked.) Parts of this poem are reproduced here:

Come listen to me for a moment or more,
For I am a 'crim', yes, I am a 'crim';
There are records against me, yes, more than a score,
I belong to the criminal kind.

I live most by plundering other men's goods,
For I am a 'crim', yes I am a 'crim';
My home is in the jungle way off in the woods,
Oh, I am of the criminal kind.

I watch out for travellers 'long lonely bye roads,
Oh, I am a 'crim', yes I am a 'crim';
And many a 'hold up' I've done on the road,
That's the life of the criminal kind...

Away to the jungle and off to the fair,
I'm only a 'crim', I'm only a 'crim',
There is booty and plenty awaiting me there,
I belong to the criminal kind.

The reader would have noticed that there is first person address used here—the 'I' dominating the narrative. The Salvation Army poet here is putting forward the supposed point of view of the Yerukulas, but from the point of view of an individual.

Coming to the second edition of the poem which is written about a decade later, it is found to be much edited, changed and added to. It appears in a book of over 300 pages, written for an international audience by Booth Tucker, now the head of the Salvation Army. The book in which it appears is called *Mukti Fauj or Forty Years with the Salvation Army in India.*[2] It is a part of the chapter called 'Criminocurology', and has a long prose narrative before and after. The content of this narrative is almost entirely the unfolding of a success story that Booth Tucker has to tell.

The interesting point about the location of this poem is that it is surrounded with prose which has important details. Here there is discussion of the tremendous resistance that the Yerukulas offered to their sedentarisation, to conversion to Christianity, or work on land or in factories. The poem, however, is quite beatific and ecstatic in tone, as if the Salvation Army just came and conquered. Perhaps the problems could now be talked about, once it is a success story, a story with a happy ending. But still, lack of any resistances in the poem is interesting as this poem, in all essential particulars, represented the myth which the Yerukulas accepted and continue to accept; the resistance which actually took place on the ground was never a part of the myth.

Reproduced here are parts of the poem which are newly added to the earlier version, most likely not by the original author but some more senior bard in the Salvation Army.

I've oft been to prison and tasted their fare,
For I am a Crim, yes, I am a Crim!
Learned more of my business profession while there,
Seeing mine is a criminal mind.

And when I get out into freedom again,
I, who am a Crim, I, who am a Crim!

I fool the police, with their cleverest men,
Oh, I'm of the criminal kind!

The longer I follow, the more I delight,
In this life of a Crim, this life of a Crim!
To rob and to plunder, by day and by night,
This life of a criminal kind.

Here the criminal is shown to be a worse one than in the original version—he fools the police with his cleverness, he even learns new tricks of the trade in prison, and in fact he also takes a perverse delight in his pursuit of crime—'the longer I follow, the more I delight'.

This is an important development—the criminal is now shown to be much more dangerous in retrospect, though he has in fact been steadily reforming for the last decade in the settlement! At one level this is understandable—the Salvation Army had to show its international audience how unpromising the initial raw material was, to heighten the fact of its success. Alternatively, perhaps the settlers seemed more criminal as they were actively resisting the Salvation Army when this poem was being rewritten. But in real terms, the new version was an improvement on the earlier one, as far as the ostensible degree of Yerukulas' criminality was concerned.

In the second edition of the poem, there is an actual break in the narrative when the Salvation Army enters the picture, both symbolically and literally. This break, separating the earlier and later lives of the criminals, is achieved on paper by the device of having the old and the new sections separated by asterisks and it is the newly added section which heralds the new man. It is interesting that this break, symbolic and literal, was absent in the earlier poem written a decade ago; this in some ways shows that even the Salvation Army was aware of the rupture that took place in the interim period, as far as the Yerukulas' past and present was concerned. The new section goes thus:

The Salvation Army now comes to our aid;
With work for the Crim—yes, work for the Crim!

And for us a pathway to Heaven has made,
For Tribes of the criminal kind...

They give us an offer of work we accept
'Tis work for the Crim—yes, work for the Crim;
And soon at our task we become quite adept,
We tribes of the criminal kind...

At last we wake up to the fact, and the thought,
I'm no longer a Crim! I'm no longer a Crim!!
I'm living by industry, honestly wrought,
And have changed from the criminal mind!

The reader will note here that the 'I' of the earlier poem has changed to 'we': there has been great progress made in the intervening years. In fact, the 'we' now includes not only the whole community of say, the Telugu country, but also 'we, tribes of the criminal kind'. (There were at least 3-4 million criminal tribe members in India.) The poem, in fact, is no longer called The Crim as we Find Him in the Telegu Country, but simply, 'The Crim', signifying a more general category rather than a region specific phenomenon. Moreover, the 'we' of the poem now includes not just those who have been reformed but includes the Salvation Army as well:

So all hands to work, through the storm, or the calm,
We will rescue the Crim, we will rescue the Crim,
And rid this fair land from a menace and harm,
The Tribes of the criminal kind.

There is not only distancing of the reformed ones from the unreformed ones, there is now total identification the reformed members feel with the projects and plans of the Salvation Army on behalf of all Indian criminal tribe members. The newly reformed man is grateful that the Salvation Army has given him an opportunity to work honestly, and give up a life of crime.

This is quite interesting, as when I had spoken to the Yerukulas in the 1980s, I found that the content of the two poems is exactly what they also believed: We were dangerous criminals, the Salvation Army came along, gave us work, and we were reformed!

One can only speculate on what happened. Did they really mean what they said? Did they believe their own stories? Where were their earlier tales? Why is their present memory devoid of their past? There are some possible explanations for their assertions of past criminality.

Firstly, the contemporary Yerukulas would not have any stakes in their past of half a century ago, and so they would not be keen on challenging even untrue versions of that past. Their energies would be better deployed in fighting their *present* crises, like retrenchment from ILTD. Equally likely, their emphasis on past criminality is to bring to others' notice their present non-criminality—a sign that they are still not free of the earlier stigma. It is also possible that talking about their earlier dangerous criminality, their ability once to 'hold up' those in authority and terrorise them, gives them a sense of power today. This remembering of past power, however, is also an indication of their powerlessness in the present.

Another possibility is that this is myth-making of their own. Belief in their earlier criminality rationalises in their minds their current situation of vulnerability and poverty: because they were criminals in the past, they deserve their present miserable fate. There is also a touch of not just defiance, but relief in their loud assertions of a criminal past: today, at least, no one can harm them. And finally, perhaps by resigning themselves to this version of their history, they will be left in peace by the Salvation Army, or the ILTD, or whoever else might be threatened by an authentic memory of their history.

About their inability or refusal to remember their itinerant past, this is probably an expression of their discontent with that way of life. As discussed earlier, they were becoming increasingly marginalised, and had begun to be dispensable to the local communities. Even before the CTA was formally instituted, (at least two or three decades), they had become vulnerable to police harassment and extortion. Perhaps they finally found peace once they were sedentarised (though a criminal tribe settlement was not the place they would ideally have chosen to become sedentary), and do not wish to be reminded of the agony of the past.

These are mere speculations. The explanation for the collective denial of a collective history, and blanking out of a collective memory of their folklore reflecting an earlier life, is probably a combination of all these but around one major fact: there was a severe rupture in the continuity of their lives once they came to Stuartpuram settlement. Folklore and songs and tales can only survive in a lived community life, and one with some continuity, however flimsy, with an earlier life. Under the Salvation Army, in a criminal tribe settlement, community life was totally broken up and their forced transformation into disciplined wageworkers took an absolute toll of their cultural resources.

As we have seen, first and most important, from being considered useful if not honourable people, they were officially declared predators on the larger society. Then, their itinerant mode of existence was replaced by settled life. The community as a unit was broken into families, which were now the operational social and economic units. The men's trading activities were replaced by forced work on land and later in the tobacco factory, and the women were first forcibly confined to the home, and then forced to become factory workers. Their earlier social practises were considered barbaric and substituted with ones more acceptable to Victorian and Brahmanical notions of respectability; the women lost their relative egalitarian position in the community, and became increasingly subordinated to the men. And then, their children were taken away from them—to whom then could they tell their stories, or sing their songs? It was a fractured community life, with broken bonds and ties. The settlement discipline allowed no meetings larger than six people at a time, except under the Salvation Army's eyes. In any case, there was no leisure, which must be there for the telling of tales or the singing of songs—both men and women worked upto 16 hours a day.

As a result, there were several drastic, sudden and deliberately engineered changes in the continuity of their lives, and therefore breaches with their immediate past. What remained of a community was more a confederacy, created by the punitive discipline and the application of the CTA. The social and cultural resources, gathered over generations were probably irreparably destroyed with the violence of the changes that each of the breaches implied. The system of relationships and other social balances that communities evolve to sustain themselves seem to have been wiped out in this particular case because of a lack of continuity between the present and the past. Ironically, it was not until both men and women began work in the tobacco factory that some semblance of a collective or community identity began to emerge again, because of a shared environment, however restrictive. By then, however, it appears that their past history had already been rewritten in their memories.

There is a clue to the gradual way in which a rupture from their past took place. Once they were labelled criminals, their real, lived experience was at complete variance with their earlier existence as legitimate traders. There was the Salvation Army inside the settlement, and if they managed to escape, they had to contend with the police. In fact, the police were a major constituent of their new psyche, as the possibility of a life outside the settlement, if they managed to escape, was clouded by their ubiquitous presence.

They hunted me, haunted me, hounded me ever,
I was a 'crim', they said I was a 'crim';
And my honest intentions were scorned all the more,
I was branded the criminal kind.

So I gave up my struggle and thought it my lot,
For I was a 'crim', yes, I was a crim,
With the rest of my fellows, the Sircar I fought,
Being marked as the Criminal Tribe.

The rupture is also expressed in a telling manner in the following two instances that Booth Tucker told his international audience in an amused manner, fully aware that absconding from the settlement spelt terror for the settlers:

> One of our women officers was conducting a meeting amongst a number of tribesmen. She had been speaking to them...about the necessity of resisting the temptations of Satan. 'Who is your greatest enemy?' she asked. 'The Police.' 'But, I mean, your spiritual enemy, the enemy of your souls.' They persisted, however, in repeating the answer. The officer was forced to change the subject and had to give them a chorus to sing instead.[3]

Recounting another instance, he recalled that a Salvation Army officer asked his Yerukula pupils, 'I have a Friend that's ever near—never fear. What does that mean?' 'Don't be afraid of the Police, God will look after you', came the prompt reply.[4]

But the most poignant of all is the way, before the rupture became complete, their prayers, which used to be for the peace of their dead and the health of their children, changed:

> Spirits of our fathers, help us. Save us from the government and shut the mouths of the police.[5]

So this was the mental soil on which so powerful a myth, so convincing a version of another history could be sown. The important point to emphasise here is that the Salvation Army had consciously spun it, improved upon it, and intended to plant it years before it was actually made their own by members of the Yerukula community. As indicated earlier, there was resistance on the ground to the components of this version while it was being spun.[6] Now being passed on to new generations, this new history shows no signs of that resistance.

Ironically, the official records of the British administration, the ILTD factory, and the Salvation Army contradict much of what the Yerukulas believe today. These sources not only grant the Yerukulas an 'honourable' past, they speak of the resistance that the community offered to forces which challenged the legitimacy of its existence at various stages. Equally ironically, it is the official sources which acknowledge the lack of any real bases for branding the community a criminal one. The oral traditions of the community, which are supposed to 'recover' an 'authentic' past, reconstruct over and over again the criminal that the larger society had once invented, by passing on a constructed version of their history to their children and grandchildren. This version, as this chapter attempts to show, did not originate out of the way their actual lives were lived, but was purposefully introduced into the oral culture of the community about seven decades ago.

Interestingly, when a nationalist enquiry committee visited the settlement in the 1940s, the settlers openly declared themselves to be 'Congress and Hindu' knowing exactly which way the political wind was blowing, and when they could safely defy the Salvation Army. In other words, not only ten years ago, but even forty years earlier than that, the Yerukulas had an accurate assessment of their present: it was the reading of their *past* which had been successfully tainted by the myth of their criminality.

It will be appropriate to end with what the 'Crims' in the 1920s were meant to be thinking of themselves and their situation:

> Now [work] is our watchword, from day unto day,
> There is hope for the Crim; there is hope for the Crim,
> *We wipe from our minds our sad record away,*[7]
> We Tribes of the criminal kind.

Notes

1. *The War Cry*, February, 1916.
2. F. Booth Tucker, *Mukti Fauj*, p. 229.
3. F. Booth Tucker, *Criminocurology*, p. 13.
4. *Ibid.*
5. *Ibid.*, p. 12.
6. Even according to the Salvation Army, 'We encountered many difficulties. The tribe was nomadic and resented internment, nor did they like the work in the quarries...In fact, they objected to everything. Even the six hundred donkeys which they brought with them entered into the spirit of their non-cooperating masters.' F. Booth Tucker, *Mukti Fauj*, p. 228. Another account speaks of their 'resentful mood', 'arguments and scuffles', 'protestation and threats of violence' towards the Salvation Army officials. W. Bramwell Baird, *The Call of the Jackals*, p. 131. The records at the ILTD,

factory, Guntur and the official documents record the assertion and resistance of the Yerukulas as workers in the factory, especially after they got organised as the ILTD Workers' Union. Meena Radhakrishna, 'From Tribal Community to Working Class Consciousness: Case of Yerukula Women', Review of Women's Studies, *Economic and Political Weekly*, April 29, 1989.

7. Emphasis added.

Conclusion

I

As far as the CTA as a legislative measure is concerned, it is worth pointing out that in its enactment, the principle of individualism, one of the ostensible main features of the British legal system, was completely abandoned: Indians were deemed to be community or caste-based collectivities. Whole communities were registered under the Act if some members were merely suspected of being criminals. The CTA was meant to check crime by a criminal caste or tribe, not by individuals. David Arnold's has been a pioneering attempt to contribute to an understanding of this phenomenon, by explaining the basis of the stereotypes invented by the British.

> ...(J)ust as the army produced handbooks to aid its recruiting officers in the selection of the finest 'fighting races', so the police department produced works ... which listed 'criminal' communities, identified their social and physical characteristics, recounted their myths and criminal lore, and described the hallmarks of their criminal trade.

The 'lawless Maravan', the 'skulking Kallar,' the 'licentious Pariah' and the 'restless Kuravan' were some of these categories. This use of the singular to typify an entire community of so many thousands of men, women and children was a common aspect of colonial categorisation.[1]

This book grapples with a number of questions: how did the

British legislatively operationalise these categories of criminals? The 'restless Kuravan' needed to be policed, but how was it actually to be done? Apart from the notified communities, which were the other sections indirectly affected by the Act? Clearly the CTA was a political act on the part of the British, if the intention was to manipulate social relations with powerful sections of the society like the landlords, or private entrepreneurs who were to employ these communities. What is interesting, however, is the successful selling by the administration of the idea of *social reform* implicit in the CTA to the public, both British and Indian, while it was actually conceived to serve quite different ends. In fact, the book concerns itself seriously with the administration's perception of the Act's potential for larger political purposes, while the British could pose it primarily as social reform rather than social control legislation.

This book, then, is not concerned so much with the day to day operation of the CTA but with the historical context in which a decision to institute the Act was taken. For this reason, the sources consulted are not the court records, but records of the various departments of the British administration—Home, Police, Revenue and so on. Interesting divergences and disagreements emerge with a study of these records, as the British administrative machine was far from homogenous. There were differences of opinion within the Governing Council itself on the usefulness or criminality of some of the communities being considered for notification under the CTA. Further, there were perceptions of local situations, which were not similar in different provinces. A uniform policy especially in matters of social control could never have been successful.

The differences in the approach of different provincial governments to the CTA were apparent in 1870 itself, when the Revenue Department in Madras sturdily resisted the impending CTA. This department depended on the itinerant Koravas to distribute salt in far-flung areas, and any surveillance would have effectively curbed their movements and hampered distribution of this very important item. Salt was, after ali, the main source of revenue in the Presidency in the nineteenth century for the

British. Individual district collectors, responsible for specific quotas of revenue in their districts, also resisted this Act for the same reason. Only when the railways and a road network had assured an alternative distribution system, could the Madras government be ready to even consider an Act like this.

What originated from one province was thus totally unacceptable to the administration in another—there was a spirited and well-argued opposition to the idea of extension of CTA, 1871, to Madras. Even suggestions made by a kindred branch of the administration—Punjab police—were not accepted by the Madras police on the grounds that the social situation was quite different in the two provinces. It took another 40 years for this piece of legislation to be applied to Madras Presidency, and that for quite different reasons to the ones enumerated in the Punjab.

As far as perception of criminality of particular groups was concerned, what is equally striking is the difference in bureaucratic perception from one department to another, and from one arm of the administration to the other in the *same* province. For instance, the very need for a CTA arose in 1871 as a result of the judiciary in the Punjab objecting to registration of 'wandering' communities by the police administration and confining their movements to prescribed areas. The Court questioned the validity of these practices by the police administration and held them to be illegal. An overarching piece of legislation was required to iron out some of the differences in perception of who precisely was a criminal community, and what measures were to be taken to control them.

There were related issues that arose from this analytical approach—political or economic requirements were not uniform or consistent over time, nor were they similar in different provinces during a given period. The revisions in the CTA should then reflect, at least partly, some of the political changes taking place during the period, as also a pattern of differential operation of the CTA in different regions. A cross-checking with Sanjay Nigam's study, which is concerned with a different historical period and focusing on communities of northern India which were not itinerant, bears this point out well. As expected, the CTA followed quite a different trajectory here, faced as the administration was with the effects of the 1857 events and a different land revenue system. Here an attempt was made through the CTA to separate out those notified under the Act on the one hand and the moral subjects of the Raj on the other i.e. the honest peasants and the landholders.[2]

It is in this significant context that the CTA originated in the north of India as early as 1871. The Bhils formed into a Corps in 1841 had already exhibited 'remarkable fidelity and military steadiness' during the 1857 battles. This only confirmed the possibility of conversion of large numbers of similar groups into loyal subjects of the government. The criminal tribe settlements in the north were to serve precisely this end. In Madras Presidency, on the other hand, the CTA became applicable only in 1911 and was operationalised with a very different end in view. With the ryotwari system in force in Madras, the landlords were an important political ally in the governing of the Presidency, and very considerable judicial, revenue and police powers were assigned to this section. Their wishes had to be taken into account as far as surveillance powers and functions under the CTA were concerned. The CTA, 1911 made the Madras headman—invariably a high caste landlord—responsible for the surveillance of criminal tribe communities, giving them a ready captive workforce at a time when breaking down of traditional caste hierarchies, as also migration of vast numbers to places like Ceylon was giving rise to an alarm over labour shortage in the fields.[3]

There were, however, inherent tensions in the relationship between the landlords and the British both in the zamindari and the ryotwari areas. On the one hand, the government needed powerful political allies, and on the other, it had to contain them from threatening the authority of the state.[4] In the north, the events of 1857 brought these tensions to the surface in a number of areas. In Madras Presidency, however, such contradictions became more obvious during the second decade of the twentieth century, with the advance of the nationalist movement. With this new dimension, the existing structures, including legal ones, had to be modified to serve immediate political needs of the British: changes made in the CTA during this period reflect these compulsions.

Concretely, after a decade or so of the operation on the CTA in Madras Presidency, the surveillance powers over the CT members were shifted from landlords to the police after the formers' active role in the non-cooperation movement. Collection of revenue was becoming increasingly difficult as the landlord-cum-village officers had formed associations and given in their resignations in large numbers. When the police had to be deployed for collecting taxes, a serious reappraisal of the roles of the landlords and police began to take place during this period.[5] This, in turn, dictated the changes in the clauses under the CTA. The police being entrusted with surveillance powers is particularly significant in the light of recurring evidence of its earlier abuse that the administration had.

Because attitudes towards criminality are culture-bound and contexual, changes in perceptions of crime lead to accompanying modification in operations of existing institutions.[6] A study of the CTA, however, shows that even political imperatives can dictate major changes in enactments like the CTA, ostensibly instituted to check social crime.

II

The purpose of criminal tribe settlements in Madras Presidency, as implied earlier, was different to that in the north. The book explores just one of the CT settlements in Madras, and studies its functioning and logic. However, some general conclusions are drawn about CT settlements under missionaries in colonial India as a whole. Formed mostly under the guidance of the Salvation Army, a missionary organisation, these settlements mirrored what the founder—William Booth—had visualised for the British unemployed and poor. It is significant that the concept of criminal tribe settlements became the meeting ground for the Salvation Army and the British administration: both felt that these settlements signified in practice the notion of 'curocriminology'. The views of both converged on the issue of reform of a section of the Indian population—the agenda of reforming the whole of Indian society was by now clearly given up.

The basic principles for handling of CTs were learnt from experiments with mill work in Bombay Presidency, and subsequently sought to be applied all over British India. Work had to be found for the CTs in order to reform them. The work had to be regular, which could be given by private enterprises which had a chronic shortage of labour. These employers actually preferred CT members as they could be reasonably sure of their continued attendance and recovery of training costs. Since this was possible only if the CT members were captive and not free labour, the whole logic of the Criminal Tribes Act could be pressed into the service of these employers.

The Salvation Army made efficient managers of criminal tribe settlements. They combined in their work the role of the landlords (they collected rent from the settlers), the police (they watched over their movements day and night), and the government (they duly inculcated a respect for law and property that the British administration wished to see imbibed by all its subjects). In fact, the settlements turned out to be quite successful from the administration's point of view, with the Salvation Army steadily working through a 'dense mass' of criminal tribe population and turning them out into either productive workers for private enterprises or industrious peasants.

III

This book also looks into the policy of land reclamation by the British government, which was the basis of the work on land in the so-called agricultural settlements for criminal tribe members. The process of land reclamation—an activity designed to raise revenue from wasteland by making it cultivable—became synonymous with material and moral progress of the settlements of this nature. Cultivation itself—the 'most appropriate industry for Indians' was then put forward as the epitome of respectable, sedentary life. The hub of the entire logic of this improved level of respectability was a settled life for itinerants— 'to break them of their idle, vicious, restless habits by holding out hopes of an independent life as farmer or artificer'. Agricultural settlements embodied this concept more or less perfectly. In fact, a definite sign of desire for reformation in the settlers was deemed to be their eagerness for any available land. These ideas of the government, of course, had plenty of adversaries.

The opposition by the Hindu high caste community to itinerant communities' work on any land except their own is a persistent trend all though the early decades of the twentieth century. The landlords, who welcomed the CTA, opposed agricultural settlements run by missionary organisations and could not be cajoled into accepting them. The high caste landlords' hostility was not only due to the 'Christian' factor, but also to losing free labour provided by the criminal tribe members whom they were supposed to watch under the powers given to them by the CTA. Moreover, the missionary-run settlements threatened to disturb, in the landlords' view, the smooth operation of traditional caste relations. There was also the additional resistance by the landlords to the lowly criminal tribe members cultivating land even in the capacity of tenants, let alone becoming patta holders.

The possibility of the itinerant communities 'reaching the pastoral stage of life' threatened the landlord sections so much that they preferred to have these communities removed from the agricultural fields altogether and advocating work for them as wageworkers in private enterprises. In fact, they tried to persuade the government that

> ...[the] roaming habits of these criminal tribes...[and] their disinclination to own property...demonstrate that they have not reached the pastoral stage of life... The best means, therefore, of reforming these criminal tribes is to engage them under loving supervision in mining work or in tea plantations of Assam.[7]

This view seems to have been shared by the administration too, in their open refusal to turn reformed criminal tribe members into 'agriculturists' when a real opportunity to do so presented itself, and instead, sending them to work for a wage in the factories. When the option of criminal tribe members actually joining the supposed mainstream came up through ownership of their own pieces of land, the haste with which they were ejected from settlement land would constitute a study in bureaucratic efficiency: they were shifted to their newly constructed homes within days to start full time work in a tobacco factory. Not just the landlords, but the Salvation Army and the British administration too found it unacceptable that criminal tribe members become owners of valuable land.

IV

Not recognising the notion of a community-based life, the Salvation Army and the administration systematically broke up the community into identifiable units—families—comprising of man, wife and children. The reclamation process to be set into motion by the Salvation Army had two vital components: moral education and 'honest' labour. The Salvation Army operationalised it by deciding that the children of criminals needed the first, and the adult men the second for true reclamation. Women, once in settlements, could be found indoor work, but more importantly, tutored in wifely and matronly qualities. The most important point in this context to note is that though the Salvation Army did not regard either women or children of criminal tribe communities as potential wage workers, women sometimes did end up forming a large part of the workforce in an enterprise. Women, thus, were the 'permanent' workforce at the ILTD Company, and as the last chapter discusses, made desireable workers. The mode of settlement life had been preparing them (and the men) for successful factory work.

The children, however, were the major attraction of the project. The Salvation Army had an enduring view of the essential corruptibility of children, especially those belonging to the criminal tribe communities, and they made special efforts to further break up the family and isolate the children from their parents. There were special separate dormitories in the settlement for boys and girls, and the day schools were far removed from the huts of the parents. While the adult settlers would be at agricultural work, mat making, or factory work, the children would go through a rigorous routine of reading, writing, singing of prayers and hymns, marching to music and so on. They were to be morally uplifted, and the hope was that they would at some point not only try and influence their parents, but tutor the wider community of criminal tribes in their capacity as teachers and promoters.

The interesting point, however, is the difference in perception of the Salvation Army and the employers of criminal tribe members as far as the issue of the children was concerned. The Salvation Army was keen on working with these communities on the plantations except for one snag: the planters insisted that the children were not to be separated from their parents as stipulated by the Salvation Army. The planting community made it quite clear that

> from the planters' point of view, the brightness and intelligence of the children and the chance of their ultimately forming a settled labour force [was] the most attractive part of the whole thing...[8]

It is a poignant historical fact that from the point of view of the settlers, the attractiveness of the initial decision to go to the inhospitable hills, also lay in the prospect of keeping their family together: in the settlements managed by the Salvation Army, they would have had their children taken away from them. It is worth mentioning here that while the jail authorities did not make the families of criminals accompany them to the jail, in the case of criminal tribe settlements, women and children were made to do so as policy.

It is also significant that neither the plantations, nor enterprises like the Parry's sugar factory were able to acquire the 'permanent workforce' which they so wanted, while ILTD, a tobacco factory, managed to do so very successfully over the years. This is possibly because the stability of the workforce which some managements sought to achieve through application of the CTA was acquired by the ILTD by virtue of the pressures of the workers' union. The organised workforce *wanted* to stay as the wages and working conditions at the factory continued to improve. It was the union which prevented the children from working in the ILTD factory on the one hand, and at the same time stabilised the adult workforce by providing a forum for redressal of their grievances. The estate owners and Parry's management on the other hand, tried unsuccessfully to 'breed in captivity' a regular, permanent workforce.

V

Within the general framework of colonial law, using the CTA as a vantage point, there is thus also an attempt to understand firstly, the factors responsible for disintegration of traditional communities over a period of time and secondly, forced fashioning of a wage workforce out of such communities during the critical decades of the early twentieth century. A close study of some of the CT settlements run by the government shows that any low caste, vulnerable section of the people could be declared a CT and forced to work in an enterprise; any person including a manager of an enterprise could be made responsible for their control; and any site including an enterprise itself could be declared a CT settlement.

The course followed by one of the CT settlements—Stuartupuram settlement in Guntur district is studied in detail. Also studied are the labour recruitment methods used by various employers of criminal tribe members through the agency of the CTA. This, incidentally, was in an era when the indentured form of labour was sought to be legally abolished; the resilience of this form of labour, which sprang up in different forms, and the furtive course it took shows itself clearly in study of the CTA. In a novel and surreptitious way, the CTA effectively replaced the repealed Workmen's Breach of Contract Act.

Booth Tucker of the SA made a graphic distinction between what he called Free Labour as opposed to Forced Labour by those settlers who were made to work in an enterprise. He had clarified that

> Free Labour (in a factory) was what might be called extremely volatile and unreliable...because the severe physical strain of.... long hours, frequently without any Sunday or other interval for rest, was more than the strongest constitution could endure. The case was widely different with the Forced Labour of our settlers. They could only relieve the strain by absconding, which was a punishable offence...[it] was the fact that they could not get away like the Free Labour that made this class of workmen appear so desirable to the [factory] manager.[9]

As he said, even in jails, the work hours were limited to eight with Sundays off, (as the government was unable to extract longer hours from their supervisory staff), but not so in CT settlements.

There are other related issues explored in the book, some at greater length than others. As the book progresses, it touches in passing on the troubled relationship between different agencies responsible for the 'care' of the criminal tribe members in Madras Presidency—the headmen of the villages, the Salvation Army, the police and the private employers.

The focus of the book, in other words, is on the historical context in which the Criminal Tribes Act originated. The aim is to analyse the way a set of social polices in the colonies were formulated, and modified under political and economic pressures. To that extent, this work is a study of legislation and of the administrative mind, as opposed to a narrative of resistance or defiance offered by the disadvantaged community of those declared criminal by the British administration.

In this book, then, an attempt is made to identify some of the strands which wove into the ideological perception, or construction of a criminal in the early twentieth century, as distinct from actual legislation to deal with criminality on the ground. Attitudes to itinerant communities are hence important, as also the details of Yerukulas' particular experiences with the British administration, the missionaries and the factory management, in addition to the sedentary community at large with which they were forced to interact. However, events never unfolded in the way desired by the authorities. Ironic, unpredicted and unplanned processes were a natural corollary, by the sheer logic of accretion, to the manipulation by those in charge of the Yerukulas' collective destiny.

The final chapter is based on an analysis of a poem that is a part of the Yerukula's oral culture even today, and which is at complete variance with the officially recorded version speaking of a useful, honourable past of the earlier generations. In the process, the chapter raises some methodological questions about the validity of oral sources as means of writing 'alternative histories'.

In the end, it is worth mentioning the point that today's category of Scheduled Castes comprises largely of those socially disadvantaged groups which were a creation of the historically disabling caste system. Today's administrative category of Denotified Tribes, however, now comprises those people who were declared criminal tribes under the British. In that sense, not just the criminal tribes of yesterday, but even millions of members of the denotified tribes today, haunted by the stigma of criminality and the spectre of the police, are a creation of the British.[10]

Notes

1. Arnold (1985, 1986).
2. Nigam 1990: I,161.
3. C.P. Ramasami Aiyar, *District Problems*, Home Rule Series No. 17, Madras, 1916.
4. Anand Yang, 'Between British Raj and Saran Raiyat' in Peter Robb (ed.) *Rural India: Land, Power and Society under British Rule*, London, 1983, p. 155; Nigam 1990: I, 161-63.
5. Christopher Baker, 'Madras Headmen' in K.N. Chaudhary and Clive Dewey (eds.) *Economy and Society: Essays in Indian Economic and Social History*, Delhi, 1979, pp 38-39; Arnold 1986: 196.

6. Freitag 1991: 228.
7. Memorandum by landlords, Judl. GO 2509, 14.10.1915.
8. The desire for a permanent workforce, incidentally, is what made British Indian planters look after their pregnant women workers. They gave their female workers half pay before and after confinement for a period and also a lumpsum cash bonus. Geraldine Forbes, 'Managing midwifery in India' in Dagmar Engels and Shula Marks (ed.) *Contesting Colonial Hegemony—State and Society in Africa and India,* London, 1994, p. 165.
9. F. Booth Tucker, *Mukti Fauj or Forty years with the Salvation Army in India and Ceylon,* London, p. 225.
10. Meanwhile, the charge of criminality against these communities continues in the writings by well-meaning anthropologists. Jakka Parthasarthy, *The Yerukula: An Ethnographic Study,* Anthropological Survey of India, Calcutta, 1988; M.A. Ansari, *Tribals in Criminal Web,* Jaipur, 1987; Y.C. Simhadri, *Denotified Tribes,* New Delhi, 1991; Gauri Shankar, *Born Criminals,* Varanasi, 1979; Y.C. Simhadri, *The Ex-Criminal Tribes of India,* New Delhi, 1979. The most noteworthy example of this genre is the monumental national level effort to understand India's communities—the *People of India* series—which is otherwise an invaluable source of baseline data. It faithfully reproduces colonial attitudes towards the denotified and nomadic communities, lifted not just verbatim from British ethnographic writings, but often held by the field researchers themselves. This is particularly unfortunate as researchers of the future generations will imagine that these communities 'continued' to be criminal a hundred years after they were first identified as criminal tribes. See K.S. Singh (ed.), *People of India,* National Series, Vols. IV, V, VI: India's Communities, Calcutta, 1998.

Afterword

After independence, the Criminal Tribes Act (CTA) was repealed, and the concerned communities, many of them nomadic, were now 'denotified'. Before describing the way the new Indian state dealt with them, it is important to re-emphasise certain points brought out by recent research, or touched upon in the book.

As described elsewhere, the Indian nomadic communities carried the negative associations historically attached to an European gypsy, a vagabond, a lower race, a savage tribe, a colonial Irish subject, a vagrant and even an immigrant/migrant.[1] At the same time, it is interesting to note the contradictory views about nomadic communities in the records of the British Indian government in the nineteenth century. While one section of British administrators discussed the nomadic tribes as 'dangerous classes' of India, another section was well aware that many of the traditionally 'wandering' groups were law-abiding and productive visitors to village society. Even the outcastes were recognised as communities that were 'exceedingly industrious and not at all given to crime.'[2] However, through a process of accretion of labels, nomadic communities, as a category, had been progressively moving towards being declared as criminals. It is important to mention here that this was made possible partly because *the definition of 'work' itself had changed significantly by the twentieth century*, with the changes wrought by colonialism in Indian society and economy. The category of the Indian nomad increasingly consisted of people employed in different kinds of menial/

casual/low-paid work.[3] Many of the nomadic communities in question collected forest produce like medicinal herbs and honey, made a variety of goods like baskets and brooms, bartered or sold these goods in villages through which they passed, and devised a hundred other diverse ways to eke out a living while being on the move. Many also continued to practice their traditional occupations and skills as acrobats, musicians, tight-rope walkers, street-singers and dancers and so on. It is in this context that the statement by Booth Tucker of the Salvation Army becomes significant: 'When we asked them to till the land, or work in a factory, they were shocked. Work? They said, we never work, we just sing and dance.'[4]

Booth Tucker did not mention that when these words were being attributed to the concerned communities, their traditional occupations were already seen by the administrators to be undesirable aspects of an underclass which should have been gainfully employed in the colonial economy by then. Street entertainment through singing and dancing, for instance, was no longer considered 'work' or a legitimate way of earning a livelihood. In effect, as mentioned elsewhere in the book, what was being discussed here was not whether these communities worked or not, but the nature of their work: their work was independent, not time bound and, most importantly, was not *wage* work. That is why, as the book discusses in detail, such communities were slowly 'weaned' away from their traditional occupations through the operation of certain sections of the CTA, 1911, and were forced to work in British-owned factories, mines, plantations, quarries and mines.

A particular view of what qualifies as 'work' is important as will become clear in the following sections.

Denotified Tribes as Habitual Offenders

There seems to be a gradual process by which gypsies and nomadic tribes, who form part of the marginalised sections in all societies, get declared criminals by law. The process in all cases is one of stark dispossession, with traditional livelihoods becoming redundant at times of rapid economic change. The process of destitution compounds the customary hostility that such communities suffer from mainstream and sedentary groups.

Within a few days of India gaining independence, a new category of 'vagrancy: nomadic and migratory tribes' was suggested and adopted as an entry under the concurrent list.[5] This entry has remained intact as a part of the Constitution adopted in 1950. The important point for our purposes is that like the European lawmakers, their counterparts in independent India too conflated vagrancy, nomadism and migration.[6] They associated the migratory tribes with vagrancy, on the one hand, and nomadism, on the other. Consequently, the concerned communities and people ended up carrying the individual and collective legal baggage attached to each of these terms.

The new entry under the concurrent list signalled that colonial British attitudes were going to be replicated amongst the lawmakers in independent India as well. Predictably, this is what the Criminal Tribes Enquiry Committee, 1949-50 had to say:

> As regards Gipsies, we feel that till they settle down on land, they will continue the life of crime. We propose that effort should be made under sanction of law, (suitable provision may be made in the Habitual Offenders and *Vagrants* Act) to settle them and teach them a life of industry and honest calling as against idleness, prostitution and crime to which their conditions of existence make them prone.[7]

The Vagrancy Act, 1824 in England served as a model for a potential Habitual Offenders and Vagrants Act in post-independent India of the 1950s. Following English law, the officials in India considered vagrancy to be a serious enough offence for it to be clubbed together with 'habitual offending' of other kinds. The Committee envisaged a Habitual Offenders and Vagrants Act that was meant to contain provisions for dealing with Habitual Offenders of different categories, one of which was 'vagrants without any settled occupation, who lead a life of crime, prostitution and idleness.'[8] Once again not only was the nomad or the gypsy treated as a synonym to the vagrant, Indian vagrancy was being again defined in much the same way as European one: *lack of occupation, shirking honest work* and *proneness to criminality.*

Such an Act actually never materialised; what did emerge was a Habitual Offenders Act, which left the vagrants out of its purview, the reasons for which will be speculated upon below. At any rate, the Habitual Offenders' Act of the 1950s in free India was successor to the colonial CTA, 1871, except that it assumed an individual to be a criminal rather than whole communities.[9] The Habitual Offenders' Act replicated all the victimising sections of the colonial Criminal Tribes Act, showing that the legal edifice of the independent Indian state did not treat the concerned marginalised people any differently.[10]

Nomadic Tribes as Beggar Offenders

The intention to introduce an Indian law to deal with the 'vagrant' part of the problem is clear in one of the Constituent Assembly debates. The Constituent Assembly in 1949 considered whether there should be a separate amendment to control beggary but then the amendment was withdrawn as Ambedkar pointed out that the concurrent list contained a provision to address the problem of vagrancy, which included beggary.[11]

The changing perception of what constituted work was just one of the reasons why nomads either got forcibly transformed into wage workers or got defined as criminals. One of the milestones in the metamorphosis of a gypsy/nomadic community to offenders in the eyes of the law also drew from the official conflation of the 'vagrant' into a 'beggar'—a lazy, wilful shirker whom Henry Mayhew would have happily classified amongst those who will not work.[12] As recent research has argued, the so-called vagrants in European societies were a heterogeneous lot, and included gypsies.[13] They were categorised summarily as the 'poor', mostly eking out a precarious living through low-paid work. Obviously, such groups and communities of people were not always able to find work, which was as sporadic in nature as it was varied.

It is interesting to note in this context that for centuries there has been a consensus in the administration, in India, England and elsewhere, that such 'vagrants' have no occupation because they do not *want* to work, and it then followed that in order to sustain themselves such people will be drawn either to criminality, or to beggary, or to both. The same train of thought that concludes that a gypsy is a vagrant can then declare, as a corollary, that a gypsy is a shirker and hence must live by crime. This logic was applied to the beggars as well, who were also seen to be perennial shirkers. A perceptive commentator on this subject had this to say:

> The distinction between the man who is unemployed because he cannot get work and the man who is unemployed because he does not want to work, requires a modicum of knowledge and reflection which even at the present day is not always forthcoming.[14]

In independent India too, as in many other societies across the world, the common ground between the vagrant and the beggar was provided by the ostensible fact that both consisted of people who committed the offence of not working, or were seen to be not working. The connection between vagrancy and beggary in the administrative mind in India is evident from the laws that were instituted in colonial India to check vagrancy and beggary. The Bengal Vagrancy Act, 1943 was a model for the Mysore Prevention of Begging Act, 1944 and the Madras Prevention of Begging Act, 1945.

The member of the Constituent Assembly, who had proposed the amendment to control beggary, considered it to be a result of the 'rot of lethargy.'

> In fact in most countries they have legislation prohibiting beggary; but in our country this evil continues as a stigma on our fair name and reputation... our climatic conditions also result in lethargy and laziness in the habits of our people. This has also accounted for this abnormal number of beggars in the land. Some people turn beggars only because they are too lazy to work. They fill their stomach without earning their livelihood by honest work. They simply live on alms and do not work. They are a burden on Society.[15]

The institution of the anti-beggary legislation with all its implications shows that the newly independent Indian state failed to address the issue of acute impoverishment of certain sections of Indian society. This impoverishment, caused by the gradual loss of traditional means of livelihood, probably *did* many a time leave begging as the sole means of survival for an ever-expanding social section. But the study of anti-beggary legislation shows something sinister: it appears that by the way this particular piece of legislation was defined, it actually targeted the nomadic tribes, prohibiting them from practicing some of their earlier occupations, and criminalising them in case they continued to practice them. This made anti-beggary legislation, in effect, profoundly anti-nomadic tribe. Beggars were seen to be a subset of the 'vagrants', and vagrants synonymous with nomadic tribes. In addition, homelessness as well as lack of means of subsistence were seen as factors serious enough to invoke anti-beggary legislation against nomadic tribes.[16]

The newly-independent Indian state found that the nomadic tribes were a mixed lot. Some were settled and engaged in intermittent, casual/wage work; many were still nomadic and supplemented casual work with their traditional occupations as itinerant traders, small artisans and street performers. Most were grievously impoverished, and all were severely persecuted by the police, being still on the list of 'Criminal Tribes' prepared by the British lawmakers.

However, that the Bombay Prevention of Begging Act, 1959 was written with the nomadic communities in mind can be seen seen by the definition of begging itself. Begging is defined as:

> Soliciting or receiving alms, in a public place whether or not under any pretence such as singing, dancing, fortune telling, performing or offering any article for sale;... Having no visible means of subsistence and wandering about or remaining in any public place in such condition or manner, as makes it likely that the person doing so exist soliciting or receiving alms.[17]

As can be seen clearly, such a definition will qualify the nomadic tribes almost to the last detail as a beggar. The Act also includes the concern about vagrancy by including the statements about 'having no visible means of subsistence' and 'wandering about'. The nomadic communities had included amongst them singers, dancers, street performers, acrobats, fortune tellers, religious mendicants and also those who earned a living by selling items like medicinal herbs, iron implements, items made from bamboo or leaves like baskets, mats, brooms and so on. As the excerpt from the Act above shows, anyone who is is found to be performing any of these earlier legitimate activities, and then expecting payment for entertaining the public or 'offering any articles for sale' is seen to be 'soliciting or receiving alms'—

meaning begging—under the supposed *pretence* of earning a livelihood through these means.

The Bombay Prevention of Beggary Act, 1959 served, and has continued to serve, as the model for anti-beggar legislation in 15 states in free India.[18] The clue to a most important missing link in our understanding of the slow but inexorable construction of a gypsy or nomad into a criminal in the Indian case is provided by a current statement on the official website of the Social Welfare Department in Maharashtra under the subject 'Social Defence':

> In Maharashtra State there are five pieces of social legislation the aim of three of which is to protect children and to prevent juvenile adolescents and young adults from becoming habitual criminals. They are the Bombay Children Act, 1948, the Bombay Borstal Schools Act, 1929 and the Bombay Probation of Offenders Act, 1938. The remaining two viz., *Bombay Prevention of Begging Act, 1959 and the Bombay Habitual Offenders Act, 1959, deal with prevention of crime and treatment of offenders.*[19]

In other words, the anti-beggary Act is not meant for the prevention of *begging* as the nomenclature in the Act suggests, but for prevention of *crime*. This is not because of any confusion in the administrative mind; by now begging and crime are seen to be synonymous. More significantly, rounding up beggars is expected to prevent crime, as beggars are deemed to be criminals in disguise. The two separate Acts mentioned above in a single breath—one for begging and another for treatment of offenders—are put together to create the notion of a 'beggar offender' in the eyes of law.[20]

The situation has continued to worsen for the nomadic communities as far as the perception of the lawmakers go. The geographical areas in which anti-beggary laws are in force have been extended and expanded by repeated amendments.[21] This is possibly because of more intensified migration of nomadic communities into new areas in search of work, and equally because they traverse new territories in order to find customers for their precarious services and goods. A random study of the operation of anti-beggary laws in Delhi shows that a large section of the communities regularly rounded up and criminalised under the Act are the denotified and nomadic communities.[22]

The extent to which the nomadic people in India have actually become impoverished enough to have genuinely degenerated to beggary for a livelihood needs to be studied further. But, from the perspective of lawmaking, intensive further research needs to be done to understand the precise judicial processes by which nomadic communities that are still practicing their earlier occupations for a livelihood are now the target of the officials enforcing anti-beggary laws. Changes in legal perceptions about poverty, and criminalisation of the poor in general, and nomadic tribes in particular, is only one of these processes that need urgent research attention.

The CTA, 1871 was instituted by the colonial administration and applied to a large number of nomadic and other communities in India. It has been studied in the book as a colonial piece of legislation, though its clear connections to caste interests have also been explored. As far as the treatment of the subaltern sections by Indian lawmakers is concerned, it is obvious that they have repeatedly taken leaves out of the colonial law books. Research has shown that as far as the gypsies and nomads are concerned, there is a startling similarity between the attitudes of the ruling classes in England in the 1850s and the views of independent India's lawmakers since the 1950s. Indian laws relating to nomadic communities have, in fact, hardened by the beginning of the twenty-first century.[23]

The foregoing discussion, then, forces us to rethink and refine some of the concepts developed in this book. It makes out a compelling case for further research that will explore 'class' as vigorously as 'colonialism' while studying legislative paradigms in countries like India, and for a comparative study of legislation across colonial, imperial and 'democratic' societies.

Notes

1. Meena Radhakrishna, 'Laws of Metamorphosis: From Nomad to Offender' in Kalpana Kannabiran (ed.) *The Rule(s) of Law: Critical Essays on Criminology in India*, Sage Publications, 2007 (forthcoming).

2. *Ibid.*, section 8. This point has also been made in chapter 1, section 1 of the book.
3. *Ibid.*, section 6.
4. F. Booth Tucker, *Criminocurology or the Indian Crim and What to Do with Him—A Report of the Work of the Salvation Army among the Criminal Tribes, Habituals and Released Prisoners in India*, London, n.d., p. 43.
5. Seventh Schedule (Article 246), Concurrent List, item no.15, *Constitution of India*. Also see debate on 20 August 1947, *Constituent Assembly of India—Volume V.* [http://parliamentofindia.nic.in/ls/debates/vol5p3b.htm]
6. Subsequent debates suggest that a special law was needed to control this multidimensional category of people moving across states.
7. Extracts from the *Report of the Criminal Tribes Enquiry Committee*, United Provinces, 1947, quoted in *Report of the Criminal Tribes Act Enquiry Committee (1949-50)*, Government of India Press, New Delhi, n.d., pp 142–3. Emphasis added.
8. It was recommended by the Committee that 'the decision whether a person comes under the definitions of "Habitual Offender" or "Vagrant" should be made by Court on recommendation of the prosecuting authority.'
9. Versions of this Act were enacted in various states mostly between 1952 and 1959.
10. Different states in independent India instituted their own legislation to deal with Habitual Offenders. For commonalities with the Criminal Tribes Act, see the case of Karnataka Habitual Offenders' Act, 1961. Karnataka Habitual Offenders' Act, 1961, Government of Karntaka, [dpal.kar.nic.in 24%20of% 201961%20(E).pdf] retrieved on September 4, 2007.
11. Raj Bahadur debating with B.R. Ambedkar, Constituent Assembly of India—Volume IX, 1 September 1949. [http://parliamentofindia.nic.in./ls/debates/vol9p23b.htm] as retrieved on 12 December 2006. Raj Bahadur, however, withdrew the amendment for a separate consideration of beggary when it was suggested that he put it to vote.
12. Henry Mayhew, *London Labour and the London Poor: The Condition and Earnings of Those that Will Work, Cannot Work, and Will Not Work* (3 Volumes), Griffen, Bohn and Company, Stationer's Hall Court, London, 1851. Electronic Text Center, University of Virginia Library, [http://etext.virginia.edu/toc/modeng/public/MayLond.html] as retrieved on 15 November 2006. Co-editor and founder of the satirical *Punch*, with a wide readership, Mayhew had written a series of influential articles on the London poor in the *Morning Chronicle*, which were later published in three volumes. A fourth 'Extra Volume' in 1861, co-written with Bracebridge Hemyng, John Binny and Andrew Halliday, covered the lives of prostitutes, thieves and beggars, though it departed from the interview

format to take a more general and statistical approach to its subject.

13. Meena Radhakrishna, 2007, op.cit.
14. R.H. Tawney, *The Agrarian Problem in the Sixteenth Century* (new edn.), 1967, p. 269, quoted in Beier, op. cit., p. 64. Research shows that the official perception that vagrants and beggars do not want to work has echoes across different time periods, especially in England. Beier has challenged some of the assumptions about vagrants in sixteenth century England being 'work shy' and 'wilfully idle'. See A.L. Beier, 'Vagrants and the Social Order in Elizabethan England', *Past and Present,* 64, 1974, p.4. The 1881 Poor Law Conference in London deemed tramps 'pedigree bred... a race which has the very genius of not working in its bones and sinews.' See Rachel Vorspan, 'Vagrancy and the New Poor Law in late-Victorian and Edwardian England', *English Historical Review,* XCII, 1977, p. 72, quoted in Hansen. Interestingly, of nineteenth century Egypt it has been written that begging by the able-bodied poor was indicative of the laziness of the peasantry. Here, one of the factors bringing *migrants* to the cities was perceived to be the 'fact' that a career of begging was much easier than the difficult work of agriculture in the countryside. 'The justifications for arrests (in Egyptian cities) were...that able bodied but "lazy" peasants were engaging in begging.' Mine Ener, 'Prohibitions on Begging and Loitering in Nineteenth Century Egypt', *Die Welt des Islams*, New Series, Vol. 39, Issue 3, November 1999.
15. Raj Bahadur debating with B.R. Ambedkar, *Constituent Assembly of India*—Volume IX, 1 September 1949. Op. cit. Emphasis added.
16. 'When the law defines begging (Bombay Prevention of Begging Act, 1959), it also takes into its gambit... any one *having no visible means of subsistence* and, *wandering about* or remaining in any public place in such condition or manner, as makes it likely that the person doing so exists by soliciting or receiving alms. This broad definition allows the police to arrest anyone who *looks poor* and unfairly targets those who are *houseless* and live in public places such as pavements or parks.' Pushkar Raj, General Secretary, People's Union for Civil Liberties (PUCL), Delhi, 'Criminalising Poverty: Houseless and Anti-beggary Law in Delhi', *PUCL Bulletin*, January, 2005. Emphasis added.
17. *Bombay Beggary Prevention Act,* Notification, Ministry of Home Affairs, 2 June 1960. [http://socialwelfare.delhigovt.nic.in/beggpreventact1.html] retrieved on 28 August 2007.
18. In fact, this Act is in force in Delhi since 1960, without adaptation to the special 'needs' of Delhi. In addition, there is the Bihar Prevention of Beggary Act, 1959; the Jammu & Kashmir Prevention of Begging Act, 1960; the Andhra Pradesh Prevention of Begging Act, 1964; the Haryana Prevention of Begging Act, 1971; the Punjab Prevention of Begging Act, 1971; the Goa, Daman & Diu Prevention of Begging Act, 1972; the

Cochin Vagrancy Act, 1974; the Uttar Pradesh Prohibition of Begging Act, 1975; and recently, there is the amended Karnataka Prevention of Beggary Act, 1975, amended in 2003. Trudy Brasell-Jones, 'Beggars Can't be Choosers: The Injustice of Anti-beggary Laws in India', unpublished paper, courtesy Indu Prakash Singh, Ashray Adhikar Abhiyan.

19. *District Gazetteer*, Nasik District: Law, Order and Justice—Social Welfare Department (Correctional Administration Wing and Non-Correctional Wing), Executive Editor and Secretary, Gazetteers Department, Government of Maharashtra, 2000. [www.maharashtra.gov.in/english/gazetteer/nasik/015%20Law/005%20Social%20WelfareDepartment.html] as retrieved on 10 December 2006.
20. A study of the Bombay Prevention of Beggary Act shows that from the time a beggar is apprehended, the terminology that is in use treats the beggar as an offender, even before it is proven that the person was indeed begging. Once it is 'proven' that the 'accused' was guilty, the Act itself clearly defines a system of 'penalty for begging after detention as beggar.' This includes detention in a certified institution upto a period of three years when a person is convicted for the first time, and this detention can be converted into imprisonment upto 10 years for a second-time conviction. What officially and progressively qualifies a beggar to become a 'beggar offender' are clauses that permit a beggar in a certified institution to subject himself to the taking of his fingerprints, refusal to do which would lead to extension of the detention or imprisonment period. Moreover, the court may legally 'order detention of persons wholly dependent on beggar.' *Bombay Beggary Prevention Act*, op. cit. Some additions have been inserted in 2003 into the latest amended Karnataka Prohibition of Beggary Act, 1975, modelled almost verbatim on the Bombay Act viz. refusal of a beggar to go to an institution or to a Magistrate punishable with imprisonment or fine or both, and every person detained in any of the institutions made subject to such rules of discipline as may be prescribed. The elaboration for the term 'discipline' includes the enforcement of manual and hard labour, which brings to mind the logic behind the criminal tribe settlements described in the book. *The Karnataka Prohibition of Beggary Act, 1975* (As Amended by Acts 7 of 1982, 12 of 1988 and 26 of 2003) [http://dpal.kar.nic.in/pdf files%5CPRO-HIBITION%20OF%20BEGGARY-B.pdf], Government of Kar-nataka, retrieved on 10 December 2006.
21. To cite just one instance, see *The Karnataka Prohibition of Beggary (Amendment) Act, 2003,* op. cit.
22. The study was conducted by this researcher, with the invaluable help provided by Jaishree Suryanarayanan and Sushil Kumar Singh , two young lawyers who are a part of a lawyers' group, which volunteers to give legal aid to the beggars in the Beggars' Court, Delhi. This research was carried

out under the aegis of the National Commission on Denotified, Nomadic and Semi-Nomadic Tribes, Ministry of Social Justice and Empowerment, Government of India, December 2006. *The Bombay Prevention of Begging Act, 1959* was extended to the Union Territory of Delhi by Government of India, Ministry of Home Affairs on 2 June 1960.

23. Some more laws like the Wild Life Protection Act, 1972, and societies set up under the Prevention of Cruelty to Animals (Establishment and Regulation of Societies for Prevention of Cruelty to Animals) Rules, 2001 also continue to target nomadic communities which used to traditionally entertain the public with birds, bears, monkeys and snakes.

APPENDIX I (A)

List of 'Criminal Tribe' Communities

(**Source:** *Bhasha Sanshodhan Prakashan Kendra, Baroda*)

Madras Presidency

1. *Adi-Dravidas*: Chingelput District.
2. *Ambalgars*: Trichinapalli District.
3. *Banjaras/Lambadas.*
4. *Bhattu Turkas*: Chittoor District.
5. *Bowas* (*Peddas and Dongas*): in Kurnool; Belrarvi; Ananthapur; Cuddapah and Chittoor, also known *Bedars/Berad.*
6. *Buda Bukkalas*; *also Ghakalas and Pamulas*: Guntur District of Madras.
7. *Dasaris* (*Dongas and Gudas*): notified all over the Presidency.
8. *Dommars or Damars* (*Reddis and Arais*).
9. *Ghasis*: Vasakhapattanam District in Madras.
10. *Irulars*: North and South Arcot; Trichinopoly and Madras City.
11. *Jogis/Jogulas.*
12. *Kaladis, also 'Parayars'*: Ramanad District.
13. *Kallars* (*Peramalais*; *Kooterpals and Periya Suriyurs*): C.T. in Madura North and South; Tanjore and Trichanapoly Districts.
14. *Kanjars.*
15. *Kepumaris*: Mainly in Kurnool; Salem; Coimbtoor and South Arcot Districts.
16. *Kintali Kalingas*: were declared C.T. in 6 villages in Pondur P.S. Limits of Vizagapattanam District.
17. *Konda Doras*: South Vizagapatanam District.
18. *Koravars*: All over Madras Presidency under different local names *Koracha*; *Yerukula*, *Erukula.*

19. *Karumbaravas*: Ramnad District.
20. *Modigas*: Kurnool District.
21. *Malas*:
22. *Maravars* (*Sambanads and Appanad-Kondayan-kottai Maravars*): Tinnevelly and Ramnad Districts of Madras.
23. *Mutharachas/Muthurians*:
24. *Nakkalas*: East Godavari District.
25. *Nokkars/Nokkans*: Chingleput District.
26. *Oddars/Woddars*.
27. *Picharis/Pardhis*: Bellary District.
28. *Pichiguntalas*: Cuddapah District.
29. *Poligars*: Chittoor District.
30. *Pariyas/Renganoor*: Parayias of Chittoor District, and *Reppur Parayias* of South Arcot District.
31. *Reddikas*: Only a small section notified in East Godavari District.
32. *Rellis*: Vizagapatanam District.
33. *Talyaris* (*Dvagudis*): Cuddapah District.
34. *Talega Pamulas, or Peddati Gollas or Thella Pamawads: Talega Pamulas or Peddati Gollas.* Also known as *Yerra Gollas; Peddeti Gollas, Parikinokkallas and Guru Dasaries.*
35. *Tellungappalatti Chattis*: Madras Presidency.
36. *Thottia-Naicks*: also known as *Kambalathans or Jathi Pillays, or Tottiyans*: Madras Presidency.
37. *Uraligaundans*: Tanjor District.
38. *Valayars*: Madura and Coimbatoor Districts.
39. *Vallayankuppam Padaychis*: South Arcot district.
40. *Vattaikarans*: Tanjor District.
41. *Vettuya Goundans*: Trichinapoly District.
42. *Yatas/Donga Yatas*: Vizagapattanam District.
43. *Yenadis*: Madras Presidency.
44. *Yerukulas*: Madras Presidency'.

APPENDIX I (B)

List of Criminal Tribe Communities

(Source: *Report of the Criminal Tribes Act Enquiry Committee, 1949-50*)

British India

Adi Dravidas
Aheria or Behelia or Aheris
Ambalgars (Moottakampatti Ambalgars and Ambalgars of Suriyamur)
Badaks and Badhiks
Behelias
Bairagis
Banjaras
Banchhadas
Barrars
Barwars
Bauriahs or Baories, Baurias, Bawaryas, Bawari, Marwaris, Baurios, Moghia
Bedyas
Bengalis or Bhangalis
Berads or Bedars
Berias
Bhamtas (Takari)
Bhamtas (Rajput)
Bhanmates
Bhantus
Bhars
Bhata
Bhattu Turkas
Bhedkuts

Bhils
Bhura Brahmans
Bijorias
Boriyas
Boyas (Peddas and Dongas)
Buda Bukkalas (Chakala or Pamulas)
Chamars
Chandravedis, Sanorias or Sanaurias
Chhuras or Chuhras
Daleras or Dalarias
Dandasis
Dasaris (Dongas and Gudus)
Dharis
Dheas or Dhes
Dhekarus
Dhenwars
Domars or Dommars (Reddis and Arais)
Doms (Maghaiyas, Oriyas, Audiniyas and Bansfores)
Donga Yatas
Donga Yerukulas
Dusadhs (Chakais, Palwars and Magahiyas)
Gandhillas
Gantichor or Gantukollars
Gidhias
Ghasis
Ghosis
Gondas
Gujars
Haburas
Handijogis
Hingoras
Irulars
Jaintra Pans
Jats (Gutkas and Dillons)
Jogis or Jogulas
Kaikadis
Kaladis
Kallars (Peramalais, Koottapals and Pariya Suriyurs)
Kanjars
Karwal Nats
Kepumaries

Kewars
Khatis
Kintali Kalingas
Komakapus
Konda Doras
Korachas and Karavas
Kuchbands
Karumbaravas
Labanis or Lamanis or Lambadis
Lodhas or Lodahs
Madigas
Mahatams
Malas
Mallahs
Mang-garudis
Maravars (Sambanada/Appanad-Kondayankottai Maravars)
Mewatis
Mianas
Minas
Moghias
Multanis
Munda Pottas
Mutharachas
Musahars
Naiks
Nakkals
Nirshikaris
Nokkars
Nuts or Nats
Oddars
Oudhias
Paidis
Pardhis
Parnas or Pernas
Pasis
Picharis
Pichguntlas
Poligars
Paraiyas
Rachbands
Reddikas

Rellis
Sansis
Sanorias
Singhikats
Sugalis
Sanghedias, Sardhis and Surmas
Tadvis
Tagus
Taga Bhats
Talayaris (Devagudi)
Talega Pamulas or Peedaty Gollas or Thella-Pamawads
Tellugappalatti Chatts
Thottia Naicks
Uraligaundans
Valayars
Vallayankuppam Padaychis
Vettaikarans
Vettuya Goundans
Waddars, Waddewads or Woddars
Yatas
Yenadis or Yenadiwads
Yerukulas

APPENDIX II (A)

Excerpts from Criminal Tribes Act, 1871

(Source: *Waiting for Freedom*, Report of the Technical Advisory Group, Ministry of Social Justice and Empowerment, Government of India, 2006)

The Criminal Tribes Act of 1871, passed by the Governor of India in Council (Received the assent of the Governor General on 12 October 1871).

'Whereas it is expedient to provide for the registration, surveillance and control of certain criminal tribes and eunuchs, it is thereby enacted as follows:

This Act may be called "The Criminal Tribes' Act, 1871". (Commencement, repealed by Act XVI of 1874, section 1 and Schedule, Part I.)

This section and section 20 extend to the whole of British India: the rest of this act extends only to the interiors under the governments of the Lieutenant Governors of Bengal, the North–Western Province and the Punjab respectively, and under the administration of the Chief Commissioner of Oudh.

Provided that any local Government, with the previous sanction of the Governor General in Council, may, by notification in the local official Gazette, declare all or any of the provisions of this act as amended by subsequent legislation. To be in force in the whole or any part of the territories under its government.'

'Definition of the Tribe, Gang and Class

1A. In this Act the words tribe, gang, and class shall be deemed to include any portion or members of a tribe, gang or class.

Part I, Criminal Tribes:

Local Government to report what tribes should be declared criminal.'

'If the local government has reason to believe that any tribe, gang, or class of person is addicted to the systematic commission of non-bailable offences, it may report the case to the Governor General in Council, and may request his permission to declare such tribe, gang or class to be a criminal tribe.

The report shall state the reason why such tribe, gang or class is considered to be addicted to the systematic commission of non-bailable offence, and as far as possible, the nature and the circumstances of the offence in which the member of the tribe are proposed to have been concerned; and shall describe the manner in which it is proposed that such tribe, gang or class shall earn its living when the provision hereinafter contained have been applied to it.

If such tribe, gang or class has no fixed place of residence, the report shall state whether such tribe, gang, or class follows any lawful occupation, and Government, the real occupation of such tribe, gang, or class, or a pretence for the purpose of facilitating the commission of the crimes, and shall set forth the ground on which such opinion is based; and the report shall also specify the place of residence in which such wandering tribe, gang, or class were proposed to be made for enabling it to learn its living therein.

If upon the consideration of such report, the Governor-General in council is satisfied that the tribe, gang, or class to which it relates ought to be declared criminal, and that the means by which it is proposed that such the tribe, gang, or class shall earn its living are adequate, he may authorize the local government to publish in the local Gazette a notification declaring that such the tribe, gang, or class is a criminal tribe, and thereupon the provision of this act shall become applicable to such the tribe, gang, or class.

No court of justice shall question the validity of any such notification on the ground that the provision therein before contained, or any of them, have not been complied with, or entertain in any form whatever the question whether they have been complied with; But every such notification shall be conclusive proof that the provision of this act are applicable to the tribe, gang, or class specified therein.

When the notification mentioned in section 5 has been published, the local government may direct the magistrate of any district in which such tribes, gang or class, or any part thereof. The declaration of the local government that any such tribes, gang or class, or any part of it, is resident in any district, shall be conclusive proof of such residence.

Upon receiving such direction, the said magistrate shall publish a notice in the place where the register is to be made, calling upon all the members of such tribes, gang or class, or of such portion thereof as is directed to be registered, to appear, at a time and place therein specified, before such person as he appoints, and to give those persons such information as may be necessary to enable them to make the register.

Any member of any such tribes, gang or class, who, without lawful excuse, the burden of proving which shall be lie upon him, shall fail to appear according to such notice, or shall intentionally omit to furnish such information, or who shall furnish, as true, information on the subject which he knows or has reason to believe to be false, shall be deemed guilty of an offence under the first part of section 174 or 176 or 177 of the Indian Penal Code (a), respectively, as the case may be.

The register, when made shall be kept by the district superintendent of police, who shall, from time to time, report to the said magistrate any alterations which ought to be made therein, either by way of addition or erasure.

No alteration shall be made in such register except by or order of the said Magistrate, and he shall write his initials against every such alteration. Notice shall be given of any such intended alteration, and of the time when, and place where, it is to be made, to every person affected thereby.

Any person deeming himself aggrieved by any entry made, or proposed to be made, in such register either when the register is first made or subsequently, may complain to the said Magistrate against such entry, and the Magistrate shall retain such person's name on the register, or enter it therein, or erase it there from, as he may see fit. Every order for the erasure of any such person's name shall state the grounds on which such person's name is erased. The commissioner shall have power to review any order of entry, retention or erasure, passed by the said magistrate on any such complaint, either on appeal by the person registered or proposed to be registered or otherwise.

Any tribes, gang or class, which has been declared to be criminal, and which has no fixed place of residence, may be settled in a place of residence prescribed by the local government.

Any tribes, gang or class, which has been declared to be criminal, or any part thereof, may, by order of the local government, be removed to any other place of residence.

No tribes, gang or class, shall be settled or removed under this act until such arrangements as the local government shall, with the concurrence of the Governor General in council, consider suitable, have been made for enabling such tribes, gang or class, or such part thereof, as is to be so settled or removed, to earn a living in the place in or which it is to be settled or removed.

When the removal of persons has been ordered under the Act, the register of such persons' names shall be transferred to the district superintendent of police of the district to which such persons are removed, and the commissioner of the division in which it is situated, shall there be empowered to exercise the powers provided in sections 11 and 12.

The Local Government may, with the sanction of Governor General in council, place any tribe, gang or class, which has been declared to be criminal, or any part thereof, in a reformatory settlement.'

'17A. (1) The local government may establish and maintain settlement for children and may separate and remove them from their parents and place in such a reformatory settlement the children of the registered members of any tribe, gang or class, which has been declared to be criminal.

(2) For every reformatory settlement for children established under sub-section (1) a superintendent shall be appointed by the local government.

(3) The superintendent of a reformatory settlement for children shall be deemed to be the guardian, within the meaning of Act No. XIX of 1850 (concerning the binding of apprentices), of every child detained in such settlement; and such superintendent, may if he shall think fit, and subject to any ruler which the local government may make in this behalf, apprentice such child under the provision of the aforesaid act.

"Explanation – the term children in this section includes all persons under the age of 18 and above the age of four years."

The local government may, with the previous consent of the Governor General in council, make rules to prescribe –

(1) the form in which the register shall be made by the said Magistrate;

(2) the mode in which the said Magistrate shall publish the notice prescribed in section 8, and means by which persons whom it concerns, and the headmen, village watchmen, and land owners or the occupiers of the village, in which such persons reside, or the agents of such land owners or occupiers, shall be informed of its publication;

(3) the mode in which the notice prescribed in the section 11 shall be given;

(4) the limits within which persons whose names are on the register shall reside;

(5) conditions as to hold passes, under which such persons may be permitted to leave the said limits;

(6) conditions to be inserted in any such pass as to (a) the places where the holder of the pass may go or reside; (b) the officers before whom, from time to time, he shall be bound to present himself; (c) and the time during which he may absent himself;

(7) Conditions as to answering at roll-call or otherwise, in order to satisfy the said magistrate or persons authorized by him, that the reasons whose names are on the register are actually present at given times within the said limits;

(8) The inspection of the residences and villages of any such tribes, gang or class, and the prevention or removal of contrivances for enabling the residents therein to conceal stolen property, or to leave their place of residence without leave;

(9) The terms upon which registered persons may be discharged from the operation of this Act;

(10) The mode in which the criminal tribes shall be settled and removed;

(11) The control and supervision of reformatory settlement;

(12) The works on which and the hours during which persons placed in a reformatory settlement shall be employed, the rates at which they shall be paid, and the dispersal, for the benefit of such persons, of the surplus proceeds of their labor, after defraying the whole or such part of the expenses of their supervision and control as tot he Local Government shall seem fit;

(13) The discipline to which persons endeavoring to escape from any such settlement, or otherwise offending against the rules for the time being in force, shall be submitted; the periodical visitation of such settlement, and the removal from it of such persons as it shall seem expedient to remove;

(14) And generally, to carry out the purposes of this act.'

'(1) Any person registered under this act violating a rule made under clause (4), clause (5) or clause (6) of section 18 shall be punishable with rigorous imprisonment for a term which may extend, on a first conviction, to one year, on a second conviction, to two years, and, on any subsequent conviction, to three years, and shall also, whether on the first or any subsequent conviction, be liable to whipping.

(2) Any such person being a member of a proclaimed tribe violating a rule made under any other clause of section 18 shall be punishable with rigorous imprisonment for a term which may extend to six months, or with fine, or with whipping or with all or any two of those punishments; and on any subsequent conviction for a breach

of any such rule, with rigorous imprisonment for a term which may extend to one year, or with fine, or with whipping, or with all or any two of those punishments.

A. Whoever, being a member of any tribe, gang or class which has been declared criminal, and having been convicted of any of the offences under the Indian Penal code specified in the schedule to this act, shall therefore be convicted of the same or any other offence specified in the said schedule, then he shall, in the absence of special reason to the contrary to be mentioned in the judgment of the court, be punished, on such second conviction, with rigorous imprisonment for a term of not less than seven years, and on a third conviction, with transportation for life.

Nothing in this section shall affect the liability of such persons to any further or other punishment to which he may be liable under the Indian Penal Code or any other law.

B. Whoever, being a registered member of any tribe, gang or class which has been declared criminal, is found in any place under such circumstances as to satisfy the court that he was about to commit, or aid in the commission of theft or robbery, or that he was waiting for an opportunity to commit theft or robbery, shall be punishable with rigorous imprisonment for a term which may extend to three years, and shall also be liable to fine.'

'21. Any person registered under the provision of this Act, who is found in any part of British India, beyond the limits so prescribed for his residence, without such pass as may be required by the said rules, or in place or at a time not permitted by the conditions of his pass, or who escapes from a reformatory settlement, may be arrested without warrant by any police-officer or village watchman, and taken before a Magistrate, who on proof of the facts, shall order him to be removed to the district in which he ought to have resided, or to the reformatory settlement from which he has escaped (as the case may be), there to be dealt with according to the rules under this Act for the time being in force. The rules for the time being in force for the transmission of prisoners shall apply to all persons removed under this section: provided that an order from the local government or from the Inspector General of prisons shall not be necessary for removal of such persons.

22. It shall be the duty of every village headman and village watchman in a village in which any persons belonging to a tribe, gang or

class which has been declared criminal reside, and of every owner or occupier of land on which any such person reside, give the earliest information in his power at the nearest police station. (1) The failure of any such person to appear and give information, as directed in section 8(2) the departure of any such person to appear and give or form such land (as the case may be). And it shall be the duty of every village headman and village watchman in a village, and of every owner or occupier of land, or of the agent of such in his power at the nearest police station of the arrival of any persons who may reasonably be suspected of belonging to any such tribe, gang or class.

Any village headman, village watchman, owner or occupier of land or agent of such owner or occupier, who shall fail to comply with the requirements of section 21, shall be deemed to have committed an offence under the first part of the section 176 of the Indian Penal Code.'

APPENDIX II (B)

Excerpts from Criminal Tribes Act, 1911

(Source: *Waiting for Freedom*, Report of the Technical Advisory Group, Ministry of Social Justice and Empowerment, Government of India, 2006)

Passed by the Governor General of India in Council (Received the assent of the Governor General on 1 March 1911).

'Contents

Preliminary

Sections

1. Short title and extent.
2. Definitions.

Notifications of Criminal Tribes

3. Power to declare any tribe, gang or class a Criminal tribe.

Registration of Members of Criminal Tribes

4. Registration of members of Criminal Tribes
5. Procedure in making register.
6. Charge of register.
7. Alterations in register.
8. Complaints of entries in register.
9. Power to take finger-impressions at any time.
10. Members of Criminal Tribes to report themselves or notify residence.

11. Procedure when deemed expedient to restrict movement of, or settle, criminal tribes.
12. Notification restricting movements of, or settling, tribe.
13. Power to vary specified area or place of residence.
14. Verification of presence of members of tribe within prescribed area place of residence.
15. Transfer of register in certain cases.

Settlement and Schools

16. Power to place tribe in settlement.
17. Power to place children in schools and to apprentice them.
18. Power of Local Government to discharge or remove persons from settlement or school.
19. Power of Governor General in Council to direct use of any settlement or school in British India for reception of persons.

Rules

20. Power to make rules.

Penalties and Procedures

21. Penalties for failure to comply with terms of notice under section 5 or 7.
22. Penalties for breach of rules.
23. Enhanced punishment for certain offences by members of criminal tribe after previous conviction.
24. Punishment for registered members of criminal tribe found under suspicious circumstances.
25. Arrest of registered persons found beyond prescribed limits.

Sections

26. Duties of village-headman, village-watchmen, and owners or occupiers of land to give information in certain cases.
27. Penalty for breach of such duties.

Supplemental

28. Bar of jurisdiction of Courts in questions relating to notifications under sections 3, 12 and 13.
29. Repeals.'

'The Act

An Act to amend the law relating to the registration, surveillance and control of Criminal Tribes.

Whereas it is expedient to amend the law relating to the registration, surveillance and control of criminal tribes; it is hereby enacted as follows :

Preliminary

1. (1) This Act may be called the Criminal Tribes Act 1911; and
   (2) **It extends to the whole of British India.**
2. In this Act, unless there is anything repugnant in the subject or context, -
   (1) "Criminal tribe" means a tribe, gang or class of persons declared to be a criminal tribe by a notification under section 3;
   (2) "prescribed" means prescribed by rules under this Act; and
   (3) "tribe", "gang" or "class" includes any part or members of a tribe, gang or class.

Notification of Criminal Tribes

3. If the Local Government has reason to believe that any tribe, gang or class of persons is addicted to the systematic commission of non-bailable offences, it may, by notification in the local official Gazette, declare that such tribe, gang or class is a criminal tribe for the purposes of this Act.

Registration of Members of Criminal Tribes

4. The Local Government may direct the District Magistrate to make or cause to be made a register of the members of any criminal tribe or of any part thereof within his district.
5. Upon receiving such direction the District Magistrate shall publish a notice in the prescribed manner at the place where the register is to be made and at such other places as he may think fit, calling upon all the members of such criminal tribe, or of such part thereof as is directed to be registered:-
   (a) To appear at a time and place therein specified before a person appointed by him on this behalf;
   (b) To give that person such information as maybe necessary to enable him to make the register; and
   (c) To allow their finger impressions to be recorded:

Provided that the District Magistrate may exempt any individual member of such Criminal Tribe or part thereof from registration.

6. The register, when made, shall be placed in the keeping of the Superintendent of Police, who shall, from time to time, report to the District Magistrate any alterations which ought in his opinion to be made therein, either by way of addition or erasure.

7. (1) After the register has been placed in the keeping of the Superintendent of Police no person shall be added to the register, and no registration shall be cancelled except by or by the order in writing of the District Magistrate.

(2) Before the name of any person is added to the register under this section, the Magistrate shall give notice in the prescribed manner to the concerned person:-

(a) to appear before him or a person appointed by him in this behalf at a time and a place therein specified;

(b) to give him or such person such information as may be necessary to enable him to make the entry; and

(c) to allow his finger impressions to be recorded.

8. Any person deeming himself aggrieved by any entry made, or proposed to be made, in such register either when the register is first made or subsequently, may complain to the District Magistrate against such entry, and the Magistrate shall retain such person's name on the register, or enter it therein, erase it there from, as he may see fit.

9. The District Magistrate or any officer empowered by him in this behalf may at any time order the finger-impressions of registered member of a criminal tribe to be taken.

10. The Local Government may, by notification in the local official Gazette, direct in respect of any criminal tribe that every registered member thereof shall, in the prescribed manner:-

(a) report himself at fixed intervals; or

(b) Notify his place of residence and any change or intended change of residence and any absence or intended absence from residence.

Restriction of Movements of Criminal Tribes

11. (1) If the Local Government considers that it is expedient that any criminal tribe should be -(a) restricted in its movements to any specified area, or (b) settled in any place of residence, it may report the case for the orders of the Governor General in Council.

(2) Every such report shall state -

(i) the nature and the circumstances of the offences in which the members of the criminal tribe are believed to have been concerned, and reasons for such belief;

(ii) whether such criminal tribe follows any lawful occupation, and whether such occupation is in the opinion of such criminal tribe, or a pretence for the purpose of facilitating the commission of crimes, and the grounds on which such opinion is based;

(iii) the area to which it is proposed to restrict the movements of such criminal tribe, or the place of residence in which it is proposed to settle it; and

(iv) The manner in which it is proposed that such criminal tribe shall earn its living within the restricted area or in the settlement and the arrangements which are proposed to be made therefore.

12. If on the consideration of any such report the Governor General in Council is satisfied -

(a) that it is expedient to restrict the movements of such criminal tribe or to settle it in a place of residence, and

(b) That the means by which it is proposed that such criminal tribe shall earn its living are adequate.

He may authorize the Local Government to publish in the local official Gazette a notification declaring that such criminal tribe shall be restricted in its movements to the area specified or shall be settled in the place of residence specified, and the Local Government may publish a notification accordingly.

13. The Local Government may at any time by a like notification vary the terms of any notification published by it under section 12 by specifying another area to which the movements of the criminal tribe shall be restricted, or another place of residence in which it shall be settled.

14. Every registered member of a criminal tribe, whose movements have been restricted or which has been settled in a place of residence, shall attend at such place and at such time and before such person as may be prescribed in this behalf.

15. When the area to which the movements of a criminal tribe or any members thereof area restricted, or the place of residence in which a criminal tribe is settled is situated in a district other than that in which the register mentioned in section 4 was prepared, the register shall be transferred to the Superintendent of Police of the district in which the said area is situated, and the District Magistrate of the said district shall thereupon be empowered to exercise the powers provided in sections 7, 8 and 9.

Settlements and Schools

16. The Governor General in Council or the Local Government may establish industrial, agricultural or reformatory settlements and may

place therein any criminal tribe or any part thereof, in respect of which a notification has been published under section 12.

17. (1) the Local Government may establish industrial, agricultural or reformatory schools for children and may separate and remove from their parents or guardians and place in such schools the children of members of any criminal tribe in respect of which a notification has been published under section 12.

(2) For every school established under sub section (1), a Superintendent shall be appointed by the Local Government.

(3) The provisions of section 18 to 22 (both inclusive) of the Reformatory Schools Act, 1897, shall, so far as may be, apply in the case of every school from children established under this section as if the Superintendent of such school were a Superintendent and the children placed in such school were youthful offenders within the meaning of that Act.

(4) For the purposes of this section, "children" includes all persons under the age of eighteen and above the age of six years.

(5) The decision of the District Magistrate as to the age of any person for the purposes of this section shall be final.

18. The Local Government may at any time, by general or special order, direct any person who may be in any industrial, agricultural or reformatory settlement or school in the Province -

(a) To be discharged, or

(b) To be removed to some other like settlement or school in the Province.

19. The Government General in Council may, by like order, direct that any person to whom the provisions of section 16 or section 17 are applicable may be placed in, or transferred to, any industrial, agricultural or reformatory settlement or school in any part of British India.

Rules

20. (1) The Local Government may make rules to carry out the purposes and objects of this Act.

(2) In particular and without prejudice to the generality of the foregoing power, such rules may provide for and regulate -

(a) the form and contents of the register prescribed in section 4;

(b) the mode in which the notice prescribed in section 5 shall be published and the means by which the persons whom it concerns, and the village-headmen, village watchmen and landowners or occupiers of the village in which such persons reside, or the agents of such landowners or occupiers, shall be informed of its publication;

(c) the addition of names to the register and the erasure of names therein and, the mode in which the notice prescribed in section 7 shall be given;

(d) the mode in which persons mentioned in section 10 shall report themselves, or notify their residence or any change or intended change of residence or any absence or intended absence;

(e) the nature of the restrictions to be observed by persons whose movements have been restricted by notification under section 12 or section 13;

(f) the conditions as to holding passes under which persons might be permitted to leave the place in which they are settled or confined or the areas to which their movements are restricted;

(g) the condition to be inserted in any such pass in regard to-

(i) the places where the holder of the pass may go or reside;

(ii) the persons before whom from time to time, he shall be bound to present himself; and

(iii) the time during which he may absent himself;

(h) the place and time at which and the persons before whom members of a criminal tribe shall attend in accordance with the provisions of section 14.

(i) the inspection of the residences and the villages of any criminal tribes;

(i) the teams upon which registered members of criminal tribes may be discharged from the operation of this Act;

(j) the management, control, and supervision of industrial, agricultural or reformatory settlements and schools;

(k) the works on which, and the hours during which persons placed in an industrial, agricultural or reformatory settlement shall be employed, the rate at which they shall be paid, and the disposal, for the benefit of such persons, of the surplus proceeds of their labour; and

(l) the discipline to which persons endeavoring to escape from any industrial, agricultural or reformatory settlement or school, or otherwise offending against the rule for the time being in force, shall be subject, the periodical visitation of such settlement or school and the removal from it of such persons as it shall seem expedient to remove.

Penalties and Procedures

21. Whoever, being a member of a criminal tribe, without lawful excuse, the burden of proving which shall lie upon him-
    (a) fails to appear in compliance with a notice issued under section 5 or section 7, or
    (b) intentionally omits to furnish any information required under those sections, or
    (c) when required to furnish information required under either of those sections, furnishes are true any information which he knows or has reason to believe to be false, or
    (d) refuse to allow his finger impressions to be taken, may be arrested without warrant, shall be punishable with imprisonment for a term which may extend to six months, or with fine which may extend to two hundred rupees, or both.

22. (1) Whoever, being a registered member of a criminal tribe, violates a rule made under clause (e), clause (f) or clause (g) of section 20 shall be punishable for imprisonment for a term which may extend -
    (a) On a first conviction, to one year.
    (b) On a second conviction, to two years, and
    (c) On any subsequent conviction to three years.

    (2) Whoever being a registered member of a criminal tribe, violates a rule made under any, clause of other Section 20 shall be punishable, —
    (a) on a first conviction , with imprisonment for term which may extend to six months, or with fine which may extend to two hundred rupees, or with both ; and
    (b) on any subsequent conviction, with imprisonment for a term which may extend to one year, or with fine which may extend to five hundred rupees, or with both.

23. (1) Whoever, being a member of any criminal tribe, and, having been convicted of any of the offences under the Indian Penal Code specified in the Schedule is hereafter convicted of the same or any other offence specified in the said schedule, shall, in the absence or special reasons to the contrary to be mentioned in the judgement of the Court, be punished -
    a) on a second conviction, with imprisonment for a term of not less than seven years, and
    b) on a third conviction, with transportation for life.

(2) Nothing in this section shall affect the liability of such person to any further or other punishment to which he may be liable under the Indian Penal Code or any other law.

24. Whoever, being a registered member of any criminal tribe, is found in any place under such circumstances as to satisfy the Court-
(a) that he was about to commit, or aid in the commission of theft or robbery, or
(b) that he was waiting for an opportunity to commit theft or robbery, shall be also punishable with imprisonment for a term which may extend to three years, and shall be liable to fine which may extend to one thousand rupees.

25. (1) Whoever, being a registered member of a criminal tribe,-
(a) is found in any part of British India, beyond the area, if any, prescribed for his residence, without the prescribed pass, or in a place or at a time not permitted by the conditions of his pass; or
(b) escapes from an industrial, agricultural or reformatory settlement or school, may be arrested without warrant by any police officer, village headman or village watchman, and taken before a Magistrate, who, on proof of the facts, shall order him to be removed to the district in which he ought to have resided or to the settlement or school from which he has escaped (as the case may be), there to be dealt with in accordance with this Act or any rules made there under.

(2) The rules for the time being in force for the removal of prisoners shall apply to all persons removed under this section or under any other provision of this Act.

Provided that an order from the Local Government or from the Inspector General of Prisons shall not be necessary for the removal of such persons.

26. (1) Every village headman and every village watchman in a village in which any persons belonging to a criminal tribe reside, and every owner or occupier of land on which any such persons reside or the agent of any such owner or occupier shall forthwith communicate to the officer in charge of the nearest police station any information which he may obtain of-
(a) the failure of any such person to appear and give information as directed in section 5; or
(b) the departure of any registered member of a criminal tribe from such village or from such land (as the case may be).

(2) Every village headman and watchman in a village, and every owner or occupier of land or the agent of such owner or occupier of land or the agent of such owner or occupier, shall forthwith communicate to the officer in charge of the nearest police station any information which he may obtain of the arrival at such village or on such land (as the case may be) of any persons who may reasonably be suspected of belonging to any criminal tribes.

27. Any village headman, village watch man, owner or occupier of land or the agent of such owner or occupier, who fails to comply with the requirements of section 26, shall be deemed to have committed an offence punishable under the first part of section 176 of the Indian penal Code.

Supplemental

28. No Court of justice shall question the validity of any notification published under the provisions of section 3, section 12 or section 13 on the ground that the provisions herein before contained or any of them have not been complied with, or entertain in any form whatever the question whether they have been complied with; but every such notification shall be conclusive proof that it has been issued in accordance with law.

29. The Criminal Tribes Act, 1871, the Criminal Tribes (Amendment) Act, 1876 and the Criminal Tribes Act Amendment Act, 1897, are hereby repealed.'

'The Schedule for Section 23

Chapter XII

Sections

231. Counterfeiting coin.
232. Counterfeiting Queen's coin.
233. Making or selling instrument for counterfeiting coin.
234. Making or selling instrument for counterfeiting Queen's coin.
235. Possession of instrument or material for the purpose of using the same for counterfeiting coin.
239. Delivery of coin, possessed with the knowledge that it is counterfeit.
240. Delivery of Queen's coin possessed with the knowledge that it is counterfeit.

242. Possession of counterfeit coin by a person who knew it to be counterfeit when he became possessed thereof.
243. Possession of Queen's coin by a person who knew it to be counterfeit when he became possessed thereof.'

'Chapter XVI

299. Culpable homicide.
307. Attempt to murder.
308. Attempt to commit culpable homicide.
310. Being a thug.
322. Voluntarily causing grievous hurt.
324. Voluntarily causing hurt by dangerous weapons or means.
326. Voluntarily causing grievous hurt by dangerous weapons or means.
327. Voluntarily causing hurt to extort property or to constrain to an illegal act.
328. Causing hurt by means of poison, etc, with intent to commit an offence.
329. Voluntarily causing grievous hurt to extort property or to constrain to an illegal act.
332. Voluntarily causing hurt to deter public servants from his duty.
333. Voluntarily causing grievous hurt to deter public servant from his duty.
369. Kidnapping child under ten years with intent to steal from its person.'

'Chapter XVII

382. Theft after preparation made for causing death, hurt or restraint, in order to the committing of the theft.
383. Extortion.
385. Putting person in fear of injury in order to commit extortion.
386. Extortion by putting a person in fear of death or grievous hurt.
387. Putting person in fear of death or of grievous hurt in order to commit extortion.
390. Robbery.
391. Dacoity.
393. Attempt to commit robbery.
394. Voluntarily causing hurt in committing robbery.
397. Robbery or dacoity, with attempt to cause death or grievous hurt.
398. Attempt to commit robbery or dacoity when armed with deadly weapon.

399. Making preparation to commit dacoity.
402. Assembling for the purpose of committing dacoity.
457. Lurking, house-trespass or house-breaking by night in order to the commission of an offence punishable with imprisonment.
458. Lurking, house-trespass or house-breaking by night after preparation for hurt, assault or wrongful restraint.
459. Grievous hurt caused whilst committing lurking, house trespass or house breaking.
460. All persons jointly concerned in lurking, house-trespass or house-breaking by night punishable where death or grievous hurt caused by one of them.'

References and Bibliography

Primary Sources

Records including Government Orders of the following departments of the Secretariat in Tamil Nadu and Andhra Pradesh Archives were consulted:

1. Judicial, Public, Public Works and Labour, Revenue, Law (General), Development, Home, Home (Judicial). While giving the reference in the endnotes, the name of the department, Government Order (GO) number, and the date when it was issued by the concerned department is mentioned (e.g. Revenue GO 326, 15.4.1944. The 'GO' is for all practical purposes a file with a collection of papers on the subject, and may contain several rounds of correspondence.)
2. Selected District Records of Madras Presidency

Records of the Salvation Army were consulted at the International Heritage Centre, London and at Stuartpuram Settlement, Guntur, Andhra Pradesh

Secondary Sources

A Gentleman with a Duster (author), *Painted Windows: A Study in Religious Personality*, Mills and Boon Ltd., London, 1922.

Achariar, M.C. Tiruvenkata, *History of the Aziznagar Settlement*, Dass Press, Viriddhachalam, 1926.

Aiyar, C.P. Ramasami, *District Problems*, Home Rule Series No. 17, Commonweal Office, Adayar, Madras, 1916.

Aiyyappan, A, *Report on the Soda-economic Conditions of the Aboriginal Tribes of the Province of Madras*, Government Press, Madras, 1948.

Ambirajan, S. 'Political Economy and Indian Famines', *South Asian Studies*, No. 1, August 1971.

Ansari, M.A., *Tribal in Criminal Web*, Publication Scheme, Jaipur, 1987.

Arnold, David, 'Bureaucratic Recruitment and Subordination in Colonial India: The Madras Constabulary, 1859-1947' in Ranajit Guha (ed.) *Subaltern Studies IV: Writings on South Asian History and Society*, OUP, Delhi, 1985.

Arnold, David, 'Dacoity and Rural Crime in Madras, 1860-1940', *The Journal of Peasant Studies*, Vol. 6, No. 2, January, 1979.

Arnold, David, *Famine: Social Crisis and Historical Change*, Oxford, Basil Blackwell, 1988.

Arnold, David, *Police Power and Colonial Rule, Madras 1859-1947*, OUP, Delhi, 1986.

Asad, Talal, The Beduin as a Military Force: Notes on some aspects of power relations between nomads and sedentaries in historical perspective' in Cynthia Nelson (ed.) *The Desert and the Sown: Nomads in the Wider Society*, Berkeley: Institute of International Studies, U.C. Berkeley, 1973.

Bailey, V., 'Salvation Army riots, the "Skeleton Army" and Legal Authority in the Provincial Town' in A.P. Donajgrodzki (ed.), *Social Control in Nineteenth Century Britian*, Croom Helm, 1977.

Baird, W. Bramwell, *The Call of the Jackals*, Salvation Army Archives, London, n.d.

Baker, C.J. and Washbrook D. (eds.), *South India: Political Institutions and Political Change, 1880-1940*, Delhi, 1975.

Baker, Christopher, 'Madras Headmen' in, K.N. Chaudhary and Clive Dewey (eds.) *Economy and Society: Essays in Indian Economic and Social History*, OUP, Delhi, 1979.

Barth, Frederick, *Nomads of South Persia—the Basseri Tribe of Khamesh Confederacy*, Oslo University Press, Oslo, 1961.

Baugh, Commr., *The CT Work in India: an Economic Experiment*, Salvation Army Archives, International Heritage Centre, London, 1930.

Bayley, D., *Police and Political Development in India*, Princeton University Press, 1969.

Beatrie, John, 'The Pattern of Crime in England 1600-1800', *Past and Present*, 72, 1974.

Beier, A.L., 'Vagrants and the Social Order in Elizabethan England', *Past and Present*, 64, 1974.

Bhargava, B.S., *The Criminal Tribes: A Social and Economic Study of the Principal Criminal Tribes and Castes in North India*, Ethnographic and Folk Culture Society, Lucknow, 1949.

Bhattacharya, Sabyasachi, 'Laissez Faire in India', *Indian Economic and Social History Review*, Vol. II, No. 1 January 1965.

Bickers, Robert A. and Seron, Rosemary (eds.), *Missionary Encounters: Sources and Issues*, Curzon Press, Great Britain, 1996.

Biswas, P.C., *The Ex-Criminal Tribes of Delhi State*, Unpublished Ph.d. thesis, University of Delhi, 1960.

Blackburn, Stuart H., 'The Kallars: A Tamil "Criminal Tribe" Reconsidered', *Journal of South Asian Studies*, New Series, Vol. 1, No. 1, March, 1978.

Booth Tucker, F., *Criminocurology or the Indian Crim and What to do with him—A Report of the Work of the Salvation Army among the Criminal Tribes, Habituals and Released Prisoners in India*, London, n.d.

Booth Tucker, F., *Mukti Fauj or 40 years with the Salvation Army in India and Ceylon*, Marshall Brothers, London, n.d.

Booth, William, *In Darkest England and the Way out: A Study of Poverty and Vice in England and a Scheme by the Salvation Army for Reclamation of Criminals and Prevention of Crime*, Salvation Army, London, 1890.

Brewer, John and Styles, John (eds.), *An Ungovernable People: The English and Their Law in the Seventeenth and Eighteenth Centuries*, Hutchinson, London, 1980.

Briggs, A., 'The Salvation Army in Sussex 1883-1892' in M.J. Kitch (ed.) *Studies in Sussex Church History*, Leopard's Head Press, 1981.

Chaman Lal, *Gypsies, Forgotten Children of India*, Publications Division, 1962.

Chapman, Denis, *Sociology and the Stereotype of the Criminal*, Tavistock Publications, 1968.

Chapman, Terry, 'Crime in Eighteenth Century England: EP Thompson and the Conflict Theory of Crime' *Criminal Justice History* 1, 1980.

Cobb, Richard, *The Police and the People: French Popular Protest 1789-1820*, OUP, 1970.

Cockburn, J.S. (ed.), *Crime in England 1550-1800*, Methuen, 1977.

Comaroff, Jean and Comaroff John, *Of Revelation and Revolution: Christianity, Colonialism and Consciousness in South Africa* (Vol. 1), The University of Chicago Press, Chicago and London, 1991.

Confino, A., 'Collective Memory and Cultural History: Problems of Method'. *American Historical Review*, 102(5) December, 1997.

Criminal Justice History: An International Annual, John Jay Press, 1980.

Dalton, E.T., *Tribal History of Eastern India*, Office of the Superintendent of Government Printing, Calcutta, 1872 (Reprinted Cosmo Publications, Delhi 1973).

Dasgupta, Uma, 'Crime, Law and the Police in India, 1870-1880', *The Indian Economic and Social History Review*, X (1973).

Davies, C.S.L., 'Slavery and Protector Somerset: the Vagrancy Act of 1547', *Economic History Review*, second series, 19, 1966.

Dena, Lal, *Christian Missions and Colonialism*, Vendrame Institute, Shillong, 1988.

Donovan, Bill M., 'Changing Perceptions of Social Deviance: Gypsies in Early Modern Portugal and Brazil', *Journal of Social History*, Vol. 26, No. 1, Fall, 1992.

Edwardes, S.M., *Crime in India*, OUP, London, 1924.

Ellis, Havelock, *Tht Criminal*, London, 1890.

Emsley, Clive, *Crime and Society in England 1750-1800*, Longman, London & New York, 1987.

Ener, Mine, 'Prohibitions on Begging and Loitering in Nineteenth Century Egypt', *Die Welt des Islams*, New Series, Vol. 39, Issue 3: State, Law and Society in Nineteenth Century Egypt, November, 1999.

Engels, Dagmar and Marks Shula (ed.), *Contesting Colonial Hegemony—State and Society in Africa and India*, British Academy Press, London, 1994.

Fabian, J., *Time and the Other: How Anthropology Makes Its Object*, Columbia University Press, New York, 1983.

FICCI, *Monograph on Common Salt*, Calcutta, 1930.

Forbes, Geraldine, 'Managing midwifery in India' in Dagmar Engels and Shula Marks (ed.) *Contesting Colonial Hegemony—State and Society in Africa and India*, British Academy Press, London, 1994.

Freitag, Sandra B., 'Crime in the Social Order of Colonial North India', *Modern Asian Studies*, 25, 2 (1991).

Frietag, Sandra B., "Sansiahs and the State: The changing nature of 'crime' and 'justice' in 19th century British India", Introduction, unpublished SOAS/Nehru Library conference paper, March 1994.

Gadgil, D.R., *The Industrial Evolution of India in Recent Times 1860-1939*, OUP, Delhi, 1971.

Gaitskell, Deborah, 'At Home with Hegemony?' in Dagmar Engels and Shula Marks (ed.) *Contesting Colonial Hegemony—State and Society in Africa and India*, British Academy Press, London, 1994.

Gardiner, A.G., *Prophets, Priests and Kings*, J.M. Dent and Sons Ltd., London, 1914.

Gatrell, V.A.C., 'Crime, Authority and the Policeman State 1750-1950' in Thompson F.M.L. (ed.), *The Cambridge Social History of Britain* 1750-1950, Cambridge University Press, Cambridge, 1990.

Gatrell, V.A.C., *Hanging Tree: Execution and the English People 1700-1868*, OUP, New York, 1994.

Gatrell, V.A.C. et al (eds.), *Crime and the Law: The Social History of Crime in Western Europe Since 1500*, Europa Publications, 1980.

Gauri, Shankar, *Born Criminals*, Kishor Vidya Niketan, Varanasi, 1979.

Ghani, Mohammad Abdul, *Notes on the Criminal Tribes*, Provincial Police Training School, Vellore, 1915.

Gordon, P.R.T., *The Khasis*, 1907 (Reprinted Cosmo Publications, Delhi 1975).

Gordon, Stewart N., 'Bhils and the Idea of a Criminal Tribe in Nineteenth Century India' in Anand A. Yang (ed.), *Crime and Criminality in British India*, The University of Arizona Press, Arizona, 1985.

Government of Bombay, *Report of the Criminal Tribes Act Enquiry Committee.* Government Central Press, Bombay, 1939.

Government of Delhi, *Bombay Beggary Prevention Act*, Ministry of Home Affairs, Notification, New Delhi, 2 June 1960. [http://socialwelfare.-delhigovt.nic.in/beggpreventact1.htm]

Government of India, *Constitution of India*, Seventh Schedule (Article 246), Concurrent List, Item no.15.

Government of India, *Constituent Assembly of India*, Volume V. [http://parliamentofindia.nic.in/ls/debates/vol5p3b.htm]

Government of India, *Constituent Assembly of India*, Volume IX, 1949. [http://parliamentofindia.nic.in/ls/debates/vol9p23b.htm]

Government of India, *A Collection of the Acts Passed by the Governor General of India in Council in the Year 1911*, Superintendent, Government Printing, Calcutta, 1912.

Government of India, *Abstract of the Proceedings of the Governor General of India in Council Assembled for the Purpose of Making Laws and Regulations*, Vol. IX, 3.10.1870, Government Press, Simla.

Government of India, *Report of the Commissioner appointed to enquire into and report upon the manufacture and sale and tax upon salt in British India, 1856*, Government Press, Calcutta, 1857.

Government of India, *Report of the Indian Famine Commission*, 1878, Parts I, II and III, Vol. I, Calcutta.

Government of India, *Report of the Indian Jail Committee, 1919-20*, Government Press, Simla.

Government of India, *Report of the Indian Police Commission, 1902-03*, Government Central Press, Simla, 1904.

Government of India, *Report of the Criminal Tribes Enquiry Committee*, United Provinces, 1947.

Government of India, *Report of the Criminal Tribes Act Enquiry Committee (1949-50)*, Government of India Press, New Delhi, n.d.

Government of India, *Report on the Census of India, 1891*, Vol. XIII, Calcutta.

Government of Karnataka, *The Karnataka Prohibition of Beggary Act, 1975.* (As amended by Acts 7 of 1982, 12 of 1988 and 26 of 2003) [http://dpal.kar.nic.in/pdf files%5CPROHIBITION% 20OF%20-BEGGARY-B.pdf]

Government of Karnataka, *Karnataka Habitual Offenders' Act, 1961.* [dpal.kar.nic.in/24%20of%201961%20(E).pdf]

Government of Madras, *A Memorandum on the Madras Famine of 1866*, Appdx., Madras, 1867.

Government of Madras, *Administration Report for Criminal Tribe Settlements and Kallar, Koravar and Yenadi Reclamation for 1940*, Madras.

Government of Madras, *Administration Report of the Forest Department (Southern and Northern Circles)*, Madras Presidency for 1885-90, Madras.

Government of Madras, *Administration Reports of the Labour Department*, 1924-35, Madras.

Government of Madras, *Administration Reports of the Stuartpuram Settlement*, 1915-28, Madras.

Government of Madras, *Nellore Manual*, Vol. II, 1868.

Government of Madras, *Note showing the Progress made in the Settlement of Criminal Tribes in the Madras Presidency upto September, 1916*, Madras, 1917.

Government of Madras, *Note showing the Progress made in the Settlement of Criminal Tribes in the Madras Presidency upto January 1925*, Madras, 1927.

Government of Madras, *Report of the Administration of the Department of Salt Revenue in the Madras Presidency and Orissa, Madras, 1894-95.*

Government of Madras, *Report of the Forest Committee*, Madras, 1912, Vol. II.

Government of Madras, *Report of the Salt Commission 1876*, Government Press, Madras, 1877.

Government of Madras, *Report on the Census of the Madras Presidency, 1871*, Vol. 1, 1874.

Government of Maharashtra, District Gazetteers, Nasik District: Law, Order and Justice—Social Welfare Department (Correctional Administration Wing and Non-Correctional Wing), Executive Editor and Secretary, Gazetteers Department, 2000. [www.maharashtra.gov.in/english/gazetteer/nasik/015%20Law/ 005% 20Social%20Welfare-Department.html]

Guenter, Lewy, 'Himmler and the "Racially Pure Gypsies"', *Journal of Contemporary History*, Vol. 34, No. 2, April, 1999.

Guha, Ranajit (ed.) *Subaltern Studies: Writings on South Asian History and Society*, Oxford University Press, Vol. I-VII.

Gunthorpe, E.J., *Notes on Criminal Tribes*, Bombay, 1882.

Gurr, T.R., *Rogues, Rebels and Reformers: A Political History of Crime and Conflict*, Sage, Beverly Hills, California, 1976.

Haikerwal, Bejoy Shanker, *Economic and Social Aspects of Crime in India*, George Alien and Unwin Ltd., London, 1934.

Halbwachs, M., *On Collective Memory*, Editor and Translator L. Coser, Chicago, IL, University of Chicago Press, 1992.

Hanawalt, Barbara A., 'Fur Collar Crime: the Pattern of Crime Among the Fourteenth Century English Nobility', *Journal of Social History*, 8, 1975.

Hansen, Adam, 'Exhibiting Vagrancy, 1851: Victorian London and the "Vagabond Savage",' CFP, Literary London, Interdisciplinary Studies in the Representation of London (e-journal), February, 2005. [http://cfp.english.upenn.edu/archive/Cultural-Historical/0180.html]

Hartog, F., *The Mirror of Herodotus: The Representation of the Other in the Writing of History*, University of California Press, 1988.

Hatch, W.J., *The Land Pirates of India*, Seeley, Service and Company, London, 1928.

Hay, Douglas, Linebaugh, Peter, Thompson, E.P. (ed.), *Albion's Fatal Tree: Crime and Society in Eighteenth Century England*, Alien Lane, London, 1975.

Hay, Douglas, 'War, Dearth and Theft in the Eighteenth Century: The Record of the English Courts', *Past and Present*, 95, 1982.

Hefner, Robert W. (ed.) *Conversion to Christianity: Historical and Anthropological Perspectives on a Great Transformation*, Berkeley, University of California Press, 1993.

Hervey, H., *Cameos of Indian Crime*, Stanley Paul and Company, London, n.d.

Hindu The, Madras.

Hunter, W.W., *England's Work in India*, Smith, Elder and Company, London, 1881.

Idem, *The Task of Social Hygiene*, London, 1912.

Ignatieff, Michael, *A Just Measure of Pain: The Penitentiary in the Industrial Revolution 1750-1850*, Macmillan, London, 1978.

Indian Patriot, Madras.

Irons, William, 'Nomadism as a Political Adaptation: The Case of the Yomut Turkmen' in *American Ethnologist*, 1:635-58.

Jones, David, *Crime, Protest, Community and Police in nineteenth century Britain*, Routledge & Kegan Paul, London, 1982.

Journal of Social History, 8, 1975.

Judges, P.V., *The Elizabethan Underworld*, London, 1930.

Kawashima, Koji, *Missionaries and a Hindu State: Travancore 1858-1936*, OUP, Delhi, 1998.

Khazanov, A.M., *Nomads and the Outside World*, Cambridge, 1983.

Khodarkovsky, Michael, 'Not by Word Alone: Missionary Policies and Religious Conversion in Early Modern Russia', *Comparative Studies in Society and History*, Vol. 38, No. 2, April 1996.

Kirk, E. (Staff Captain), *Unveiled—A Study of the Salvation Army from Within*, London, 1915.

Kloss, C. Boden, *In the Andaman and Nicobars*, John Murray, London, 1903.

Knapp, S., 'Collective Memory and the Actual Past', *Representations*, 26, Spring, 1989.

Kuper, Leo (ed.), *Race, Science and Society*, The Unesco Press, Paris, 1975.

Lawson, James Gilchrist, *Deeper Experiences of Famous Christians*, Herald Publishing House, Ohio, 1911. (Reprinted by Pyramid Books, New York, 1970).

Le Goff, J., *History and Memory*, trans. S. Rendall and E. Claman, Columbia University Press, New York, 1992 (1986).

Le Goff, Jacques and Nora, P. (eds.), *Constructing the Past: Essays in Historical Methodology*, Cambridge, CUP, 1985.

Lindholm, Charles, 'Images of the Pathan: The Usefulness of Colonial Ethnography', *European Journal of Sociology*, 21: 350-61.

Lodhi, Abdul and Tilly, Charles, 'Urbanisation, Crime and Collective Violence in Nineteenth Century France', *American Journal of Sociology*, 79, 1973.

Ludden, D. 'Who Really Ruled Madras Presidency?', *The Indian Economic and Social History Review*, XV (1978), 4.

Macfarlane, Alan, *Reconstructing Historical Communities*, CUP, 1977.

Macmunn, George, *The Underworld of India*, London, n.d.

Madras Mail The, Madras.

Major, Andrew J., "State and Criminal Tribes in Colonial Punjab: Surveillance, Control and Reclamation of the 'Dangerous Classes'" *Modern Asian Studies*, 33, 3 (1999).

Mayall, David, *Gypsy Travellers in Nineteenth Century*, Cambridge University Press, Cambridge, 1988.

Mayaram, Shail, 'Criminality or Community? Alternative Constructions of the Mev Narrative of Darya Khan', *Contributions to Indian Sociology* (n.s.), 25, 1 (1991).

Mayhew, Henry, *London Labour and the London Poor: The Condition and Earnings of Those that Will Work, Cannot Work, and Will Not Work* (3 volumes), Griffen, Bohn and Company, London, 1851. Electronic Text Center, University of Virginia Library. [http://etext.virginia.edu/toc/modeng/public/MayLond.html].

Mayhew, Henry and Binny, John, *The Criminal Prisons of London and Scenes of Prison Life*, Griffin, Bohn and Company, London, 1862.

Megill, Allan, 'History, Memory, Identity', *History of the Human Sciences*, Vol. II, No. 3, August 1998.

Melossi, Dorio and Pavarini, Massimo, *The Prison and the Factory: Origins of the Penitentiary System*, Macmillan, 1981.

Morrison, W.D., *Crime and its Causes*, London, 1891.

Murdoch, Norman H., 'Salvation Army Disturbances in Liverpool, England, 1879-1887', *Journal of Social History*, Vol. 25, No. 3, 1991.

Naidu, M. and Paupa Rao, *The Criminal Tribes of India, No. II, A History of Korawars, Erukulas or Kaikaries*, Madras, 1905.

Natarajan, Nalini, *The Missionary Among the Khasis*, Sterling Publishers, New Delhi, 1977.

Nigam, Sanjay, 'Disciplining and Policing the "Criminal by Birth", Part I and II, *The Indian Economic and Social History Review*, 27, 2, (1990).

Noel, Conrad, *Byways of Belief*, Frank Palmer, London 1912.

Oddie, G.A., 'Protestant Missionaries, Caste and Social Change in India, 1850-1914, *The Indian Economic and Social History Review*, VI (1969), 3.

Okley, Judith, *The Traveller-Gypsies*, Cambridge University Press, Cambridge, 1983.

Parsons, Gerald, *Religion in Victorian Britain*, Vol. I (Traditions), Vol. II (Controversies), Manchester and New York, 1988.

Parthasarthy, Jakka, *The Yerukula: An Ethnographic Study*, Anthropological Survey of India, Calcutta, 1988.

Passerini, Luisa (ed.), *Memory and Totalitarianism*, International Yearbook of Oral History and Life Stories, Volume 1, OUP, Oxford, 1992.

Pearson, Geoffrey, *Hooligan: A History of Respectable Fears*, Macmillan, London, 1983.

Peel, J.D.Y., 'For who hath despised the day of small things? Missionary Narratives and Historical Anthropology', *Comparative Studies in Society and History*, vol. 37, No. 3, July, 1995.

Perks, Robert and Thomson, Alistair (eds.) *The Oral History Reader*, Routledge, London and New York, 1998.

Philips, David, *Crime and Authority in Victorian England: The Black Country 1835-1860*, Croom Helm, London, 1977.

Portelli, Alessandro,'The Peculiarities of Oral History', *History Workshop Journal*, issue 12, Autumn, 1981.

Proctor, Tammy M., 'Uni(forming) Youth: Girl Guides and Boy Scouts in Britain, 1908-39', *History Workshop Journal*, 45, Spring 1998.

Radhakrishna, Meena, 'Laws of Metamorphosis: From Nomad to Offender' in Kalpana Kannabiran (ed.), *The Rule(s) of Law: Critical Essays on Criminology in India*, Sage Publications, New Delhi, 2007 (forthcoming).

Radhakrishna, Meena, 'Colonialism, Evolutionism and Anthropology—A Critique of the History of Ideas 1850-1930', Research-in-Progress Papers, *History and Society*, Nehru Memorial Museum and Library, New Delhi, June, 1997.

Radhakrishna, Meena 'Surveillance and Settlements under the Criminal Tribes Act in Madras', *The Indian Economic and Social History Review*, 29, 2 (1992).

Radhakrishna, Meena, 'Colonial Construction of a Criminal Tribe: The Itinerant Trading Communities of Madras Presidency' in Neera Chandhoke (ed.) *Historical Trajectory: Essays in Honour of Ravinder Kumar*, Tulika, New Delhi, 2000. Also in *Economic and Political Weekly*, Vol. XXXV, No. 28, 29, 15 July 2000.

Radhakrishna, Meena, 'From Itinerant Communities to Wage workers—The Criminal Tribes of Madras Presidency, 1910-1947', paper presented at the first annual conference of Association of Indian Labour Historians (AILH) in March, 1998. Research-in-progress paper, *History and Society*, Third series. No. LVII, March 2000. Nehru Memorial Museum and Library, New Delhi.

Radhakrishna, Meena, 'From Tribal Community to Working Class Consciousness: Case of Yerukula Women', Review of Women's Studies, *Economic and Political Weekly*, April 29, 1989.

Radhakrishna, Meena, 'The Criminal Tribes Act in Madras Presidency: Implications for Itinerant Communities', *The Indian Economic and Social History Review*, 26, 3, 1989.

Rafael, Vicente L., *Contracting Colonialism: Translation & Christian Conversion in Tagalog Society under Early Spanish Rule*, Cornell University Press, Ithaca, 1988.

Raghaviah, V., *Nomads*, Swarajya Printing Works, Secunderabad, 1968.

Raghaviah, V., *The Problem of Criminal Tribes*, Akhil Bhartiya Adim-Jati Sevak Sangh (BASS), Delhi, n.d.

Raj, Pushkar, 'Criminalising Poverty: Houseless and Anti-beggary Law in Delhi', *PUCL Bulletin*, January, 2005.

Ramaswami, N.S. and Muthiah, S., *Parrys 200*, Affiliated East West Press, Madras, 1988.

Rao, S, Venugopala, *Facets of Crime in India*, Allied Publishers, New Delhi, 1982.

Reclus, Elie, *Primitive Folk: Studies in Contemporary Ethnology*, The Contemporary Science Series, Walter Scott, 1892.

Richards, J.F. and Rao, V.N., 'Banditry in Mughal India: Historical and Folk Perceptions', *The Indian Economic and Social History Review*, XVII (1980), 3.

Rude, George, *Criminal and Victim, Crime and Society in Early Nineteenth Century England.*

Ruhela, Satya Pal, *The Children of Indian Nomads*, Sterling Publishers, New Delhi, 1984.

Rule, John G., 'Social Crime in the Rural South in the Eighteenth and Early Nineteenth Centuries', *Southern History*, 1, 1979.

Rusche, George and Kirchheimer Otto, *Punishment and Social Structure*, New York, 1939.

Rylands, Gordon, *Crime: Its Causes and Remedy*, London, 1889.

Salvation Army, *All the World*, International Heritage Centre, London, 1908-1918.

Salvation Army, *Social Problems in Solution*, (Papers read at the International Social Council, London), 1921.

Salvation Army, *Some Aspects of Salvation Army Social Work*, papers read at the International Social Council, London conducted by the Founder, 1911, The Salvation Army Printing Works, 1917.

Salvation Army, *The War Cry*, International Heritage Centre, London, 1909-19.

Sharpe, J.A., *Crime in Early Modern England 1550-1750*, Longman, New York, 1984.

Shaw, Bernard, Preface to 'Major Barbara', *The Complete Prefaces of Bernard Shaw*, Paul Hamlyn, London, 1965.

Sher Singh 'Sher', *The Sansis of Punjab: A Gypsy and Denotified Tribe of Rajput Origin*, Munshiram Manoharlal, Delhi, 1965.

Simhadri, Y.C., 'Changing Criminal Behaviour of an ex-Criminal Tribe in an Indian Village', *Indian Journal of Criminology*, 1976, 4(1) 23-26.

Simhadri, Y.C., *Denotified Tribes*, Classical Publishing Co., New Delhi, 1991.

Simhadri, Y.C., *The Ex-Criminal Tribes of India*, National Publishing House, New Delhi, 1979.

Singh, K.S., *People of India*, National Series, Vols. 4-6: *India's Communities*, Anthropological Survey of India. Calcutta, 1998.

Singha, Radhika, *A Despotism of Law*, Oxford University Press, 1998.

Singhal, D.P., *Gypsies: Indians in Exile*, Folklore Institute, Archana Publications, Meerut, 1982.

Slack, P.A., 'Vagrants and Vagrancy in England 1598-1664, *Economic History Review*, 2nd series, 27, 1974.

Smith, Solveig, *By Love Compelled*, Salvationist Publishing, London, 1981.

Spooner, Brian, *The Cultural Ecology of Pastoral Nomads*, Addison-Wesley Module in Anthropology no. 45, Reading, Mass: Addison-Wesley, 1973.

Srivastava, S.P., *A Social Psychological Study of Barawara: An Ex-criminal Tribe of U.P.*, Unpublished Ph.D. thesis, Lucknow University, 1970.

Stepan, Nancy, *Idea of Race in Science: Great Britain 1800-1960*, Oxford, 1982.

Stuart, H.A., *Census of India*, 1891, Vol. XIII, Madras, 1893.

Taylor, C., *Sources of the Self: The Making of the Modern Identity*, Cambridge MA, Harward University Press, 1989.

Taylor, Howard, 'Rationing Crime: the Political Economy of Criminal Statistics since the 1850s', *The Economic History Review*, Vol. LI, No. 3, August 1998.

Terdiman, R., *Present Past: Modernity and the Memory Crisis*, Ithaca, Cornell University Press, NY, 1993.

Thakkar, A.V., *Tribes of India*, BASS, Delhi, 1950.

Thompson, E.P., *The Making of the English Working Class*, Penguin, Harmondsworth, 1963.

Thompson, E.P., 'The Moral Economy of the English Crowd in the Eighteenth Century', *Past and Present*, 50, 1971.

Thompson, E.P., *Whigs and Hunters: The Origin of the Black Act*, Alien Lane, 1975.

Thurston, Edgar, *Castes and Tribes of Southern India*, Madras, 1909, reprinted Cosmo Publications, Delhi, 1975.

Thurston, Edgar, *Ethnographic Notes on Southern India*, Government Press, Madras, 1907.

Titus, Paul, 'Honour the Baloch, Buy the Pushtun: Stereotypes, Social Organisation and History in Western Pakistan', *Modern Asian Studies*, Vol. 32, Part 3, July 1998.

Tobias, J.J., *Crime and Industrial Society in the Nineteenth Century*, Penguin, Harmondsworth. 1972.

Tolen, Rachel J.,'Colonising and Transforming the Criminal Tribesmen: The Salvation Army in British India', *American Enthologist*, 18{1), February 1991.

Varady, R.G., 'North Indian Banjaras: Their Evolution as Transporters', *South Asia*, II (1979), 1 and 2.

Walsh, Cecil, *Crime in India with an Introduction on Forensic Difficulties and Peculiarities*, Ernest Benn Ltd., London, 1930.

Washbrook, D., *The Emergence of Provincial Politics: Madras Presidency 1870-1920*, Cambridge, 1976.

Washbrook, David, 'Economic Development and Social Stratification in Rural Madras: The Dry Region, 1878-1929' in Dewey and Hopkins (ed.) *The Imperial Impact: Studies in the Economic History of Africa and India*, London, 1978.

Watson, Bernard, *A Hundred Years' War*, Hodder and Stoughton, London, 1964.

Weisser, Michael R., *Crime and Punishment in Early Modern Europe*, Harvester, 1979.

White, Arnold, *Problems of a Great City*, London, 1886.

Wiener, Martin J., *Reconstructing the Criminal: Culture, Law, and Policy in England, 1830-1914*, CUP, Cambridge, 1990.

Wilson, Nerissa, *Gypsies and Gentlemen: The Life and Times of the Leisure Caravan*, Columbus Books, London, 1986.

Wright, Gordon, *Between the Guillotine and Liberty: Two Centuries of the Crime Problem in France*, OUP, New York, 1983.

Yang, Anand A. (ed.), *Crime and Criminality in British India*, The University of Arizona Press, Arizona, 1985.

Yang, Anand A., 'Between British Raj and Saran Raiyat' in Peter Robb (ed.) *Rural India: Land, Power and Society under British Rule*, Curzon Press, London, 1983.

Zehr, Howard, *Crime and the Development of Modern Society: Patterns of Criminality in Nineteenth Century Germany and France*, Croom Helm, 1976.

Index

Aborigines, 17
American Baptist Mission, 79, 92*n*, 104, 126*n*
Anthropology and CTA, 3–4, 23*n*
anti-beggary legislation, 175
Aziznagar settlement, 87

Banjaras *see* Brinjaries
beggars, xiv, 174–75
Bhils, 161
Booth, Bramwell, 15, 16
Booth, William, 17, 72, 73–77, 162
  In Darkest England, 17, 73–77
Borstal Prison, Lahore, 72
Brinjaries, 11, 27
  salt trade, 24*n*, 27, 31, 34, 35, 41*n*

CTA, *see* Criminal Tribes Act
caste system and criminal tribes, 34–35, 48, 102, 164, 169
Central Legislative Assembly, 88
children of CT communities, 99, 111, 114, 115, 117, 118, 119, 125*n*, 128, 130, 141, 165–7
Christian Association, 138
Church Panchayat, 104
crime and criminality
  administrative criteria, 51–56
  alcoholism and, 3
  changing notions of, 2–3, 5–7, 19, 26*n*
  famine and, 7, 8, 34, 35
  forest policy and, 8
  hereditary, 2–6, 8, 17, 34, 35, 72, 98
  individual and group, 54–55
  livelihood means, loss of, 6–7, 14, 24*n*, 31–34, 35–36, 53, 86, 98
  poverty and, 2, 3, 78, 152
  prejudices and, 12–15, 36
  railways and, 8, 33, 34, 35
  salt policy and, 8, 30–34
  Salvation Army's views on, 16–18
  social causes of, 2–8
  unemployment and, 3, 5, 77
  urbanisation and, 2
Criminal Procedure Code, 53
criminal tribes
  criteria for identification of, 49–51
  Government of India and, 28, 57, 86, 88
  in private enterprises, 105–14
  proof of criminality of, 52–56
  settlement schemes, failure, 101–05
  social context and, 4, 8, 10, 13, 36, 55, 129, 154, 159

Criminal Tribes Act (CTA), 1871, 1–2, 4, 5, 12, 16–21, 27–30, 37, 45, 71–72, 160
- Anthropology's input into, 3–4
- Criminal Tribes Act, 1911, 2, 6, 8, 15, 20, 27, 75, 77, 79–82, 86–89, 100, 103, 112, 114–17, 119, 128, 135–36, 142, 146, 152, 154, 158–60, 161–64, 167–68
- indiscriminate use of, 55–56
- nationalist activity and, 18, 39
- notification and surveillance, 45–49, 51–64
- openendedness of, 49–51
- powers to private enterprises, 105–10, 114–17
- protests against, 62, 64
- provisions, 37–39
- Salvation Army's role in formulating, 72–75

Criminal Tribes Act Enquiry Committee Report, 1939, 65*n*

Criminal Tribes Settlements
- abscondings from, 85, 95*n*, 96*n*
- Bijapur, 111–12
- Brandt and Company, Nellore, 106, 107
- forced and underpaid labour in, 87–89, 96*n*, 104, 107, 168
- Gorakhpur, 72–73
- Guntur, 47, 81, 102, 104
- Garvey's Cotton Mills, Madura, 106
- Magnesite Syndicate Ltd., 106, 109
- opposition by landlords, 10–105, 121*n*, 122*n*, 127, 161, 164
- Parrys' factory, 84, 87, 95*n*, 106, 108–09, 115, 124*n*, 166, 167
- plantations, 116–19, 123*n*, 126, 164, 166
- reformation in, 73–74, 79, 98, 99–100, 111, 131, 134, 163
- Sitanagaram, 80–81, 82, 94*n*, 96*n*
- Stuartpuram, 21, 78, 80, 81, 94*n*, 96*n*, 102, 104, 128, 135, 136, 141, 146, 148, 153
- surveillance in, 82–85, 95*n*
- unofficial settlements, 92*n*
- Vizianagaram Mining Company, 106

crimnocurology, 17, 72, 149, 163

dakaiti, 1

Darkest England, 17, 73–77

Denotified Tribes, 169

Denotified and Nomadic Tribes Rights Action Group (DNTRAG), 170*n*

Dasaris, 35, 106, 107

Dommars, 107

Doms, 72, 73, 94*n*

East India Company, 31, 32

Emigration Act, 1911–12, 122*n*

Factories Act, 86, 136, 141
- relaxation for CT workers, 136–37

Gandhi, M.K., 63

genetics and crime, 5, 6, 8, *see also* hereditary crime
- biological determinism, 5
- caste system and, 4–5
- Eugene, 3
- Galton, Francis, 3
- genetic traits, 2, 5

Gokhale, G.K., 39

Gounders, 48

Government of India and criminal tribes, 28, 57, 86, 88

Government of India Act, 1919, 47, 57, 81, 102, 104

gypsies, *see* itinerant communities

Habitual Offenders, 172–73
hereditary crime, *see also* genetics and crime, 2–6, 34, 35, 72, 98
Hunter, W.W., 1

ILTD *see* Indian Leaf Tobacco Development Company
Indian Jails Committee, 83
Indian Leaf Tobacco Development company, 21, 124*n*, 129–41, 146–47, 152, 155, 165–67
  retrenchment, 146
  Salvation Army and, 130–39
  Staff Association, 138
  Workers' Union, 137–42
Indian National Congress, 57, 138–39
Indian Penal Code, 53, 81
Indian Public Commission, 1902–03, 37, 46, 49
International Labour Organisation, 86, 88
itinerant communities
  ambivalence towards, 11
  charges against, 9–12, 13–15
  contemporary, 25*n*, 174
  legislation enactment for, 28–30
  livelihood means, loss of, 6–7, 14, 31–34
  marginalisation, 9–11
  notification and surveillance, 47–69, 147
  occupations, 12, 14–15, 23*n*, 24*n*, 30–35, 50–51
  prejudices against, xiv, 9–1 5, 36
  relationship with sedentary communities, 9–12
  resistance to settling, 156–57
  Salvation Army and, 80
Kallars, 19
Kapus, 48
Kathiars, 107
Kilagudi Kallas, 106
Korachas, 2, 27, 66*n*
  salt trade, 31, 34
  see also Koravas
Koravas, 2, 7–9, 20, 45, 49, 54, 68*n*, 106, 107, 127, 159
  charges against, 12
  kinship relations, 49
  livelihood means, loss of, 14–15, 32
  notification and registration, 80
  salt trade, 31–34, 41*n*, 42*n*
  social organisation, 13
Korava Reclamation Scheme, 101
Koravars, 2, 15, 27, 48, 53–55, 61–62, 64, 68*n*, 71, 95*n*, 107–09, 115, 122*n*, 124*n*
  Dabbai, 15, 51, 52, 66*n*
  Gandarvakottai, 50, 101
  Inji, 15, 51, 52, 66*n*
  Kal, 15, 51, 52, 66*n*
  Oppression and harassment, 48, 63, 101
  Salem Melurnad, 50, 51, 65*n*, 66*n*, 92*n*
  salt trade, 27, 31, 34
  settlements, 87, 101
  Togamalai, 51, 62, 92*n*
  Uppu, 15, 51, 66*n*, 116
  see also Koravas

laissez faire policy, 34, 43*n*
Lambadis *see* Brinjaries
Landlords, *see also* village headman
  abuse of CTA, 47–49, 65*n*, 97*n*, 122*n*
  opposition to CT settlement, 102–05, 121*n*, 122*n*, 1??, 164
  surveillance powers of, 45, 37–39, 56–57, 59–61, 69*n*
Land reclamation policy and agricultural settlements, 98–101, 163–65

reasons for failure, 101–105
livelihood means, loss of and criminality, 6–7, 14, 31–34, 35–3?, 53, 86, 98
London Mission, 72

Madigas, 105, 143
Madras Government Committee of Enquiry, 48
Madras Legislative Council, 88–89
Madras Salt Commission, 1876, 33
Malas, 105, 142

Nakkalas, 106
nomads *see* itinerant communities
North West Provinces (NWP), criminal communities, 27
legislative enactment for, 28–31
powers, 28–30, 37, 57–63, 81, 83, 105–10, 152
Salvation Army and, 78–79
use of CTA for wage work, 105–10

Pachappas, 107
Paidis, 35
Parayas, 35, 54
Parrys' factory as a CT settlement, 84, 87, 95*n*, 106, 108–09, 115, 124*n*, 166
patta (title deed), 100, 104, 134
Pillai, Kesava, 114
Plantations and CT workers, *see also* labour, wage; criminal tribes settlements, 116–19, 164, 166
police administration
Criminal tribe members and, 45, 47–49, 53–61, 65n, 66*n*, 67–68, 94*n*, 152, 154, 162
powers, 28–30, 37, 57–63, 81, 83, 105–10, 152
Salvation Army and, 78–79
use of CTA for wage work, 105–10
Punjab
criminal communities, 27
legislative enactment for, 28–29
Salvation Army, 72–78

railways and salt trade, 33, 34, 42*n*
reformation and CT members, 73–74, 79, 98, 99–100, 111, 131, 134, 163
Rellis, 35
religion
and reclamation process, 105
and trade unions, 138–39

salt policy, 8, 30–34
railways and, 33, 34, 42*n*
Salvation Army (SA)
Criminocurology, 17, 72, 149, 163
ILTD and, 130–139
in England, 73–78
in India, 13, 15–18, 20–22, 71–75, 78–85, 88, 98–103, 110, 117, 127–36, 139–41, 146–55, 162–63, 165–66, 168
Major Anandham, 148–49
Major Barbara, 77
social credentials of, 15–17, 73–78, 91*n*
Shaw, Bernard, 77, 78
Tata's contribution, 78
Starte, 111, 113
Stuart, Harold, 78, 102–103, 112, 15–16
Stuartpuram CT settlement, 21, 78, 80, 81, 94*n*, 96*n*, 102, 104, 128, 135, 136, 141, 146, 148, 153

Thugee and Dacoity Department, 29, 71
Tucker, Booth, 13, 16, 73, 82, 117, 149, 154, 168

United Planters Association of South India (UPASI), 106–107, 116–18

vagrancy, xiv, xv
village headman, *see also* landlords, powers, 45–49, 104, 109

wage work, 22
- arranged by administration, 111–14
- arranged by police, 105–110
- forced and underpaid, 87–89, 104, 107, 168
- plantations, 115–20, 123*n*, 125*n*, 164, 166, 170*n*
- Salvation Army settlements, 76–77, 87, 90*n*, 117

wanderers, xiii, xv
War Cry, The, 15
Women, itinerant
- attitudes of sedentary women to, 10, 11
- brideprice, 13, 133
- changes in gender roles, 129, 131, 132, 140, 143*n*
- changes in social position, 130–37, 153, 154
- charge of immorality, 13, 36, 67
- confinement in settlements with men, 81–82, 92*n*, 93*n*, 128
- Police and, 60–63, 69*n*, 70*n*
- polygamy, 13, 55
- reformation, 131–33
- social customs, 13
- song by, 17–18
- work, 111, 130–41, 170*n*

workers' union, 137–43, 145*n*
- Christian Association, 138
- Staff Association, 138

Workman's Breach of Contract Act, 167

Yenadis, 35, 103
Yenadi Reclamation Scheme, 121*n*
Yercand Planters' Association, 116
Yerukulas, *see also* Koravas, 2, 20–21, 27, 52–53, 56, 66*n*, 67*n*, 71, 78, 80–81, 96*n*, 116–19, 124*n*, 126*n*, 129–30, 135–43
- declared as criminal tribe, 127, 142
- Donga, 53
- reformation, 130
- salt trade, 24*n*, 27, 31, 34
- settlements, 80–82, 85, 92*n*, 103
- women, 93*n*, 129–30, 139–41